OLD TESTAMENT TRANSLATION PROBLEMS

HELPS FOR TRANSLATORS

PREPARED UNDER THE AUSPICES OF THE

UNITED BIBLE SOCIETIES

VOLUME I

OLD TESTAMENT TRANSLATION PROBLEMS

PUBLISHED FOR THE UNITED BIBLE SOCIETIES

BY E. J. BRILL, LEIDEN

1960

OLD TESTAMENT TRANSLATION PROBLEMS

BY

A. R. HULST

IN CO-OPERATION WITH OTHER SCHOLARS

PUBLISHED FOR THE UNITED BIBLE SOCIETIES

BY E. J. BRILL, LEIDEN

1960

PRINTED IN THE NETHERLANDS

CONTENTS

Introduction vii
List of Publications Cited xi
List of General Abbreviations xiv
Hebrew Transcription xvi
Translation Problems:
- Genesis 1
- Exodus 6
- Leviticus 9
- Numbers 9
- Deuteronomy 12
- Joshua 18
- Judges 20
- Ruth 24
- 1 Samuel 25
- 2 Samuel 30
- 1 Kings 36
- 2 Kings 41
- 1 Chronicles 44
- 2 Chronicles 49
- Ezra 54
- Nehemia 57
- Job 60
- Psalms 92
- Proverbs 114
- Ecclesiastes 130
- Song of Solomon 134
- Isaiah 137
- Jeremiah 159
- Lamentations 186
- Ezekiel 190
- Daniel 223
- Hosea 230
- Joel 236
- Amos 238

Obadiah 241
Micah 241
Nahum 245
Habakkuk 248
Zephaniah 253
Haggai 255
Zechariah 256
Malachi 260

INTRODUCTION

Every Bible translator knows how difficult it is to deal adequately with serious problems of text and exegesis. This is especially true of problems posed by certain Old Testament passages which seem almost to defy intelligible rendering. One can obtain some help in commentaries and technical journals, but there is no place where all the principal problems have been gathered together in a single handy volume. Accordingly, this book is designed to remedy, at least in part, certain aspects of this situation and to provide practical suggestions for the solution of many textual and exegetical problems of the Old Testament.

Plans for this volume began in 1947 at an international conference of Bible translators meeting in „Woudschoten", Zeist, Holland, under the auspices of the Netherlands Bible Society. At this conference the problem of the Old Testament text was discussed at considerable length, and the conclusion was that a translator should wherever possible follow the Masoretic text. However, it was clearly recognized that there are a number of passages in which the Masoretic text is unintelligible and therefore untranslatable. Such circumstances reflect two different types of problems: (1) instances in which the correct meaning of an obscure word or expression is not known, and (2) those in which the Hebrew text has become irreparably corrupt. At these points Bible translators need guidance if they are to find satisfactory solutions which are in line with the highest standards of contemporary scholarship. In some cases ancient translations, e.g. in Greek and Syriac, provide significant clues. There are a number of other passages which can be interpreted in a variety of ways without violating any grammatical rules. The practical problem for the conference, however, was to determine how translators could be provided with the information which would help them find satisfactory solutions in line with contemporary scholarship.

The delegates meeting in Woudschoten felt that the Bible Societies had a key responsibility to provide the required assistance, but that existing commentaries are often of such an individualistic character as to fail to meet the translators' needs, for too often the writers of such commentaries have indulged in types of textual emendation or conjectures which have not had wide support. Bible translators, who are preparing a text to be used by all the churches, must make certain that the alternative which they select has the greatest possible weight of authority and the widest usage by the church.

At the time of the Woudschoten conference a committee in Holland was already engaged in preparing a new Dutch translation of the Old Testament. Thus it seemed appropriate for the conference to request that this committee undertake the task of drawing up a list of difficult Old Testament passages.

Accordingly, Professor A. R. Hulst, a member of the Dutch committee, was asked to assemble the data on the basis of discussions in the sessions of the Dutch translation committee. At first the problem passages were classified under three groups: (a) those texts which are very obscure and practically untranslatable; (b) those in which one or more of the ancient versions provide a clue to adequate exegesis; and (c) those in which more than one legitimate translation of the Masoretic text is possible. Later these three lists were combined into a single one for more ready reference, but the designation of *a*, *b*, and *c* is still retained and indicates to the reader something about the nature of the difficulty and certain aspects of the solution. Under the imprint of the United Bible Societies, the Netherlands Bible Society has arranged to publish this volume containing more than twelve hundred problem passages, following the order and versification of the English Bible. It must be recognized immediately that this treatment is by no means exhaustive, either in the selection of problem passages or in the citation of relevant background data. Many other texts could have been added, especially in such books as Hosea, Job, and Ezekiel. The practical limitations of a publication of this nature have made it necessary to eliminate a number of these passages, especially some in class *c*. This, however, is not as serious as it might seem, since commentaries generally provide helpful suggestions for these types of difficulties.

Another element of "incompleteness" in this volume is the fact that no attempt has been made to cite in a comprehensive manner all translations or textual authorities which might be relevant on a particular point. At first the committee dealt with these passages only in terms of the Dutch translation. Later, however, in order to make this document more useful to English-speaking translators, relatively full citations have been made from the Revised Standard Version.

This treatment of difficult Old Testament texts is not primarily technical, but practical. Thoroughly comprehensive and scientific discussions of these problem passages belong to a textual commentary or scientific jounal. Nevertheless, as will be observed, Professor Hulst has made full use of technical publications which contain extensive treatments of textual data. However, he has purposely not included numerous highly hypothetical solutions since these would be too subjective and tentative. It must be recognized, of course, that this type of treatment cannot be ultimate and definitive. As new light on these problems becomes available, especially from the Qumran material, it is inevitable that many difficult passages will be clarified. However, the committee has been purposefully conservative in its adopting of new evidence, for it has seemed better to "lag" a little, rather than to be found guilty of accepting attractive, but unproved, solutions.

It will be evident to anyone using this volume that the committee has no mere theoretical or "armchair" interest in the problems of Bible translation. This is the work of men who have grappled with these problems firsthand and who have had a very practical goal in mind, namely, the effective communication of the Word of God to increasing numbers of men and women through new translations and revisions.

Bible translators are deeply indebted to the Netherlands Bible Society for having sponsored this project of textual and exegetical study. Our thanks must be extended to the Dutch translation committee which has given special attention to these hundreds of problems in order that their findings and judgments might be properly recorded. We are particularly indebted to Professor Hulst, who not only kept the minutes of these discussions, but who has supplemented the data, rewritten the material in book form and added the bibliographical information. We are no less indebted to Mr. Cullen Story and Dr. Robert Bratcher of the American Bible Society for giving their most valuable assistance in the editing of this volume.

U.B.S. Subcommittee on Translation.

LIST OF PUBLICATIONS CITED

1. *Bibles*

Authorized Version, 1611
Die Bybel in Afrikaans, 1953
Biblia Hebraica, 3rd ed. 1937, 4th ed. 1951
The Complete Bible, An American Translation, ed. Smith and Goodspeed, 1939
Dutch New Version, 1951
Echter-Bibel, Das Alte Testament herausgegeben von D.Dr. Fr. Nötscher, 1947-
La Sainte Bible, traduite par L. Segond, ed. 1948
Revised Standard Version, 1952
Zürcher Bibel, 1935 (= Zwingli-Bibel)

2. *Periodicals*

Bulletin of the American Schools of Oriental Research
Hebrew Union College Annual
Journal of Biblical Literature
Journal of Theological Studies
Journal of the Palestine Oriental Society
Syria
The Bible Translator
Vetus Testamentum
Zeitschrift für die alttestamentliche Wissenschaft

3. *Lexica and Grammars*

Beer, Georg. *Hebräische Grammatik* 2., völlig neubearb. Aufl. von Rudolf Meyer. Berlin: W. de Gruyter, 1955

Dalman, Gustaf H. *Aramäisch-Neuhebräisches Handwörterbuch.* Göttingen: Eduard Pfeiffer, 1938.

Galling, Kurt. *Biblisches Reallexikon* (HAT, Erste Reihe, 1). Tübingen: J. C. B. Mohr, 1937.

Gesenius, Wilhelm, and Buhl, Frants. *Hebräisches und Aramäisches Handwörterbuch über das Alte Testament.* Leipzig: F. C. W. Vogel, 1915.

Grossman, Reuben, and Segal, M. H. *Compendious Hebrew-English Dictionary* Tel Aviv: Dvir Publishing Co., 1954².

Köhler, Ludwig, and Baumgartner, Walter. *Lexicon in Veteris Testamenti Libros.* Leiden: E. J. Brill, 1953.

——, *Supplementum ad Lexicon in Veteris Testamenti Libros.* Leiden: E. J. Brill, 1958.

4. *Commentaries*

Bertholet, Alfred. *Hesekiel* (HAT, Erste Reihe, 13). Tübingen: J. C. B. Mohr, 1936.

Cooke, G. A. *The Book of Ezekiel* (ICC). 2 vols. New York: Charles Scribner's Sons, 1937.

Eerdmans, B. D. *The Hebrew Book of Psalms* (*Oudtestamentische Studiën,* Deel IV). Leiden: E. J. Brill, 1947.

Elliger, Karl. *Das Buch der zwölf Kleinen Propheten.* Vol. II (ATD) Göttingen: Vandenhoeck & Ruprecht, 1956.

Fohrer, Georg. *Ezechiel* (HAT, Erste Reihe, 13). Tübingen: J. C. B. Mohr, 1955.

Gordis, Robert. *Koheleth — The Man and his World* (Texts and Studies of the Jewish Theological Seminary of America, Vol. XIX). New York: Bloch Publishing Company, 1955².

Harper, William R. *A Critical and Exegetical Commentary on Amos and Hosea* (ICC). New York: Charles Scribner's Sons, 1936².

Hölscher, Gustav. *Das Buch Hiob* (HAT, Erste Reihe, 17). Tübingen: J. C. B. Mohr, 1952.

Humbert, Paul. *Problèmes du livre d'Habacuc.* Neuchâtel: Secrétariat de l'université, 1944.

König, Eduard. *Das Deuteronomium.* (KAT). Leipzig: A. Deichertsche Verlagsbuchhandlung, 1917.

Kraus, H. J. *Klagelieder (Threni)* (BK, XX). Neukirchen: Verlag der Buchhandlung des Erziehungsvereins, 1956.

——, *Psalmen* (BK XV, 1-12) Neukirchen: Verlag der Buchhandlung des Erziehungsvereins, 1958.

Montgomery, James A. *A Critical and Exegetical Commentary on the Book of Daniel* (ICC). New York: Charles Scribner's Sons, 1927.

——, *A Critical and Exegetical Commentary on the Books of Kings* (ICC) (ed. H. S. Gehman). New York: Charles Scribner's Sons, 1951.

Rudolph, W. *Chronikbücher* (HAT, Erste Reihe, 21). Tübingen: J. C. B. Mohr, 1955².

——, *Esra und Nehemia* (HAT, Erste Reihe, 20). Tübingen: J. C. B. Mohr, 1949.

——, *Jeremia* (HAT, Erste Reihe, 12). Tübingen: J. C. B. Mohr, 1958².

Schmidt, H. *Die Psalmen* (HAT, Erste Reihe, 15). Tübingen: J. C. B. Mohr, 1934.

Simon, Ulrich E. *A Theology of Salvation; a commentary on Isaiah* 40-55. London: S. P. C. K., 1953.

Steuernagel, C. *Das Deuteronomium* (HKAT). Göttingen: Vandenhoeck & Ruprecht, (1900), 1923².

Volz, P. *Der Prophet Jeremia* (KAT) Tübingen: A. Deichertsche Verlagsbuchhandlung, 1928.

Weiser, A. *Das Buch Hiob* (ATD). Göttingen: Vandenhoeck & Ruprecht, 1951.

——, *Das Buch des Propheten Jeremia* (ATD) Göttingen: Vandenhoeck & Ruprecht, 1955.

Wolff, H. W. *Dodekapropheton* (BK XIV: 1-2). Neukirchen: Verlag der Buchhandlung des Erziehungsvereins, 1957-

Zimmerli, Walther. *Ezechiel* (BK 13 : 1-6). Neukirchen: Verlag der Buchhandlung des Erziehungsvereins, 1955-

5. *General Works*

Albright, William F. *Archeology and the Religion of Israel.* Baltimore: Johns Hopkins University Press, 1946².

——, *The Archeology of Palestine and the Bible.* New York: Fleming H. Revell Co., 1932.

Burrows, Millar. *The Dead Sea Scrolls of St. Mark's Monastry.* Vol. I. New Haven: The American Schools of Oriental Research, 1950.

Dalman, Gustaf H. *Arbeit und Sitte in Palästina*. Gütersloh: C. Bertelsmann, 1935.

Danby, Herbert. *The Mishnah*. London: Oxford University Press, 1954.

Gordon, Cyrus H. *Introduction to Old Testament Times*, Ventnor, N. J.: Ventnor Publishers, Inc., 1953.

——, *Ugaritic Handbook* (*Analecta Orientalia* 25). Roma: Pontificium Institutum Biblicum, 1947.

Lindhagen, Curt. *The Servant Motif in the Old Testament*, Uppsala: Lundequistska bokhandeln, 1950.

Margoliuth, David S. *The Relations between Arabs and Israelites Prior to the Rise of Islam*. London: Oxford University Press, 1924.

Montgomery, James A. *Arabia and the Bible*. Philadelphia, 1934.

North, C. R. *The Suffering Servant in Dentero-Isaiah*; *an historical and critical study*. London: Oxford University Press, 1948.

Oestreicher, Th. *Das Deuteronomische Grundgesetz*. Gütersloh: C. Bertelsmann Verlag, 1920.

Pedersen, J. *Israel, Its Life and Culture*, I-IV. London: H. Milford, Oxford University Press, 1947[2].

Thilo, M. *Der Prediger Salomo*. Bonn: A. Marcus und E. Weber, 1923.

LIST OF GENERAL ABBREVIATIONS

Accad	Accadian
acc.	accusative
adj.	adjective
Aq	Aquila
Aram	Aramaic
ARI	Archeology and the Religion of Israel (by W. F. Albright)
ATD	Das Alte Testament Deutsch
AV	Authorized Version
Babyl	Babylonian
BASOR	Bulletin of the American Schools of Oriental Research
BH	Biblia Hebraica (3rd ed. 1937, 4th ed. 1951)
BK	Biblischer Kommentar (ed. Martin Noth)
BRL	Biblisches Reallexikon
BS	La Sainte Bible (translated by L. Segond)
BSG	The Bible, An American Translation (ed. J. M. Powis Smith and E. J. Goodspeed)
cf.	compare
cod. Alex	codex Alexandrinus
cod. L	codex Leningradensis
cod. Sin	codex Sinaiticus
cod. Vat	codex Vaticanus
comm.	commentary
DNV	Dutch New Version
DSI^a	Dead Sea Scroll with the text of Isaiah (text as publ. by M. Burrows)
ed.	edited by
e.g.	exempli gratia (for example)
f., ff.	following page(s)
fem.	feminine
Ges-Buhl	Hebräisches und Aramäisches Handwörterbuch über das Alte Testament (ed. W. Gesenius and Frants Buhl)
HAT	Handbuch zum Alten Testament (ed. O. Eissfeldt)
HKAT	Handkommentar zum Alten Testament (ed. W. Nowack)
Hebr	Hebrew
hiph	hiphil
hithp	hithpael
ICC	International Critical Commentary
impf.	imperfect
impv.	imperative

inf.	infinitive
JBL	Journal of Biblical Literature
JPOS	Journal of the Palestine Oriental Society
JTS	Journal of Theological Studies
KAT	Kommentar zum Alten Testament (ed. A. T. Sellin)
KBL	Lexicon in Veteris Testamenti Libros (ed. L. Köhler and W. Baumgartner)
L	Vetus Latina (Itala)
LXX	Septuagint
masc.	masculine
Mont-Gehm	Montgomery-Gehman
ms(s)	manuscript(s)
MT	Masoretic Text
niph	niphal
op. cit.	opere citato (in the work cited)
OT	Old Testament
OTS	Oudtestamentische Studiën
part.	participle
pass.	passive
perf.	perfect
pers.	person
Pesh	Syriac Peshitta
pi.	piel
plur(s).	plural(s)
po.	poel
prep.	preposition
pron.	pronoun
pu.	pual
RSV	Revised Standard Version
Sam	Samaritan
sing.	singular
suff.	suffix
s.v.	sub voce (see under the word)
Symm	Symmachus
Syr-Hex	Syro-Hexaplar
Tg	Targum
Th	Theodotion
v.	verse
Vg	Vulgate
VT	Vetus Testamentum
ZAW	Zeitschrift für die alttestamentliche Wissenschaft (N. F. = Neue Folge)

HEBREW TRANSCRIPTION

The following is the system used in this book:

Consonants

א	— ʾ	ל	— l
ב	— b	מ	— m
ג	— g	נ	— n
ד	— d	ס	— s
ה	— h (initial)	ע	— ʿ
ה	— (h) (end of syllable)	פ	— p
ו	— w	צ	— ṣ
ז	— z	ק	— q
ח	— ḥ	ר	— r
ט	— ṭ	שׂ	— ś
י	— y (initial)	שׁ	— š
י	— (y) (end of syllable)	ת	— t
כ	— k		

Vowels

		Example:
◌ָ	= ā	yādaʿ
◌ַ	= a	yādaʿ
◌ֲ	= ă	ʾănī
◌ֵ	= ē	yēšēb
◌ֶ	= e	melek
◌ֱ	= ĕ	ʾĕlōhīm
◌ְ	= ^{e}	l^{e} (vocal shewa)
◌ְ	= no transliteration	malʾākīm (silent shewa)
◌ִי	= ī	š^{e}līšī
◌ִ	= i	higgīd
◌ֹ or וֹ	= ō	kōl
◌ָ	= o	kol
◌ֳ	= ŏ	ḥŏlī
וּ	= ū	šūb
◌ֻ	= u	huggad
◌ֵי	= ē(y)	b^{e}nē(y)
◌ָיו	= ā(y)w	b^{e}nā(y)w

; 7 (C) There are serious textual problems in both parts of this verse. In the first half, a difficulty exists in the word *śeʾēt* 'a lifting up', a *qal* inf. construct of *nāśāʾ* 'to lift up, raise'. The RSV has translated this word with the negative interrogative particle 'will you not be accepted?' (cf. also the AV). On the other hand, the DNV has sensed a close connection between the 'lifting up' of v. 7, and the 'falling' of Cain's countenance, according to verses 5 and 6. Thus, the DNV has rendered 'why has your countenance fallen?' (v. 6), and 'may you not raise it (i.e. your countenance) if you do well?' (v. 7).

The RSV translates the second part of the verse 'if you do not do well, sin is couching at the door; its desire is for you, but you must master it'. This translation is uncertain. The suff. in 'its desire', as well as the suff. in the final word of the verse *bō* 'in it', are both masc., while the word 'sin' in this verse is fem. This problem can be met by dropping the fem. ending *t* of *ḥaṭṭāʾt*, and by pointing the consonants that remain to form *ḥēṭʾ*, the masc. form of 'sin', but this change is not advisable. The DNV rendering 'sin lies like a besieger before the door', suggests a better solution. The Hebr. active part. *rōbēṣ* 'besieger', is often used of an animal that lies in wait for its prey (cf. also Arabic *rabbāḍ*). It is quite possible then, that the writer's use of the masc. suffixes has been determined by this mental image of 'the croucher'.

: 8 (B) The DNV and RSV read 'let us go out to the field'. This sentence is not a part of the MT. However, a few words must have dropped out of the Hebr. text, or from a particular recension of it, since the clause is found in the ancient versions (Samar, LXX, Pesh, Tg and Vg). From the standpoint of clarity, the insertion of the clause is necessary.

: 3 (B) Though the word 'son' is missing from the MT, it is clearly implied in the suff. 'his' attached to the word 'name' at the end of the verse.

: 3 (C) The DNV rendering 'now they have gone wrong' is the translation of the word *bešaggām* (with final *qameṣ*), a word composed of the prep. *be* with the inf. of *šāgag* and the 3rd masc. plur. suff. The plur. suff. could be connected with the sing. collective noun *ʾādām* 'man', that occurs just two words earlier in the verse. This is possible even though another 3rd masc. sing. pronoun immediately follows. The RSV follows the pointing *bᵉšaggam* (with final *pataḥ*) and translates 'for' (the AV more literally 'for that also'). This translation understands the word as composed of the prep. *bᵉ*, the relative *ša*, and the particle *gam* 'also', i.e. 'in that also' (= 'because' or 'for'). This translation connects the word with the following phrase 'for he is flesh'. The meaning would be that because man is mortal (i.e. flesh), God's vital spirit will not always abide in him. This interpretation has the support of numerous ancient versions.

9 : 26 (C) The MT, followed by the DNV and the AV, reads 'praised be the Lord, the God of Shem'. At first glance this translation appears a little strange, since God is known not as the God of all Semites, but only of Israel. But the meaning is clear when one thinks of Israel as descended from Shem, one of the three sons of Noah. The translation of the RSV and BSG 'blessed by the Lord my God be Shem', implies a different vocalization of the consonantal text, i.e. *bᵉrūk* instead of the MT *bārūk*, and *'ĕlōhay*, instead of the MT *'ĕlōhē(y)*.

11 : 31 (B) Literally the MT reads 'and they went away with them'. The DNV follows the LXX and Latin translations taking the verb as a causative sing. with Terah as the subject. Also the word *'ōtām* is read in place of *'ittām*, thereby producing the translation 'he made them go away'. Another possible rendering is given by the Pesh which understands the verb as sing. but leaves *'ittām* as it is, i.e. 'he went away with them'. The RSV has no comment on the verse and appears to have read the MT, though translating rather freely 'they went forth together'.

14 : 14 (C) The DNV and RSV translation 'his trained men', is uncertain (cf. the verb. *ḥānak*). Another possible translation is 'his followers' (BSG 'his retainers'), a form connected with *ḥanaku*, a word found in one of the clay tablets of Taanach, where it indicates the followers of Palestinean chiefs. Cf. W. F. Albright, *The Archaeology of Palestine and the Bible*, p. 141.

20 : 16 (B) The DNV has adopted a slight alteration reading *kullō* (neuter) instead of the MT *kōl wᵉ*. The RSV translates *kōl* as 'every one'. This

is possible though it has the disadvantage of repeating what has just been said in the verse.

: 13 (C) The word *ʿālā(y)w* can be translated either ‘above it’, i.e. the ladder (cf. the RSV), or ‘beside him’, i.e. Jacob (cf. the RSV margin). Thus, either God stood at the top of the ladder reaching up to heaven, or he stood beside Jacob who was lying on the ground (cf. Gen. 18 : 8 where *ʿălē(y)hem* has the sense ‘beside them’). The DNV has ‘at the top of it’, but after its revision it will translate ‘beside him’.

: 34 (B) In agreement with the Samar the DNV has ‘she named’. In this case the text must be altered to read *qār*^{e}*ʾā(h)*. Another solution is offered by the RSV which translates the form as though it were passive ‘his name was called’.

: 23 (B) The DNV translates as though the word *kōl* ‘everything’ were
.T 24) in the text. This is done on the basis of ancient versions including the Samar.

: 6 (B) The MT reads ‘to a land’. In early times something was inserted here, occasionally the name of the land to which Esau went, i.e. Seir. The MT punctuation (a separating accent in the word ‘land’) encourages the insertion of an additional word (‘another land’ in the DNV). The RSV has viewed the MT as a combined whole and connected the word ‘land’ with what follows, i.e. ‘into a land away from his brother’.

: 30 (B) The MT has *ʾallupē(y)hem* ‘their chiefs’. Both the DNV rendering ‘tribes’, and the RSV translation ‘clans’, reflect the vocalization *ʾalpē(y)hem* ‘their thousands’, i.e. their groups or clans.

: 3 (C) The meaning of *k*^{e}*tōnet passīm* is uncertain. The LXX and Vg. (cf. the AV) have interpreted Joseph’s garment as a gaily-colored one. The DNV translation ‘gorgeous dress’, implies that it was not a garment for daily use. Still another possible rendering is ‘a garment with long sleeves and which hangs down to the feet’ (RSV ‘a long robe with sleeves’ and BSG ‘a long cloak’). That royal princesses also wore such garments is indicated in 2 Sam. 13 : 18, 19. Galling

(BRL, col. 334) thinks of a *Wickelkleid* and says, *beim Wickelkleid liess man einen beträchtlichen langen Stoffstreifen . . . bis auf die Wade herabhängen und führte ihn dann von unten nach oben in sich überkragenden Spiralen um den Körper herum.*

37 : 36 (B) The DNV and RSV read 'Midianites' instead of 'Medanites'.

38 : 3 (B) On the basis of a few Hebr. mss., the Samar, and Tg. Ps.-Jonathan, the DNV translates, 'she named'. The RSV follows the MT 'he called his name'.

41 : 8 (B) The difficulty in the MT lies in the fact that the plur. suff. in the word *'ōtām* 'them' can only refer back to the noun which is in the sing. form, i.e. *ḥălōmō* 'his dream'. The LXX has understood *'ōtō* 'it' instead of the Hebr. *'ōtām*. The RSV has followed the LXX though noting the Hebr. reading in the margin. The DNV has read 'his dreams' and therefore retained the *'ōtām* that follows, as it is.

41 : 43 (C) The meaning of the word *'abrēk* is uncertain. The RSV and AV translate 'bow the knee'. The RSV footnote says that the word is probably Egyptian and that the Israelites heard in it the sound of the Hebr. verb *bārak* 'to kneel'. The DNV translation 'reverence', considers the word to be an exclamation or a call to the people to show respect for the dignitary. The DNV translation, then, is to be understood as an interpretation from the context. Gordon (*Introduction*, p. 125) views the expression as Egyptian, a compound with the meaning 'pay heed to', and thus a call to the people. Some have connected the word *'abrēk* with the Accad. *abarakku* which indicates a high official, or a person high in rank in the royal court. Thus, in Gen. 41 : 43, it would announce the person who was approaching. However, this explanation from Accad. seems not very probable here. It is better to follow the RSV (cf. the AV) or the DNV: there is little difference between them.

42 : 33 (B) The word 'corn' (RSV 'grain') is an addition to the text (cf. also 42 : 19). The insertion is justified because of the context.

45 : 7 (B) The Hebr. reads 'to keep alive for you to a great salvation' (or

'rescue'). One can regard the word *p*^{e}*lē(y)ṭā(h)* 'rescue' as an abstract form meaning 'those who escaped', or 'those who were rescued'. In some of the ancient versions, the prep. *l*^{e} 'to' is omitted. Hence, the RSV (cf. also the DNV) has 'to keep alive for you many survivors'.

6 : 23 (B) 'Son of Dan' has been read instead of 'sons of Dan' in agreement with an old conjecture. The RSV follows the MT vocalization.

7 : 21 (B) Literally the MT reads 'and, as for the people, he made them pass over unto the cities'. The DNV and RSV follow the translations of the Samar and LXX (cf. the RSV 'and as for the people, he made slaves of them'). The difference in the verbs has arisen from the confusion of two similar Hebr. letters, the *daleth* and the *resh*. In a somewhat similar way in this verse, the Hebr. word for 'cities' (*'ārīm*) has been understood as 'servants' (*'ăbādīm*) by the LXX.

9 : 4 (C) The first word, *paḥaz*, is found also in Judg. 9 : 4 where bold or audacious men are mentioned. In Gen. 49 : 4 translators generally accept the meaning 'to flood, boil over'. Though the LXX and Tg have read the form *pāḥaztā*, it is not necessary to alter the MT. The DNV has 'you, who boil up as water'; the RSV 'unstable as water' (cf. the AV); and still another translation has 'turbulent'.

9 : 5 (C) According to KBL, the last word of the verse *m*^{e}*kērōtē(y)hem*, has no explanation. Little help is given by the ancient versions. An alteration to *mikm*^{e}*rōt* 'nets', gives no sense here. The verse indicates that some instruments of force are present in the word. Thus, the DNV has 'tools', the *Zürcher Bibel* 'weapons', the RSV 'swords', and the BS and BSG 'daggers'. An explanation from the Ethiopic offers the translation 'counsel', but this is questionable in this context.

9 : 12 (C) The prep. *min* 'from', can indicate result. Thus, the RSV translates 'his eyes shall be red with wine, and his teeth white with milk'. The phrase 'red with wine' means 'red as a result of wine'. The word *ḥaklīlī* means 'dull, dark', thus, eyes that are dark (or red) from too much wine (cf. Prov. 23 : 29). But the prep. *min* can also indicate comparison, and it is interpreted in this way here by the DNV, which renders

'he shall have eyes darker than wine, and teeth whiter than milk'. Either translation is possible.

49 : 19f. (B) The DNV and RSV read 'but he shall raid at their heels'. This rendering follows the ancient versions which read the first letter *m* of the Hebr. text of v. 20 as a suff. to the last word of v. 19. This suff., then, must refer back to the word *g^edūd* which can be viewed as a collective. In this case, however, v. 20 begins with the name 'Asher'.

50 : 26 (B) The RSV and DNV on the basis of the Samar translate 'he was put'. This involves a very slight alteration of the consonantal text.

EXODUS

1 : 16 (A) The Hebr. phrase *ūr'īten 'al hā'obnāyīm* offers several difficulties in this context. First, the verb 'and you shall see' has no expressed object. An object 'them' is supplied by the AV and RSV. Then, too, it is unusual to have the prep. *'al* 'upon' connected with the verb 'to see'. But the real problem is the meaning of the word *'obnāyīm*. In Jer. 18 : 3 this word is rendered 'potter's wheel', but it obviously cannot have that sense here. The LXX translation indicates that the real meaning was lost early, for *pros to tiktein* can scarcely be called a translation. KBL still points to the opinion in the *Midrash Rabba* that the genitals are meant.

If the vocalization is correct, there is surely some definite concrete meaning. Some feel that there is an allusion to the stool on which the woman sits when giving birth to her child; others, to the stones (*'ăbānīm*) on which she supports herself. The RSV renders 'the birthstool' (cf. the AV). The DNV has chosen to give a 'sense translation' for the entire phrase, i.e. 'then, you must watch carefully at the delivery'.

3 : 19 (C) At the close of the verse the Hebr. reads 'and not by a strong hand' (cf. the AV), which is translated in the DNV 'not even by a strong hand'. This would mean that Pharaoh has so hardened his heart that, no matter what might happen, he will not let the Israelites go. Thus, the 'strong hand' of v. 19, is the utmost of human strength

that, nevertheless, is powerless to effect the release of the Hebrew slaves: much more is needed, even the very hand or power of God (v. 20). A different interpretation is given by the RSV, supported by the LXX. It understands *w*^{e}*lōʾ* 'and not' as meaning *ʾim lōʾ* 'unless', and translates 'unless compelled by a mighty hand'. The 'hand' of v. 19, in this case, is the same as the 'hand' of v. 20, i.e. the hand of God. The context of v. 20 might be said to favor this translation since Pharaoh will only let the people go after God performs His wonders (v. 20). Thus, he will not let them go unless compelled to do so by God's hand (v. 19). It is possible, however, that the RSV translation, though having ancient versional support, represents a later interpretation of the text.

8 : 10f. (B) In the DNV and RSV all the words from *ʾăšer hiṣṣīl* through the end of v. 10 have been transferred to v. 11. The word *ʾăšer* is then omitted and the other words placed after the (second) word *kī* in v. 11.

3 : 21 (B) The Hebr. has *ʾal tammēr*, the negative particle with the causative form of *mārar*, i.e. 'do not embitter'. The DNV and RSV have translated from an altered vocalization, *ʾal temer*, negative with the causative form of *mārā(h)*, i.e. 'do not rebel'.

6 : 31 (B) The MT reads the 3rd pers. masc. sing. impf. 'he shall make it'. The DNV on the basis of the LXX and a few Hebr. mss, has understood the 2nd pers. and rendered 'you shall make it'. In this case the vocalization remains the same but the initial *yod* is changed to a *tau*. The RSV retains the consonantal form of the text but reads a vocalization corresponding to the *niph.* 'shall it be made'.

7 : 11 (B) The word 'cubits' after the number 'hundred' is not found in the MT but for clarity it must be understood.

7 : 15 (B) The insertion of the word 'cubits' after the number 'fifteen' is completely in accord with the meaning of the text and is supported by the Samar and the LXX.

8 : 7 (B) The DNV understands the impf. form and translates 'must he be joined with'. This form is more suitable than the MT *ḥubbār* which is

also found in 39 : 4 where it does fit. The RSV translates 28 : 7 ‘that it may be joined together’ and 39 : 4 ‘joined to it’.

30 : 4 (B) The DNV and RSV understand *w*^{e}*hāyū* (plur.) ‘and they shall be’ instead of the sing. of the MT *w*^{e}*hāyā*(*h*) ‘and it shall be’. The plur. form is actually given in a few mss. and the Samar.

32 : 29 (C) Three textual problems are present in this verse. The first is found in the phrase ‘fill your hand today for the Lord’. This translation is a possible one (cf. the *Echter Bibel*, 1952), meaning ‘to fill the hand with a gift for the Lord’ (1 Chron 29 : 5). On the other hand, the translation ‘consecrate yourselves today to the Lord’ (AV) has support from 2 Chron 29 : 31. On the basis of ancient versions (LXX, Vg, Tg), the RSV has read the verb in the perf. form ‘you have ordained yourselves’, instead of the MT impv. form. This translation, as well as the DNV ‘be consecrated this day to the Lord’, is uncertain. The RSV rendering points to the act of ‘consecration’ as having been accomplished in the judgment that the sons of Levi carried out among the people, according to v. 28.

A second problem is found in the word *kī*, before the word *ʾīš* ‘one, man’, and in the prep. *b*^{e} before the words ‘son’ and ‘brother’. The DNV translates the *kī* as causal, and *b*^{e} in the sense of ‘against’, i.e. ‘because everybody was against his son and his brother’. The RSV has apparently omitted *kī* on the basis of the LXX and Pesh, and has taken the prep. *b*^{e} as the ‘*beth* of worth or value’, i.e. ‘each one at the cost of his son and of his brother’. Does this mean that the gifts with which one fills his hands for the Lord are his son and his brother (cf. the BS *même en sacrifiant votre fils et votre frère*)? Either the DNV or RSV translation is grammatically possible.

The third problem in the verse is related to the phrase ‘to give you a blessing today’. It is not clear from the Hebr who gives the blessing. The subject may be the Lord, who gives to the Levites the blessing of the priestly office, since they did not spare the members of their own families. Or the subject may be those ‘who fill their hand for the Lord’, and thus bring blessing upon themselves. The RSV makes the subject ‘God’, i.e. ‘that he may bestow a blessing upon you this day’ (cf. the AV), while the DNV is indefinite ‘and to bring you a blessing today’. The translation here depends upon the opinion one has formed of the behavior of the Levites in the context. The translation of the *Echter Bibel* is in the nature of a paraphrase. It is advisable to keep as close as possible to the Hebr text even though this does not make the translation fully comprehensible.

: 19 (B) The MT reads *tizzākār* 'shall be told' or 'remembered'. This does not lend itself to the context. Translations have generally understood the word as *hazzākār* 'the male' on the basis of the LXX, Th, Tg, and the Vg. The change affects one consonant and one vowel only.

LEVITICUS

: 17 (B) The verse begins *w*^{e}*ʾim nepeš kī* which means 'if anyone sins'. Since the MT is redundant it is better to read *w*^{e}*nepeš kī* (cf. 4 : 2). It is also possible to leave out the word *kī* and make the text like that of 4 : 27. This has no influence on the translation.

: 5 (B) The sing. noun *ḥămišitō* 'its fifth' should be read instead of the
MT 5 : 24) MT plur. *ḥămišita(y)w* 'its fifths'. The sing. is found in many mss, the Samar and Tg (cf. 5 : 16).

: 21 (B) The RSV word 'abomination' follows the MT *šeqeṣ*. However, since the verse has much in common with 5 : 2, the DNV has read the word *šereṣ* 'swarming creatures'. This translation is based on a few mss, the Samar, the Pesh, and Tg Onkelos.

: 47 (B) Instead of the asyndetical construction *l*^{e}*gēr tōšāb* it is preferable to read *l*^{e}*gēr ūltōšāb* 'a stranger or sojourner'. Support for this slightly altered reading is found in the Samar, the LXX, and other versions.

: 39 (B) The RSV follows the MT reading 'your enemies' lands'. The DNV, however, on the basis of numerous mss and the Samar understands the 3rd masc. plur. suff. 'their enemies' lands'.

NUMBERS

: 14 (B) The MT has *d*^{e}*ʿūʾēl* but in 2 : 14 *r*^{e}*ʿūʾēl*. Here is a further illustration of the confusion in mss of the *daleth* and the *resh* (cf. Gen 47 : 21 above). The RSV has followed the MT and thus has both spellings.

The DNV has chosen to follow the LXX which translates *r*ᵉʿ*ûʾēl* in all occurrences (1 : 14; 2 : 14; 7 : 42; 7 : 47; 10 : 20).

12 : 1 (C) There are two possible translations for the first part of the verse. The DNV has 'Miriam now spoke to Aaron about Moses in connection with the Cushite woman'. This would mean that they spoke together about the matter and not directly to Moses. Cf. v. 2 which may mean that Moses did not hear their jealous words though God did. The other possible rendering is that of the RSV 'Miriam and Aaron spoke against Moses' (cf. the AV).

14 : 11 (C) The translation 'by all the signs', or 'in all the signs' (cf. the DNV) is possible since signs are a means by which people may be encouraged to trust God. The RSV, on the other hand, has reproduced the meaning of the text well by rendering 'in spite of all the signs'.

21 : 14 (A) The Hebr is difficult to understand. First of all, the sign of the acc. *ʾet*, has no verbal predicate. Some versions have added a verb 'we took' or 'we reached', but these are only conjectures. By the use of dots in its text, the BSG assumes that something has dropped out of the Hebr before *Waheb* and after *Moab* (v. 15). A further question relates to the meaning of Waheb and Sufah. They are generally considered to be place-names, but one cannot be sure of their respective localities. Finally, one senses that the last two words should be in a construct relation, 'the valleys of the Arnon' (RSV), but 'valleys' is actually in the absolute state and is translated in that way in the DNV 'the valleys, the Arnon'. A reconstruction of the text is dubious, and thus one should simply "translate" the words that are there.

21 : 18 (C) Since, according to v. 16, Israel is in *Beer*, it is strange to read at the end of v. 18 'and from the wilderness they went on to Mattanah' (RSV). It is possible, however, that instead of being a place-name, *mattānā*(*h*) may be a noun meaning 'gift', derived from the root *nātan*. This would mean that the last two words of v. 18 *ūmimmidbār mattānā*(*h*) continue the song about the well. Thus, the translation of v. 18b would be:

'with the scepter and with their staves;
a gift from the wilderness'.

The translation fits the context, for a spring in arid land is nothing short of a 'gift'. If this translation is accepted, then the name Mattanah in v. 19a can remain unaltered; it should however, be understood as a parallel name to Beer in v. 16.

: 30 (A) The verse is full of difficulties. The first word *wannīrām* 'and we shot at them', is read as *nīnām* or *nīrām* by the LXX (= *sperma* 'seed, posterity', cf. 1 Kings 11 : 36). The RSV 'their posterity perished from Heshbon', follows the LXX. On the other hand, Heshbon may be understood as the subject of the verb *'ābad.* Some support for this possibility is found in the Samar which has the 3rd fem. sing. form of the verb, *'āb*^{e}*dā(h)*. In the second part of the verse, the word *wannaššīm* 'and they laid waste' has apparently been read *hannāšīm* 'the women' by the LXX, which has *hai gunaikes*. The word Nophah raises another question. Is it a place-name (AV)? Does it mean Nobach (cf. Judg 8 : 11)? The RSV on the basis of the LXX has evidently read *nuppaḥ 'ēš* 'fire spread' (literally, 'was blown'), in place of the MT *nōpaḥ 'ăšer* 'Nophah which'. The RSV has, however, retained the verbal form *wannaššīm* and translated this part of the verse 'and we laid waste until fire spread to *Med'eba*'.

: 10
, C) By conjecture the DNV reads *rib*^{e}*bōt* 'crowds' instead of the MT *rōbaʿ* 'a fourth'. Cf. 2 Kings 6 : 25 for the meaning 'a fourth part'. It is possible that *rōbaʿ* here in Num 23 : 10 is in some way connected with the Accad. *turbū'u* 'cloud of dust'. It would then be synonymous with *ʿăpar* 'dust' in the first part of the verse. An alternative translation therefore is 'dust clouds' mentioned in the RSV footnote. This translation deserves serious consideration. Near the close of the verse, the word *'aḥărīt* 'end', has been taken by the DNV, RSV, and other translations, as meaning 'end of life'. It is possible, however, that the LXX translation *sperma* 'seed' or 'descendants', gives the true meaning of the Hebr word here, and that the translation should be 'let my descendants be like his'. Jer 31 : 17 supports this translation.

: 21 (C) The question as to the subject of the 3rd masc. sing. verbs 'observed' and 'seen', has had no less than four varying answers. The most obvious subject in the context of this pericope is God. According to the Pesh. however, which reads the 1st pers. sing., the subject is Balaam. This is probably the easiest reading and can be readily explained. Still a third answer is furnished by the LXX, which understands 'trouble' and 'misfortune' as the subjects. Finally, it is possible to interpret the subject as impersonal, i.e. 'one'. Thus, 'one sees no evil in Jacob, one observes no trouble in Israel', because Yahweh himself is in the midst of his people. The DNV has translated the verse in this way. Likewise the *Echter Bibel* reproduces this interpretation clearly:

... nichts von Mühsal schaut man in Israel
Yahwe, ihr Gott, ist ja mit ihnen.

Cf. the *Zürcher Bibel* and the BSG for this interpretation also.

DEUTERONOMY

2 : 18 (C) Varying translations of this verse are the result of the following facts; the word *g^ebûl* can mean either 'territory' or 'boundary'; the verb *'ābar* may be rendered 'to travel through', or 'to cross'; and finally, the place name Ar can be interpreted as a parallel designation of Moab, or as a place on the border of Moab (cf. 2 : 9). Thus, the following translations are to be noted: the DNV 'today, you will cross the territory of Moab, namely Ar'; the RSV 'this day you are to pass over the boundary of Moab at Ar'; Steuernagel (*Das Deuteronomium*), *du wirst jetzt Ar, das Gebiet Moabs durchziehen*; and the BS *tu passeras aujourd'hui la frontière de Moab à Ar* (cf. also the *Afrikaans Bibel*). Consult the commentaries.

2 : 24, (B) In these two verses an impv. of the verb 'to begin' is followed by
2 : 31 an impv. of *yāraš* 'to take possession of'. Usually in Hebr the impv. of 'begin' is followed by an inf. (cf. 2 : 25). Therefore in v. 24 one is inclined to read *hāḥēl l^ehōrišō* (or *lōrišō*) 'begin to take possession' instead of the MT *hāḥēl rāš* 'begin, take possession'. In v. 31 it is possible to drop out *rāš* since there an inf. of the same verb follows the impv. 'begin'. The DNV and RSV have read the forms of *yāraš* in both verses as infinitives.

3 : 14 (C) The DNV translates 'Bashan' where it is found in the MT but prefixes the word 'namely' in an attempt to make the sentence clear. The RSV

translation implies that 'Bashan' is not in the right place since it has the phrase 'that is, Bashan', after the place-name Argob. Likewise Steuernagel (*op. cit.*, p. 62) says, '*ursprünglich wohl Glosse zu den ganzen Bezirk Argob*'.

16 (C) Two translation problems are present here. First, the words *min haggil'ād* can mean either 'from Gilead', or 'a part of Gilead' (partitive *min*). If 'a part of Gilead' is correct, the verse would agree with verses 12-13 which mention that the half-tribe of Manasseh also received a part of Gilead. A second problem is contained in the words *naḥal 'arnōn* and the word *g^ebūl* that follows later. The DNV (cf. the AV) has translated *naḥal 'arnōn* as 'the brook Arnon', and *g^ebūl* as 'border-land'. The RSV, however, translates these same words as 'the valley of the Arnon', and 'boundary'. Since the closing words of the verse indicate clearly that the brook Jabbok is the 'boundary' of the Ammonites, it may be that the verse is saying that the brook Arnon is likewise a boundary.

33 (C) The verse is parallel to 5 : 26 which reads 'the voice of the living God'. The adjective 'living' is absent in the MT of 4 : 33 but present in two Hebr mss as well as the LXX. Even without the adjective, however, it is obvious that 4 : 33 is speaking of the God whom Israel had come to know. Thus 'voice of God' is the translation of many versions (*Afrikaans Bibel*, BS, AV, Lu, and the *Dutch State Translation*). Notwithstanding this fact, the DNV, RSV and others, have translated here 'the voice of a god'.

37 (C) The Hebr reads 'and he brought you forth with his countenance' (cf. Ex 33 : 14). Some have felt that the word *pāna(y)w* 'his countenance', contains an allusion to the unusual presence of God in the pillar of cloud, but this is doubtful. The AV rendering 'in his sight' is not likely to be right, since in that case one would expect the prep. *l^e* not *b^e*.

The DNV has 'he himself has led you out of Egypt'; the BSG 'in his own person'; and the RSV 'with his own presence'. It would appear that a choice should be made from these three translations. Cf. the comments of Steuernagel (*op. cit.*, p. 69) who says that the countenance *ist seine Erscheinungsform und sein irdischer Repräsentant*.

4 : 42 (B) The MT reads *hā'ēl* which must be taken as a shortened form of the demonstrative pron. The same form is found in 7 : 22 and 19 : 11.

4 : 48 (B) The MT reads 'Sion'. Chap. 3 : 9, however, points to 'Sirion' as the correct reading here which is generally accepted.

5 : 10 (B) The MT consonantal text has a 3rd pers. sing. suff. which requires the sing. form for the word 'commandment'. The *Qere* reading of the Masoretes has the 1st pers. which is undoubtedly correct, being supported by the Samar, the LXX, and other ancient versions. Cf. Ex 20 : 6.

5 : 27 (B) The Hebr has a 2nd pers. fem. sing. personal pron. *weʾattᵉ*. However, *weʾattā(h)*, the 2nd pers. masc. sing. pron., should be read.

7 : 20 (C) The Hebr word *ṣirʿā(h)* is generally translated 'hornets' (cf. Ex 23 : 28; Josh 24 : 12). KBL does not mention this translation and instead renders the word as 'depression, discouragement'. The BSG understood the word as *ṣāraʿat* 'leprosy'.

10 : 4 (C) The DNV has interpreted the MT as meaning *kammiktāb hāriʾšōn* 'with the same handwriting as the first time'. This translation stresses the *method of writing* and this is a possible meaning (cf. Ex 32 : 16). The RSV rendering 'as at the first writing' agrees fairly well with the DNV. On the other hand, a comparison of Deut 10 : 4 with Ex 34 : 28 suggests that the *writing material*, or the *written text* on the new stone tablets, is the point of emphasis. Stone tablets were used the second time as at the first. This is the interpretation of the BSG in its clear rendering 'when the Lord had reproduced the former inscription on the tablets . . .', certainly a possible meaning.

11 : 24 (B) The Hebr reads 'from the wilderness and Lebanon'. It is obvious that the prep. 'to' should be inserted before 'Lebanon' (cf. the DNV and RSV).

15 : 9 (B) The DNV agrees with the RSV rendering 'base thought'. Similarly the *Echter Bibel* has *nichtswürdiger Gedanke*. The MT word order suggests literally 'a word with your heart belial'. In Hebr usage,

however, 'belial' is generally found immediately after the word with which it must be connected. 'Belial-word' then is 'base thought', and 'belial' itself is to be taken as 'baseness'.

: 1 (C) The 3rd masc. sing. suff. in the word *naḥălātō* 'his portion', has two possible antecedents. It can refer to Yahweh, i.e. 'the offerings by fire of the Lord and his inheritance' (DNV). This is probably the best interpretation. It has been understood, however, to refer to the tribe of Levi, i.e. the Levites shall eat the offerings by fire of the Lord which are his (i.e. their) inheritance. This second interpretation is favored by the LXX which translates 'their inheritance'. A choice should be made in translating even though it is somewhat difficult to recapture the original train of thought in this verse.

: 8 (C) The AV, DNV, and RSV are in essential agreement in translation at the close of the verse. The RSV renders 'besides what he receives from the sale of his patrimony'. While this has been the usual interpretation, Driver terms it as "nonsensical" (*Syria* 33, 1956, pp. 77f.). He cites the Code of Hammurabi which carefully distinguished between a man's own property and the property of his father's house which under no circumstances could be sold. In Babyl. the term is *makkūr bît abim* 'property derived by inheritance from his father'. Hence, here in Deut, Driver believes the meaning is "his patrimony shall not be reckoned in calculating what is due to him; he shall enjoy this as something additional."

: 3 (C) The first three words of the Hebr read *tākīn lᵉkā hadderek* which are translated in the RSV 'you shall prepare the roads'. The verb *kūn* in the *hiph.* form can mean 'to make ready', but it can also mean 'to fix the distance of (the road)'. Hence, the BSG renders 'you must so fix the distances'. Steuernagel (*Deuteronomium und Josua*, KHAT, 1900, pp. 71 f.) was apparently the first to propose this meaning. He suggested the translation *Miss dir die Entfernung ab* (cf. KBL who cites Steuernagel for this reference in Deut under the verb *kūn*). This meaning for *kūn* then, i.e. 'to fix the distance' is somewhat probable in this context.

: 8 (B) The RSV and DNV take the words 'the heart of his brothers' as the subject, even though the MT has the sign of the acc. just preceding the phrase. However, the translation is possible since the verbal form is pass. (*yimmas* is *niph.*). In such a construction the true subject can be introduced with the sign of the acc. If one prefers to take 'the heart of his brothers' as an object, the verb 'melt' must be taken as a causative, and, accordingly, the vocalization changed to *yāmēs*. The causative sense, which occurs in 1 : 28, was understood here by the ancient versions. The translation then becomes 'so that he does not melt the heart of his brothers'.

20 : 19 (C) The end of the verse takes on meaning only if it is read as an interrogative sentence. This means that, in the MT, the *h* before *'ādām* is to be taken as an interrogative particle, not as the definite article. The interrogative sense that is given in the DNV and RSV, is found also in the ancient versions (cf. also Steuernagel, *op. cit.*, p. 127). The RSV reads 'Are the trees in the field men that they should be besieged by you?'

21 : 4 (C) The MT *naḥal 'ē(y)tān* is rendered in the RSV by 'a valley with running water', and in the DNV 'valley, that always has water'. Another old translation needs to be considered, however, which is 'desolate, stony valley' (cf. the AV 'a rough valley'). The Vg has *vallem asperam et saxosam* (cf. the Tg).

21 : 14 (C) For the verb *hit'ammēr* 'to treat as a slave' (cf. the translations), one should consider the meaning 'to trade with' or 'to view as merchandise' (cf. VT 1951, pp. 219-221, and 1952, pp. 153 ff.). See also 24 : 7.

24 : 7 (C) See 21 : 14.

28 : 21 (C) The 3rd pers. masc. sing. suff. in the phrase *'ad kallōtō* can refer to the pestilence 'until it has destroyed' (DNV), or, to Yahweh, i.e. 'until he has consumed' (RSV, cf. AV).

28 : 22 (B) The MT has *ḥereb* 'sword'. The DNV, RSV, and many others have read *ḥōreb* 'drought'. The word 'drought' undoubtedly fits better with the types of punishment enumerated in this verse.

: 7 (C) The MT *qal* form *tābō'* followed by the prep. *'et* reads 'you shall enter with this people' (cf. the AV and RSV). From a grammatical point of view this translation can be supported. But a comparison of this verse with v. 23, where the causative *hiph.* form is found, i.e. *tābī'*, 'you shall bring', makes it apparent that the causative form may be the original form in 31 : 7. If so, then the prep. *'et* 'with' will naturally become the sign of the acc., and the translation will be 'you shall bring this people'. Several Hebr. mss and the Samar support this change in the MT of 31 : 7, though it is clear that the text makes sense without the change.

: 5 (C) Neither the DNV 'who are not his sons but a disgrace', nor the RSV 'they are no longer his children because of their blemish', are certain translations. Steuernagel (*op. cit.*, p. 166) alters the text. The train of thought in the verse may be as follows: if they have behaved perniciously, this does not apply to Him-it is not His fault; it is His children who have behaved disgracefully, and therefore, it is to their disgrace that they have not acted as His children. A translator can choose one of the above translations here: neither translation, however, is certain.

: 13 (B) The RSV has translated the MT exactly 'and he ate the produce of the field', the 'he' being Israel. The DNV following the LXX and Samar has translated the verb as though it were causative 'he (Jahweh) fed him the produce of the field'. In a somewhat parallel reference (Is 58 : 14) a causative form of the verb is used.

: 31 (C) The Hebr 'and our enemies judges' is somewhat elliptical. The DNV has 'our enemies may themselves judge', i.e. as to whether Israel's defeat was due to God's impotence or not. Actually, the Rock of Israel is all-powerful. Israel's enemies can compare the notes of their own history in this regard. Cf. the RSV and AV 'even our enemies themselves being judges' which agrees with the opinion of Steuernagel (*op. cit.*, p. 169) who says, *so müssen (selbst) unsere Feinde urteilen.*

: 2 (C) At the end of the verse, the DNV translation 'at his right side they saw a burning fire', is very dubious. The difficulty lies in the word *'ēšdāt*, which the AV (cf. Hebr text ed. Bombergiana) has understood as two words, *'ēš* 'fire', and *dāt* 'provision, regulation, law', i.e. 'from his right hand went a fiery law for them'. But to secure this rendering, the AV has had to supply the word 'went', which is not in the Hebr. More recently, an attempt has been made to explain *'ēšdāt* as an abstract plur. form from an old Arabic or Sabaean root *'sd* having the sense of 'strong ones' or 'warriors' (cf. the LXX 'angels'). Thus, A. F. L. Beeston (JTS, 1951, pp. 30-31, *Angels in Deuteronomy* 33 : 2) suggests the rendering 'and at his right hand angels that are His', or, 'at His right hand warriors thereof'. This implies that angelic beings are present at the coming of Yahweh. The RSV has translated 'flaming fire', but notes the reading as uncertain. Similarly, Steuernagel (*op. cit.*, p. 174) comments *unverständlich*.

33 : 3 (C) Both the DNV translation 'they sit down at your feet, catch some of your words', and the RSV rendering 'so they followed in thy steps, receiving direction from thee', are uncertain (Vg = *adpropinquant*). Cf. F. Stummer, *Bonner Biblische Beiträge I*, 1950, pp. 265-270. The RSV appears to be somewhat free in its translation, more than is necessary. Cf. the commentaries, especially König which the DNV has followed rather closely. Should *tukkū* be related to the verb *tākak*? Is the meaning 'to crouch' (cf. the French 'se presser')? *Non liquet* (the translation is doubtful)!

33 : 26 (C) Both the RSV and DNV render 'there is none like God, O Jeshurun'. This is the true translation of the MT vocalization *kā'ēl*. If one reads the vocalization *k^{e}'ēl*, the translation would be 'there is none like the God of Jeshurun' (cf. the ancient versions and the AV).

JOSHUA

4 : 24 (B) The Hebr reads 'that you may fear the Lord' (cf. RSV). However, in order to keep the MT vocalization, one must understand that there is a change in the subject of v. 24a and that of v. 24b. In 24a the subject is 'all the peoples of the earth' and, according to the MT pointing, the subject of 24b is 'you'. Yet, it would appear that the subject of both halves of the verse is the same. It is when all the peoples of the earth have learned to recognize the power of God that they will have learned to fear Him. If this then is the true sense of the verse, one must read not the MT *y^{e}rā'tem* but *yir'ātām*. The use of

the word *l*^{e}*maʿan* argues in favor of this different vocalization which lies behind the DNV translation 'so that they should fear the Lord your God'.

1 (B) The consonantal text reads 'until we were passed over' (cf. AV). The *Qere* reading of the Masoretes 'until they were passed over' is accepted by various ancient manuscripts as well as recent translations.

4 (C) The DNV rendering 'they set out upon their way as messengers', is simply an attempt to translate the Hebr word *wayyiṣṭayyārū*. A verbal form *ṣīr* is elsewhere unknown. However, on the basis of Is. 18 : 2, the verbal form in Josh 9 : 4 can be understood to be a denominative with the meaning 'to behave as ambassadors' (i.e. messengers). Cf. the AV 'made as if they had been ambassadors'. On the other hand, it is possible that the verbal form was originally *wayyiṣṭayyādū* (with a *daleth* in place of the *resh*), from *ṣīd* having the meaning here 'to supply oneself with provisions'. This is the reading that the LXX adopted. It would then parallel the description in v. 12 that presents the action of the Gibeonites in the first person. The RSV and others have accepted the LXX reading for v. 4 which does give an excellent meaning.

: 28 (B) The MT reads *ʾōtām*, the sign of the acc. with a plur. suff. Various mss have understood the sing. suff. *ʾōtāh̲* (cf. DNV). The RSV, on the other hand, has followed the text of some early versions which omit *ʾōtām* and the copula that follows. It is possible, however, that the plur. suff. of the MT can point to the following collective, i.e. *kŏl nepes*. The translation would then be 'he struck them (i.e. all living creatures who were within) with the ban'.

: 11 (C) The last two words are not clear. The word *nāpet* can be translated as 'elevation, high place', which in Josh 11 : 2 is found properly connected with Dor. Thus, the translation of the DNV (cf. also the AV). The RSV, however, in both 11 : 2 and 17 : 11 regards *nāpet* as a proper name. The LXX has evidently understood it in a similar way—at least it simply transliterates the name in both places. Mont-Gehm (*The Books of Kings*, ICC, 1951, p. 125), regards Naphath as a proper name. If it is, it may actually be a technical term for the territory that belonged politically to the town Dor, but this is not certain (cf. 11 : 2; 17 : 11; 12 : 23; 1 Kings 4 : 11).

JUDGES

1 : 16 (B) The sing. verbs in the MT 'he went and lived' can be taken as collectives and translated as plurs. as in the RSV and DNV. No alteration in the text is necessary.

1 : 19 (B) The RSV has 'he could not drive out'. The MT contains only the elliptical phrase 'but not to drive out'. In Josh 15 : 63 as well as in two mss of Judg 1 : 19 we actually find the verb *yākal*—'can, be able' used in a parallel reference. Therefore the translation in Judg 1 : 19 'he could not drive out' is a valid one.

2 : 3 (B) The MT reads 'for sides'. By altering only one consonant (*d* into *r*) the phrase becomes 'for opponents'. This is an ancient variation witnessed by the LXX, L, and Vg and it has been adopted by the DNV and RSV.

2 : 22 (B) For *lāleket bām* the DNV understands the prep. with the 3rd fem. sing. suff. *bāh* 'in it' referring to the 'way of the Lord' immediately preceding.

3:22, 23 (A) The exact meaning of the words *paršᵉdōn* and *misdᵉrōn*, is not known. Some have connected *paršᵉdōn* with the Accad. *parašdinnu* 'hole' or 'toilet'; others with the Hebr *pereš* 'the contents of the stomach' (not the 'intestines', cf. KBL). Therefore the RSV translation (cf. the AV) 'and the dirt came out', is not at all certain. The word *misdᵉrōn* may be a technical term for 'gallery' or 'vestibule'. It is rather striking that the last two words of v. 22 show a great deal of similarity to the first words of v. 23—the same verbal form, and the same ending for the substantive. In the light of this similarity, the DNV has taken Ehud as the subject of both verbs, and explained both *-ā(h)* endings as the locative or as denoting direction, expressing the places to which Ehud went forth.

5 : 2 (C) The first three words in Hebr are capable of two different trans-

lations. First, the RSV and others read 'that the leaders took the lead in Israel'. This translation has some support, in that the Hebr word 'leaders' is paralleled in Arabic by a word meaning 'a prominent man.' A second translation is found in the BSG and DNV 'when locks were worn loose in Israel'. This translation follows the meaning of the verb *pāraʿ* 'to allow to hang free', from which the noun *peraʿ* is derived meaning 'locks of hair hanging loose', i.e. not plaited or tied up (cf. KBL). It was customary in time of war for a soldier to let his hair grow until the battle was ended (cf. J. Pedersen, *Israel, its Life and Culture*, III-IV, 1940, p. 671).

5 (C) The words *ze(h) sīnay* have been reproduced in the DNV by 'even Sinai' (AV 'even that Sinai'). The RSV has 'yon Sinai'. The word *ze(h)* can be either a demonstrative pronoun 'this', or a relative pronoun 'those of'. The relative sense is seen to be possible by the use of *d̠*, equivalent of *ze(h)*, as a relative in Ugaritic (cf. Gordon, *Ug. Handb.*, I p. 31, and Albright, BASOR, 62, 1936, p. 30). The question remains, however, as to whether or not *ze(h)* is a relative in Judg 5 : 5.

7 (C) Should the translation be 'until I, Deborah arose' (DNV and AV), or 'until you arose, Deborah' (RSV)? The Hebr *qamtī* can be either 1st pers., or 2nd pers. sing. fem. The question is tied up with the problem as to whether Deborah composed this song herself, or whether it was written by some unknown singer. Cf. the commentaries.

13, (C) The word *baggibbōrīm* may be rendered 'as heroes' (DNV, BSG), understanding the prep. *bᵉ*, as the so-called '*b*-essential', or 'among the heroes', or even 'against the heroes' (cf. the RSV and AV). The *Zürcher Bibel* has *gleich Helden* in v. 13, and *unter den Helden* in v. 23.

15 (B) The MT reads 'and my princes in Issachar'. An old Jewish interpretation reads *sārē(y)* omitting the prep. before Issachar. The translation would then be 'also princes of Issachar'.

22 (B) The MT reads 'the Lord set every man's sword against his fellow, and against all the army' (cf. RSV). The cod. Vat. of the LXX omits the copula 'and'. On the basis of this version the DNV has translated

'the Lord set the sword of the one against the other in the whole camp'. The Hebr word *maḥăne(h)* can mean either 'army' or 'camp'.

9 : 31 (B) The MT reads *tormā(h)* which undoubtedly should be read *'Aruma(h)* as in v. 41.

9 : 44 (B) The Hebr reads 'companies' (plur.) but the context makes a sing. noun necessary. Abimelech has separated his men into three companies (9 : 43); one company remains with him while the other two companies take up positions elsewhere. The situation seen as a whole makes it preferable to read the sing. 'company' at the beginning of v. 44.

11 : 13 (B) Probably the word *'ōtāh* 'it' should be read for the MT *'eten* 'them', though it is possible that the word *'eten* (sign of acc. with plur. suff.) has been used because different parts of the country were in view.

11 : 19 (B) The Hebr reads 'let us pass . . . to my country'. Numerous mss read 'let me pass' which is also the rendering of the DNV. The RSV, however, reads 'our country' to parallel the plur. hortative.

11 : 26 (B) In verses 23, 24, and 25, the Ammonites are referred to by the use of the 2nd pers. *sing.* personal pron. 'you'. In v. 26, however, they are referred to in the *plur.* since the MT has the 2nd pers. plur. verb form *hiṣṣaltem*. Without change in the consonantal text this form can be vocalized to read *hiṣṣaltām*, 2nd pers. sing. with 3rd pers. plur. suff. The suff. then would refer to the towns and villages mentioned shortly before in this verse. This vocalization lies behind some of the ancient versions as well as the DNV and RSV. The RSV translates 'why did you not recover them?'

11 : 34 (B) On the basis of the context we should read 'beside her' instead of the MT 'beside him'.

12 : 7 (B) The MT literally reads 'in the towns of Gilead' which has no meaning here. Jephthah can obviously be buried in only one town (cf. the DNV). On the basis of the LXX, the RSV reads *'īrō* and

translates 'in his city in Gilead'. There is no point in trying to find the name of some town in the Hebr text.

: 2 (B) The MT has no finite verb at the beginning of the verse. The LXX supplies 'it was told', which is the basis of the DNV and RSV translations. The word *lēʾmōr* is a clear indication that a preceding verb dropped out of the Hebr text.

: 10 (C) The last two words of the verse 'and the Levite went', are rather strange in this setting, and are often omitted in translation (cf. the RSV). The DNV has taken the two words as the beginning of v. 17, and has attempted to translate them there, 'and the Levite came to the decision'.

: 30 (B) The MT reads 'Gershom, son of Manasseh'. In the text, however, the letter *n* in Manasseh is placed slightly higher than the other consonants of this word. Certain mss of the LXX and Vg omit the letter *n* and read the name as Moses and thus form the basis for the DNV and RSV translations. It is supposed that the change to the name Manassah was introduced later when men did not wish to connect the name of Moses with the priesthood of Dan. It should be added that the name 'Gershom' is associated with Moses, not with Manasseh.

: 15 (B) The MT followed by the RSV reads two sing. verbs 'and he went in and sat down'. However, since immediately preceding these sing. verbs there is a plur. verb and another plur. verb immediately after them, it is possible to translate the sing. verbs 'they went in and sat down'. The DNV does this on the basis of the LXX.

: 18 (B) The LXX and other translations, including the DNV and RSV, read 'my house' instead of the MT 'house of the Lord'. 'The house of the Lord' does not fit the context well, as may be seen by comparing v. 29.

: 19 (B) The Hebr has the plur. 'servants'. Thus the RSV 'and the young man with your servants'. But whom does the Levite mean by 'your servants'? Lindhagen, *The Servant Motif in the O.T.*, Uppsala, 1950, does not consider it necessary to read a sing. ('your servant') here because the plur. "can be used as a *commune*" (p. 57). In that case the text must mean 'and the young man whom we have with us', or something similar to this. The DNV, however, in keeping with many mss, the Vg, and Pesh has translated with a sing. 'your servant'. The Levite means himself. The plur. of the MT then could be viewed as the term used by the Levite "of himself and his concubine" (Lindhagen, *op. cit.* p. 57).

20 : 12 (B) Though the MT reads 'tribes of Benjamin', one should translate the sing. 'tribe of Benjamin'.

20 : 43 (A) The word *mᵉnūḥā(h)* 'resting place', is a problem in this context. The DNV has translated it 'restless', indicating that the pursuit was pressed against the Benjamites so that they had no time to rest. The RSV has followed cod. Vat. which has read not *mᵉnūḥā(h)*, but *min nōḥā(h)* 'from Nohah', thus a place-name. But this translation is far from certain.

20 : 48 (B) The Hebr phrase 'out of a town' gives no real meaning here and, accordingly, it is omitted by the DNV and RSV. The following word *mᵉtōm* is read *mᵉtīm* 'people' in many mss, which accounts for the translation 'men and beasts'. The word *mᵉtōm* appears in Is 1: 6, where it means 'soundness'.

RUTH

1 : 21 (B) The DNV following the MT translates *'ānā(h)* as 'testify against'. The RSV on the basis of the LXX, Pesh, and Vg has read an intensive form of the verb *'ānā(h)* having the meaning 'to humiliate, afflict' (cf. the RSV 'the Lord has afflicted me'). The difference is one of vocalization only.

2 : 7 (C) A literal translation of the last four words would be 'this her remaining at home little'. The DNV has attempted to follow the MT in translating 'she is someone who does not often remain at home', thereby understanding that the servant is praising Ruth for her dilligence and industry. The RSV translation 'without resting even for a moment', follows the LXX somewhat, i.e. 'she has not rested

in the field a little', as well as the Vg rendering which has 'she has not gone home even for a moment'. The main emphasis is clear: Ruth, the faithful gleaner, has been on the job all day long without a moment's rest.

4 (B) The MT reads 'and if he does not redeem'. It is not clear who is meant by the person 'he'. The whole context calls for a 2nd pers. sing. instead of a 3rd pers. This is the understanding of the LXX and many ancient versions, and so the phrase should be rendered 'but if you will not redeem'.

1 SAMUEL

5 (C) The translation of the phrase *mānā(h) 'aḥat 'appāyim*, is not certain. The dual form *'appāyim* means 'both nostrils' or 'anger' (neither meaning being applicable here), or sometimes 'face'. Hence the Hebr can be rendered literally 'one portion, (the portion), of the face'. Might 'the portion of the face' mean an extra share or a worthy portion? A further problem is contained in the word *kī*. Is its sense causative (DNV, AV), concessive (RSV), or something else? The entire phrase is translated 'double share' in the DNV (cf. 'a worthy portion' in the AV). This would mean that though God had not given any children to Hannah, this would be no occasion for Elkanah to neglect her, but rather demonstrate his love for her by giving her an extra share. One might compare Gen 43 : 34 where Joseph gives Benjamin a share five times larger than that of his brothers. Yet, this meaning in the Samuel passage is not at all certain. The RSV has apparently read the words *'epes kī*, in place of the MT *'appāyim kī*. The meaning then, would be that although Elkanah loved Hannah, he could give her only one share because she was childless. But since Peninnah had sons and daughters, she together with them received 'shares'.

5 (C) How may we understand the word *'ad*? It is possible to take it with the following phrase, i.e. 'even a barren one' (cf. the AV 'so that the barren'). It is likewise possible that it means here 'perpetual, forever', to be taken with the words that precede it, (i.e. 'but those who were hungry may rest for ever'. The antithetical parallelism of the verse favors this sense. Cf. the RSV 'but those who were hungry have

ceased to hunger', and the DNV 'but those who were hungry were allowed to rest'. The BSG translation 'while the hungry have ceased to toil' involves a textual alteration from the MT *'ad* to *'ăbōd* 'to toil'.

2 : 12, 13 (C) The DNV translation 'they paid no regard to the Lord, nor to the rights of the priests towards the people', implies two things. First, it suggests that the sentence of v. 12 ends in v. 13 after the word 'people', and then a new sentence begins. And second, it takes the word *mišpaṭ* 'right' as meaning that in Samuel's time there was a clear standard or law which stated exactly the priestly share in the sacrifices (cf. Deut 18 : 3 which mentions the rights of the priests in the sacrifices of the people). In a similar way the BSG has rendered 'they did not regard the Lord, nor the rightful dues of the priest from the people'. On the other hand, the RSV has understood *ūmišpaṭ* as beginning a new sentence, and has translated the word by 'custom' (cf. the AV). Since 'custom' is a regular meaning of the word *mišpaṭ*, the RSV translation must be considered to be possible. It reads 'The custom of the priests with the people was'.

2 : 14 (B) Instead of the MT *bō* 'in it' the word *lō* 'for himself' should be read (cf. the versions).

2 : 22 (C) The word *ṣōbeʾōt* is generally translated 'women who served'. Since the word can have also a cultic meaning, it is possible to translate it here as 'women who offered themselves'. Cf. the sacred prostitutes, such as were common in sanctuaries of the Ancient East, in connection with nature-worship and the cult of fertility. Cf. also Ex 38 : 8.

2 : 24 (C) What is the subject of the words *ma'ăbirīm 'am Yahwe(h)*? The DNV (cf. the AV) views 'the sons of Eli' as the subject and 'the people of the Lord' as the object. In this connection, it is not necessary to use the sign of the acc. before a direct object. The meaning, then, would be that the sons of Eli made the people of the Lord to break the law. The word *'ābar* means 'to cross a boundary, to trespass', thus, in the *hiph.* 'to cause to trespass'. The RSV and others, however, believe that the subject of the above phrase is 'the people of the Lord', i.e. 'it is no good report that I hear the people of the Lord spreading abroad'. Grammatically, there is no objection to this translation,

since *ʿābar* can have the causative sense 'to spread, scatter', and since *ʿam*, a collective noun, can be accompanied by a plur. part. As to the nature of the rumor, this translation can say only that it is not good.

29 (C) The word *māʿōn* 'habitation, dwelling', is difficult in this context. It can be regarded as an acc. of relation, as in the DNV 'why do you scorn my sacrifices and my offerings which I have prescribed in my house' (= with regard to my house). The RSV and others have vocalized the MT *māʿōn* as *meʿōyēn*, a denominative *poʿel* part. from *ʿayin* meaning here 'to look upon with an envious eye'. Thus the RSV translates 'why then look with greedy eye at my sacrifices'. Nevertheless, the MT as it stands has meaning, and a change in vocalization is not necessary.

31, (C) In v. 31, the DNV has translated *zāqēn* as 'old man' (cf. the AV and RSV). This means that in v. 33, the last word *'ănāšîm* should mean 'as men', i.e. at the age of manhood. The RSV has a footnote to this effect, yet it prints in its text, 'by the sword of men'. The word 'sword' has been inserted on the basis of the LXX and might be considered to make the verse read more smoothly in this context. A different interpretation, however, is that in v. 31, the word *zāqēn* means 'notable, elder', and that the word *'ănāšîm* of v. 33 has the sense of 'ordinary men'. This would mean that the judgment on the generation of Eli is not that they die by the sword, but that they die as ordinary men without becoming men of distinction.

19 (B) The remarkable *lālat* must stand for *lāledet* 'to give birth' (cf. the LXX).

18 (B) The Hebr reads *weʿad 'ābēl*. A literal translation does not make sense. If *'ābēl* is regarded as a substantive, it could mean 'water course', but this has no meaning here. The following adj. and the connected relative sentence lead one to think of some such word as *'eben* 'stone'. A large stone is mentioned in v. 15. From the standpoint of external witness, the reading *'eben* is supported by three Hebr mss as well as the LXX and the Tg. The word *weʿad* is likewise difficult. It should probably be vocalized to read *weʿēd* 'a witness'. Both of these proposed

readings have been accepted by the DNV and the RSV (cf. the RSV 'the great stone . . . is a witness').

9 : 24 (C) The Hebr word *wᵉheʿāle(y)hā* has usually been translated 'and what was upon it' (i.e. on the shank). At best, the translation is uncertain, since it involves a somewhat strange though not impossible construction of the article with the prep. *ʿal*. Because of this, some have accepted the reading of the Tg *hāʾalyā(h)* 'the fat tail', but this likewise is doubtful. The RSV 'the upper portion' is simply another guess.

9 : 25, 26 (C) At the end of v. 25 and at the beginning of v. 26, the Hebr reads 'and he spoke with Saul on the roof, and they arose early'. Since the MT is very clear as it stands, there is no need to follow the LXX and read with the RSV 'a bed was spread for Saul upon the roof, and he lay down to sleep'.

10 : 5 (C) The word *nᵉṣīb* is capable of several meanings. The DNV, AV, and RSV, have rendered it here as 'garrison', which translation is supported by other references (1 Sam 13 : 3 and 2 Sam 8 : 6, 14). The plur. form here in 10 : 5 could be explained in terms of the occupying forces. The word can also mean 'pillar' (cf. Gen 19 : 26) which might conceivably mean here a victory pillar which the Philistines erected in Gibeah. Still another possible meaning, in this context, is 'prefect' or 'captain', or more precisely the army 'brass' at the head of the Philistine occupation troops at Gibeah. Whatever its meaning, we find that the word was read in the sing. by the LXX, Pesh, and Vg.

12 : 11 (B) Instead of the MT 'Bedan' the DNV and RSV in agreement with the LXX and Pesh translate 'Barak', even though the sequence Jerubbaal, Barak, Jephthah, Samuel is not the order given in the book of Judg. Another suggested reading for Bedan is *ʿAbdon* (cf. Judg 12 : 13, 15). However, too little is known about him to consider his name as the possible original reading here.

13 : 1 (A) One can do little with this verse. Some have supposed that it contains two numbers, the first giving Saul's age when he became king, and the second, the length of his reign. This is what one would expect the verse to say. Both numbers, however, appear to be missing, and,

although in 1b there is the number 'two', yet, it fits neither his age nor the length of his reign. The RSV uses dots in its text to show the missing numbers, adding a footnote to this effect. Both the DNV and AV have attempted to make a connection between verses 1 and 2 by translating 'Saul reigned one year, and when he had reigned two years over Israel, Saul chose . . .' But this rendering is very uncertain in both parts. If it were the meaning, one would expect a different sentence construction with a more natural Hebr idiom.

The phrase *ben šānā(h)* 'one year old' or 'son of a year', has had two very ingenious explanations. Apparently Symm as well as Jewish tradition, took the expression as meaning that Saul was as pure as a one-year-old child when he became king. A second explanation proceeds to split up the three radicals of *šānā(h)*, the first one, *š*, standing as an abbreviation for 'year', and the second and third, *nh* indicating Saul's age, the numerical value of these two letters being 55. These explanations at best, are merely curious.

: 5 (B) The Hebr reads '30,000', followed by the RSV. A slight change produces the number '3,000' which is indicated in the LXX (ed. Lagardiana) and Pesh (cf. also the DNV). Both the number '3,000' and the following '6,000' fit the situation better. This is especially true if we translate *pārāšīm* as 'horses' rather than 'horsemen'. A detailed note about 'chariots and horses' is found in Mont-Gehm, *op. cit.*, pp. 82, 83. The question is disputed as to whether in the time suggested by 1 Sam 13, one can think of 'horsemen' as such. In any case, it is preferable to accept the number '3,000'.

: 21 (A) For a long time this verse remained unintelligible, but in recent years archeology has offered a clear solution to its problems. Cf. *The Bible Translator*, Jan 1950, pp. 14 f., where this verse is dealt with fully.

: 32 (C) The Hebr word *maʿădannōt* is rendered 'cheerfully' by both the DNV and RSV (BSG 'trembling', AV 'delicately'). The word has been associated with the stem *ʿādan* (cf. the noun *ʿēden* which means 'delight'). KBL prefers to translate 'hesitatingly, reluctantly' by presuming that the consonants *d* and *n* should actually be interchanged. This is probably the way the LXX and other versions read it (LXX *tremōn*—'trembling'). Nevertheless, the versions may not have interpreted the text correctly at this point. Is there possibly a connection with the verb *mā'ad*, to totter'?

17 : 12 (B) In the MT the phrase is found 'having come among the men'. This could mean that David's father now belonged to the most distinguished inhabitants of Bethlehem. A different reading, however, *baššānīm* gives the sense 'getting on in years, advanced in years'. This expression is found elsewhere in the OT. Both the DNV and RSV have accepted this meaning which among other versions has the support of the Pesh and an edition of the LXX. Still another possibility is to omit the word *bā'* of the MT on the theory of dittography. The translation would than be 'this man was an old man among the men'.

17 : 52 (B) For the MT *Gai* read *Gath* (cf. cod. Vat. of the LXX).

23 : 15 (C) The Hebr has 'and David saw, that', which by a slight vocalization change becomes 'and David was afraid because' (RSV). The change makes for greater meaning in the verse.

25 : 6 (C) The RSV has 'and thus you shall salute him' which agrees with the DNV, and is probably the best that can be done with the MT as it stands. The word *ḥay* in modern Hebrew means 'life', and thus, *leḥay* conveys the sense of 'your health'. Some suggest that the form should be *le'āḥī* 'to my brother', but this change is not necessary.

26 : 4 (C) The translation of *'el nākōn* is uncertain. If *nākōn* is a place name, its location is not known. The word can be taken as a *niph.* part. from *kūn*, meaning 'definite' or 'certain'. Thus, it could mean that Saul had definitely come (DNV, AV), or that David had come to know with certainty that Saul had come (RSV). Either sense is possible.

2 SAMUEL

1 : 9 (C) A question surrounds the meaning of *šābāṣ*. Does it mean 'cramp', or 'weakness', in that all the resistance is gone? The DNV has 'dizziness' and the AV and RSV 'anguish', and still others translate it by

'confusion'. An interrelated question is the meaning of the word *kī* that follows, which can have the sense of 'because', or 'yet', or 'but'. Some believe that *kī* should be rendered 'because', feeling that several words are missing from the end of the verse, the statement of Saul thus remaining unfinished. The translation in this case, would be 'because as long as I live . . .', the missing words perhaps being 'the Philistines will not touch me'. This would mean that Saul intends to say that he will not fall into the hands of the Philistines.

18 (C) The DNV translation 'song of the bow', is only a conjecture, since the Hebr text has simply the word *qešet* 'bow'. Since the word occurs in the song (v. 22), does its use in 1 : 18 form a kind of title for the lamentation? This is a possibility. Another explanation of 'to teach the sons of Judah the bow' is that it means 'to urge them to behave in a soldierly, or martial way' (cf. VT 5, 1955, pp. 232-235). On the basis of the LXX, the RSV has omitted *qešet* in 1 : 18.

12 (C) The *Kethib* reads *taḥtō* and the *Qere tahtā(y)w*. The word can be a noun, meaning 'place', or a prep. meaning 'under'. If it is a noun here, it might mean 'David's place' (literally 'his place'), or it might have the sense the DNV has given to the whole introductory clause, 'then Abner sent messengers to David at the place where he was'. This translation is somewhat dubious partly because it expresses a self-evident truth. Abner certainly would not send messengers to David to a place where David was not! If, on the other hand, the word is connected with Abner, it could have a prepositional sense. The meaning would then be that 'Abner on his part sent messengers to David', or, 'then Abner sent messengers in his place, to David', literally, 'messengers under him', i.e. 'under his order'. The RSV has chosen to follow one recension of the LXX and translate 'Hebron', i.e. 'and Abner sent messengers to David at Hebron'. This makes for a smooth reading in the context, since, according to verses 2, 5, 19, 20, David was at Hebron at this time. What the RSV translation does not do is explain the difficulties of the Hebr text.

8 (C) The DNV reads 'whoever will defeat the Jebusites, must force a way in by the water course; David has a vigorous aversion to the lame and the blind'. The crux of the difficulty is the meaning of *ṣinnōr*

in this context. It can mean 'water shaft' (cf. the RSV and DNV), a shaft leading from the well of Maria (the Gihon well) to the surface of the hill. David would thus be referring to a secret shaft entrance into the city. Excavations have unearthed such a shaft, and it is conceivable at least, that this verse in Samuel is to be connected with it. If this explanation is accepted, then the verb form of *nāgaʿ* that precedes the word *ṣinnōr*, can be translated, 'to force a way in' (cf. the DNV). It is scarcely possible, however, to force a way into a city by a water course. Possibly the translation could be 'whoever will defeat the Jebusites, must reach (i.e. 'seize' or 'conquer') the water course'. Another possible translation for *ṣinnōr* is 'throat' or 'gullet'. In this case, *nāgaʿ* could have the meaning 'to seize', and the translation could be 'whoever will defeat the Jebusites must seize (them) by the throat'. And still a third possibility is that *ṣinnōr* means a 'weapon', such as a 'trident', and that *nāgaʿ* means 'to strike'. Hence the translation, 'whoever will defeat the Jebusites must strike the blind and the lame with his trident'. In this case, *nāgaʿ* is construed with an acc., which, though unlikely, is not impossible. The RSV, though agreeing with the DNV in the translation 'water shaft', differs from the DNV in rendering the next phrase 'to attack the lame and the blind, who are hated by David's soul'.

6 : 3, 4 (B) The MT is difficult. In the first place it repeats (probably through dittography) the clause, 'and they brought it up out of the house of Abinadab which was in the hill'. In the second place it is not easy to fit the phrase of v. 4, 'with the ark of God', into the context. The DNV and RSV have met these difficulties by translating primarily from cod. Vat. which omits the last word of v. 3 'new', as well as the first part of v. 4 up to the words 'with the ark'. The BSG has gone further and supplied the words 'Uzza was walking' at the beginning of v. 4.

6 : 7 (C) The Hebr *ʿal haššal* is rendered in the DNV 'because of this thoughtlessness' (AV 'for his error'). The translation is uncertain though it has the support of the L *pro ignorantia*. The parallel passage in 1 Chron 13 : 10 is textually clearer and more detailed, and for this reason, the RSV has adopted the text of the Chron passage here in 2 Sam. In doing so, however, the remarkable character of the text

of 2 Sam is lost. It is perhaps best, then, to keep to the uncertain translation 'thoughtlessness'.

19 (C) The word *'ešpār* has been rendered 'piece of meat', but this is uncertain. KBL translates 'date cake', and compares it with the Arabic *sofrat* 'provision'. Cf. also Dalman, *Arbeit und Sitte in Palästina* IV, 1935, p. 68, from which it appears that *'ešpār* could mean a kind of cake.

23 (B) The word *lāhem* 'for them' should be read instead of the MT *lākem* 'for you'. Since the context refers to Israel in the 3rd pers., the 2nd pers. suff. is unlikely. Furthermore, in this direct address of David to God it is far more appropriate for the nation to be referred to in the 3rd pers. The word *lāhem* is also understood by the Tg and Vg.

1 (C) The AV and RSV have transliterated the words *meteg hā'ammā(h)*, thereby regarding them as a proper name. It is possible, however, that the word *meteg* which as a noun means 'rein, bridle', has the metaphorical sense here of 'power' or 'government', or 'control'. While the word *'ammā(h)* basically means 'yard' or 'cubit', it could possibly mean here 'mother city' or 'fortification'. Thus, the DNV translates the phrase 'the government of the capital', and the BSG 'the bridle of the mother city'.

13 (B) The MT reads the name 'Aram', though six mss, the LXX, and the Pesh read 'Edom'. On the basis of the context in v. 14 and the parallel account in 1 Chron 18 : 12, 'Edom' is clearly the preferred reading in this place. The difference is the well-known change between the *daleth* and the *resh* (cf. above in Gen 47 : 21 and Num 1 : 14).

: 31 (A) Three different words cause some difficulty in this verse. The verb *śīm* ordinarily means 'to lay, place, put', but here, it probably means 'to appoint to' or 'to set to'. Thus, the people were not 'put under' saws and picks' (AV), but they were 'set to work' with saws and picks, i.e. forced labor. The second problem is contained in the *Kethib* reading *malkēn* or *milkōn*, which has no meaning here. One should adopt the *Qere* reading *malbēn* to be translated 'brick kilns' (cf. the AV and RSV). And finally, the word *he'ěbīr* 'he made (them) to pass over' (or

4

'through'), which is retained by the AV and the DNV, is altered in the RSV to read *heʿĕbīd* 'he made (them) toil'.

14 : 4 (B) According to the first word of the MT *wattōʾmer* 'and she spoke', the woman is described as speaking to the king before falling down in obeisance before him. Many mss and versions (cf. also the DNV and RSV) avoid this unnatural sequence by understanding the first word as *wattābōʾ* 'and she entered'. The fact that the word *wattōʾmer* comes later in the verse is a further argument for this change. The RSV does not indicate that it has deviated from the MT in its translation.

15 : 7 (B) The 'forty years' of the MT can hardly be correct. The problem is solved by adopting the reading 'four years' found in the Pesh and the LXX (ed. Lagardiana). Only a slight change is involved.

15 : 27 (C) The simple interrogative sentence here in Hebr does not indicate whether a negative or positive answer is expected, i.e. 'are you a seer'. The AV has introduced a negative in italics to show that a positive answer is expected, i.e. 'art not thou a seer'. The DNV renders 'you are surely a seer', while the BS views the word *rōʾe(h)*, not as a noun, but as a true part. 'do you see' (= *comprends tu*). The RSV has chosen to follow the LXX and read the part. as an impv. 'look'.

15 : 31 (B) The MT *hiph.* verb in an *active* sense, *higgīd* 'and he reported', is ruled out by the context. David does not give but rather receives information. There are two possible solutions:

1. Take the construction as impersonal, i.e. 'and as for David, they told him' = 'and it was told David'.
2. Follow the suggestion of the LXX tradition and actually read the verb as a *hoph.* i.e. *ūldāwīd huggad* 'and it was reported to David'.

17 : 9 (C) The Hebr word *bāhem* together with the verb *nāpal* can be translated in two different ways. The DNV understands the prep. *bᵉ* as construed with the preceding inf. of *nāpal* meaning 'to take by surprise', i.e. 'if he takes them by surprise'. The other possibility is given by the RSV translation 'when some of the people fall', which understands the prep. *bᵉ* as independent of the verbal construction. The phrase

'some of the people' can be taken as a translation of *bāhem* (literally 'among them'), and *not* as an alteration of the text into *bā'ām* 'among the people'.

: 20 (C) The AV, DNV, and RSV, read 'they have gone over the brook of water'. However, the meaning of *mīkal* translated as 'brook' is uncertain. Some have suggested that the word should be read *mikkō(h) 'el* 'from here unto', thus making the translation 'they have gone away from here unto the water'.

: 25 (B) On the basis of 1 Chron 2 : 17 the word 'Ishmaelite' should be read here instead of 'Israelite'.

: 3 (B) The Hebr has 'but now'. Without doubt the MT *'attā(h)* 'now' should be changed to *'attā(h)* 'you' on the basis of ancient versions including cod. Vat. and cod. Alex. of the LXX. Probably the MT 'now' can be explained as influenced by the 'now' that is found four words later in the verse. The change suggested by the versions makes the verse meaningful as is seen in the RSV rendering 'but you are worth ten thousand of us'.

: 12 (B) The MT *šimrū mī* can be translated 'protect, whoever it may be, (the young man Absalom)'. Some mss, the LXX, Tg, etc. read *šimrū lī* 'for my sake protect'. The alteration is not necessary.

: 13 (C) The *Kethib* reading, followed by the RSV, suggests the translation 'if I had dealt treacherously against his life' (*napšō*). The Masoretes, however, preferred the reading *napšī*, thus 'to deal treacherously at the risk of my life' (cf. the RSV margin).

: 14 (C) The word *'ōḥīlā(h)* from *yāḥal*, is translated in the DNV and RSV by 'I will not waste time like this with you'. But it is possible to read a different vocalization, i.e. *'āḥēllā(h)* from *ḥālal* 'to bore, pierce', which would produce the translation 'I will pierce him in your presence' (cf. the RSV margin).

: 18 (C) The first two words of the MT read literally 'the ford crossed', which
T, obviously cannot be right. Neither can one accept the AV translation
: 19) 'and there went over a ferry boat', since *'ăbārā(h)* does not mean 'ferry

boat'. Since, however, in the preceding verse, there is a plur. verb with a plur. subject, it is quite possible that the verb at the beginning of v. 18 (MT 19), should be changed to a plur. instead of being a sing. as it is in the MT. The reading would thus become *wᵉʿābᵉrū hāʿăbārā(h)* 'and they crossed the ford' (RSV).

21 : 8 (B) In place of the MT 'Michal' two mss and the LXX (ed. Lagardiana) read correctly 'Merab'. Also the Pesh seems to suggest the reading 'Merab'. It is true that Michal was one of David's wives, yet, the connection of the wife named here with Adriel the Meholathite shows definitely that *Merab*, sister of Michal, is meant (cf. 1 Sam 18 : 19).

23 : 20 (C) Two textual problems confront us here. First, the *Kethib* reading *'īš ḥay* should probably be read *'īš ḥayil* 'a valiant man' (cf. the AV and RSV). A second problem is present in the words *šᵉnē(y) 'ărī'ēl* rendered 'two great heroes' in the DNV, but left untranslated in the RSV, i.e. 'two ariels'. Can it mean 'lion of God' (cf. the AV 'two lionlike men')? Or, is *'ărī'ēl* a proper name? We simply do not know. The LXX has 'the two (sons of) Ariel'. Cf. the lexica and commentaries, and also 1 Chron 11 : 22 where additional facts are given.

24 : 6 (C) The words *taḥtīm ḥŏdšī* are transliterated as a place-name in the AV. If this is correct, the location is unknown. On the basis of one recension of the LXX, the RSV has suggested 'and to Kadesh in the land of the Hittites', BSG (more probable) 'and to the land of the Hittites, to Kadesh'.

1 KINGS

4 : 28 (C) (MT, 5 : 8) There is a certain vagueness in the expression *'ăšer yihye(h) šām* which might mean 'to the place where it should be', or, 'to the place where it was required'. The subject of the verb *yihye(h)* is not clear. It could be the king ('where he, i.e. the king, would be'), or, which is more likely, the subject could be the word *'īš* that follows, i.e. 'to the place where, according to the regulation he had received, everybody ought to be'. The AV has supplied 'officers' as the subject, thereby making a connection with the officers of v. 27.

6 : 6 (B) The MT has *yāṣīăʿ* (*Qere*). This word is found also in v. 5 where the

DNV translates it as 'building' (cf. the RSV). This meaning does not suit the beginning of v. 6, where, in keeping with the context and in agreement with the LXX, we should read the word *ṣela*' 'story' (cf. the RSV). The word *ṣela*' is also found at the end of v. 5. Apparently *yāṣīăʿ* and *ṣelaʿ* were occasionally confused.

9 (A) One cannot be certain of the meaning of the words *gēbīm* and *śᵉdērōt*. The DNV has 'compartments and rows'. It is clear that the verse is concerned with roof construction, and thus the words in question may be technical building terms. A translation 'rows' for the word *śᵉdērōt* is possible, for in 2 Kings 11 : 8, 15, the same word is used to mean 'ranks' (cf. Mont-Gehm, *op. cit.*, p. 419, and the RSV translation 'ranks' in the two verses in 2 Kings). Thus, here in 1 Kings 6 : 9, the word *śᵉdērōt* may denote the all-important ceiling joists or beams that are stretched out in parallel 'rows' from one wall to the opposite side, thus criss-crossing the parallel rows of joists that span the other two walls. The *gēbīm* could then be the various 'compartments' (DNV), or 'hollow squares' or 'coffers' (Mont-Gehm, *op. cit.*, pp. 146, 149), that are formed by the intersecting rows of beams. Literally translated, the Hebr reads 'he made a ceiling in the house, compartments and rows, of cedar wood'. The prep. that is joined to the word 'cedar wood', should be construed with the verb. The RSV translates 'he made the ceiling of the house of beams and planks of cedar'.

12 (B) The second part of this verse is difficult. It is missing from certain recensions of the LXX. Is a distinction made in the text between the large outside court and the inner court? The DNV renders 'vestibule of the house' but places the words between square brackets. Some translators believe that the final word 'house' refers not to the temple, but to the palace. The RSV gives a literal rendering, but actually it is not clear whether both the inner court and the vestibule have three courses of stones.

17 (B) At the beginning of the verse, the DNV and the RSV along with other translations make the addition 'and he made two'. The addition has the support of the LXX.

8 : 31 (B) Instead of *'et* at the beginning, read *'im*. The sentence then becomes conditional 'if . . .' (cf. 2 Chron. 6 : 22).

9 : 18 (B) The final word of the verse is to be rendered 'in the land'. Its ambiguity has led the translators of the DNV to put the translation in brackets. The RSV has attempted to clarify the Hebr by translating 'in the land of Judah' (cf. the RSV in 1 Kings 4 : 19). Ancient versions likewise felt the difficulty of the Hebr. According to Mont-Gehm, however, the Hebr is clear: 'in the land' is merely "the native expression for the homeland," i.e. Judah (*op. cit.* pp. 122, 208). In this sense the Hebr is sufficient as it is.

A second difficulty in the verse lies in the place name *Tamar* (cf. Ezek 47 : 19; 48 : 28). The parallel in 2 Chron 8 : 4 reads *Tadmor* which was named in Greek *Palmyra* (*Tadmur* is the modern Arabic name for the ruined site). The preference of the Masoretes in the passage here in 1 Kings is for *Tadmor* as seen in the *Qere* reading (cf. also the Vg *Palmiram*). If Mont-Gehm is right, however, in asserting that 'in the land' = 'in the homeland', then Tamar is the better reading, to be identified with Ḳurnub, south-east of Beersheba (Mont-Gehm, *ibid*).

10 : 12 (A) The meaning of the word *mis'ād*, generally translated 'supports', or 'pillars', is unknown. The parallel verse in 2 Chron 9 : 11 has *m^{e}sillōt* usually translated 'steps'. This translation is likewise uncertain. The fact that *mis'ād* is to be related somehow to the verb *sā'ad* 'to support', does not solve the problem (cf. Mont-Gehm, *op. cit.*, pp. 219, 229).

10 : 22 (C) The RSV translates 'peacocks' with an alternative reading in the margin 'baboons'. It is probable that the last two words of the verse indicate two types of monkeys (cf. Mont-Gehm, *op. cit.*, pp. 224 f.).

11 : 24 (B) The RSV translation 'made him king' implies a *hiph.* form with suff. instead of the MT *qal* form 'they ruled'. Either translation can fit the context. Another possibility is to read the three verbal forms at the end of v. 24, each in the sing., with Rezon as the subject, 'he went to Damascus, settled there, and became king in Damascus'.

: 2 (B) At the close of the verse the MT reads ‘and Jeroboam lived in Egypt’. The reading is doubtful for two reasons: first, it introduces an awkward repetition since Jeroboam’s residence in Egypt has just been cited, and second, the parallel passage in 2 Chron 10 : 2 suggests what is undoubtedly the correct reading here ‘and he returned from Egypt’. This reading requires two slight changes in the MT of 1 Kings 12 : 2. First, the verbal form should be vocalized as a derivative of *šūb* ‘to return’ instead of a form of *yāšab* ‘to dwell’. The consonants remain unchanged. In the second place, the prep. *min* ‘from’ should be read in the place of *bᵉ* ‘in’. The Vg and cod. Alex. of the LXX are external witnesses for these changes which have been accepted by the DNV and the RSV.

: 11 (B) The MT has at the beginning of the verse ‘his son came and told him’, but at the close ‘they told to their father’. The context shows that the versions (the LXX, Pesh, and Vg) are correct in reading the plur. noun ‘his sons’ and plur. verbs ‘came’ and ‘told’. The DNV and RSV have accepted the versional renderings.

: 12 (B) The MT *qal* verb ‘they saw’ in this context should be vocalized as a *hiph.* with the 3rd masc. sing. suff. added to form the word *yar’ūhū* ‘they showed him’. This change is supported by the LXX, Tg, and Vg, as well as by the DNV and RSV.

: 10 (C) The words *‘āṣūr* and *‘āẓūb* are both pass. participles that occur together in this same order several times, e.g. Deut 32 : 36. The RSV renders ‘both bond and free’, while the DNV has ‘from high to low’. It is fairly certain that the two terms are meant to be all-inclusive, denoting everybody without exception. Various other suggested translations are; ‘unborn (shut up in the womb) and born’ (J. Lewy, *Hebrew Union College Annual*, 1937/38, pp. 99 ff.); *Unmündige und Mündige* (E. Kutsch, VT, Vol. II, 1952, pp. 57 ff., 60 ff.); ‘a helpless and worthless person’ (P. P. Saydon, VT, 1952, pp. 371 ff.). Mont-Gehm (*op. cit.*, p. 272) sense the difference in the two terms to be the difference between ‘the gentleman and the boor in the street’. This is a possible conclusion, quite similar to ‘high-born and low-born’, but the explanation seems a little strained. The BSG has attempted to adhere to the Hebr by translating ‘him that is shut up and him that is left at large’, but it is questionable whether *'āzab* can mean 'to leave at large'.

14 : 14 (A) The last five words of the Hebr text are difficult. Various attempts at explaining them are listed in Mont-Gehm (*op. cit.*, p. 272), which itself proposes the translation 'today and at once'. The DNV has turned the phrase into a question, i.e. 'this today, and what then', but the RSV suggests that while the word 'today' belongs with v. 14, the words 'and henceforth' actually begin the following verse. No translation is basically certain.

16 : 11 (B) The sing. form *rē'ēhū* in the MT can be understood in a plur. sense. No textual change is needed (cf. 1 Sam 30 : 26).

16 : 31 (B) The MT has an interrogative particle and reads literally 'and it happened, was it too little'. The LXX conveys no sense in this context 'and it was not fitting to him'. Probably the interrogative particle should be interpreted in a conditional sense 'as if it had been a light thing' (RSV). Mont-Gehm (*op. cit.* p. 291) believe that textual change is unnecessary.

17 : 1 (B) In place of the MT 'from the settlers of Gilead', the LXX has indicated that the text should read 'from Tishbe in Gilead' (cf. the RSV). The difference is one of vocalization only.

17 : 3 (C) The phrase *'al pᵉnē(y) hayyardēn* is rendered 'east of the Jordan' in the RSV, but this is not certain. Mont-Gehm (*op. cit.*, p. 294) has 'in front of the Jordan'. The DNV rendering 'which empties into the Jordan', has much in its favor since the wadi in question is identified in many places.

18 : 4 (B) Probably a second 'fifty' has been omitted by haplography. Three facts make this quite certain. First, the MT would imply that Obadiah hid only fifty of the hundred prophets instead of the full one hundred as is indicated in v. 13. Second, v. 13 has the double 'fifty' in a passage parallel to v. 4. In the third place the LXX has a distributive sense in v. 4 as it does in v. 13, i.e. 'by fifties'. This could only be possible if the translators understood 'fifty fifty' as the actual text of v. 4. The RSV translates 'by fifties' in both verses.

: 21 (C) The RSV renders 'go limping with two different opinions'. Most scholars interpret the Hebr as meaning 'to limp on both sides', thus, Mont-Gehm (*op. cit.*, p. 301) believe that the AV expresses the sense well, but add, "more exactly it means 'hopping now on one leg, now on the other, before the dilemma'."

: 34 (C) The DNV understands that Benhadad is the speaker throughout, and that the last part of the direct speech should be translated 'and I myself may bid you farewell with an alliance'. While possible, a change in speakers in the verse is likewise possible. Thus the AV and RSV understand that Ahab is the speaker in the final part of the conversation, the RSV translating thus, 'and Ahab said, "I will let you go on these terms" '.

If this is accepted as the rendering of the conversation, a translator must make it clear that Ahab is the speaker. The AV and RSV have done this.

: 32 (C) Instead of 'they called', or, 'they said', it is possible to translate, 'they thought'. The verb *'āmar* can mean either 'to say' or 'to think'.

2 KINGS

13 (B) The MT has the plur. *š^{e}lišīm* referring to the word 'fifty' (cf. the RSV 'captain of a third fifty'). The DNV, however, following the witness of the LXX (ed. Lagardiana), the Vg has understood a sing. form *š^{e}liši* 'a third' and applied it to the word 'captain', i.e. 'a third captain of fifty'. Cf. 1 Sam 19 : 21 where the Hebr *mal'ākīm š^{e}lišīm* can be translated 'a third group of messengers'.

13 (C) The Hebr phrase *'el gerem hamma'ălōt* is rendered freely in the DNV 'on the steps of the staircase'. The basic difficulty is the meaning of *gerem*. While the word means 'bone', in Aram. it came to replace the reflexive pron. If the reflexive sense is present here, one can translate 'on the steps themselves' (cf. Rashi 'on the very stairs', and the RSV 'on the bare steps'). This would mean that in their enthusiasm, the followers of Jehu threw their garments on the very steps where he stood. Mont-Gehm (*op. cit.*, pp. 404 f.), believe that *gerem* is an architectural term, but give no definite translation. The ancient

versions offer no help. At best, the meaning of *gerem* is uncertain.

11 : 6 (C) The translation of the last word *massāḥ*, is uncertain. The LXX, followed by the RSV, has omitted the word in its translation. Other ancient versions have viewed the word as a derivative of the verb 'to break away', but they give no acceptable translation. The KBL and others support the view that the word ties in with the Arabic verb *nasaḫa* 'to replace'. The form *massāḥ*, then, would mean 'replacement, relief, by turns' (cf. the DNV 'in turn'). While this explanation is not air-tight, still it is possible, and gives meaning to the verse. Furthermore, simply to omit the word as the LXX and RSV have done, means following the line of least resistance.

11 : 11 (C) At the close of the verse, the Hebr reads 'around the king'. The RSV and others have omitted the phrase, possibly because the king (i.e. 'the king's son') does not appear until v. 12. But there is no reason to omit anything, for, as Mont-Gehm comment, "the reference to the king's presence (i.e. in v. 12) may well be anticipative" (*op. cit.*, p. 420).

14 : 28 (A) The words *līhūdā(h) bᵉyisrā'ēl* are troublesome. Apparently the writer is indicating that Jeroboam of the northern kingdom Israel recovered the territory of Damascus and Hamath. But what has this to do with Judah, the southern kingdom? Some attempt to escape the problem by omitting any reference to Judah. Nevertheless, 2 Sam 8 shows that Hamath and Damascus were related to David sometime during the period of the united monarchy. It is possible, then, that the annotation here in 2 Kings 14 : 28 refers to this historical fact. Accordingly, the DNV and RSV (cf. also the AV) arrive at the translation 'which had belonged to Judah' for the word *līhūdā(h)*. However, the explanatory words 'which had belonged' should be indicated by using round brackets, as the DNV does. But a difficulty still remains in these translations. They indicate that David had conquered both Hamath and Damascus, and this point is not clear in 2 Sam 8. The reference in Samuel implies that Hamath and Damascus were related to David differently. Damascus, which was located much closer to Judah, was occupied by David's armies, and he stationed garrisons there. This, however, is not said of Hamath. The text of 2 Sam 8

reveals only that David accepted tribute from Hamath. Thus, in 2 Kings 14 : 28, the RSV and DNV translations are not certain.

C. H. Gordon in his *Introduction to Old Testament Times*, 1953, p. 209, suggests the translation 'from Jehudah to Israel', believing that Jehudah was a far-off kingdom in northern Syria. But this introduces confusion between a non-Israelite kingdom and Judah.

: 15 (C) The RSV renders the close of the verse 'but the bronze altar shall be for me to inquire by' (cf. also Mont-Gehm, *op. cit.*, p. 461). The phrase 'to inquire by' is the translation of the word *lᵉbaqqēr*. The verb *bāqar* has various meanings, such as to 'split, break through, appear, inspect thoroughly, be concerned about, let one's thoughts go over'. Does the text then mean that Ahaz will consider what he will do with the brazen altar, or that he will use the altar for consultation with someone or with something? A clear decision cannot be made here. Mont-Gehm (*ibid*) believe that "the primary meaning of the verb (*biqqēr*) is the examination of the sacrifice for omens." The altar, then, would be a kind of source object for procuring oracles.

: 11 (C) The word *parwārīm* has been variously rendered: DNV 'buildings on the outside', RSV 'precincts', AV 'suburbs'. In Aram at a later date, a word *parwārāʾ* appears, meaning 'suburb', or 'space', or 'strip around a town'. But care must be exercised in using a later Aram word to decide the meaning of the verse here. The translation 'precincts' is likewise uncertain.

Oestreicher (*Das deuteronomische Grundgesetz*, 1923, p. 54) believes that the word belongs to the sing. form *parbār* (1 Chron 26 : 18), and that *parbār* is the equivalent form of the Sumerian *barbar* 'the white house', the name for a sun temple in Sippar and elsewhere. While it is true that sun worship is found in 2 Kings 23 : 11, there are serious philological objections to Oestreicher's explanation. The connection made by KBL between *parwārīm* and the Persian *frabada* 'forecourt', is very unlikely. Rudolph (*Chronikbücher*, HAT Erste Reihe 21, 1955, p. 172) believes that the word means *ein heidnischer Kultraum*. He refers to the interpretation of Yahuda (JBL, 1947, p. 88) who claims that *parwārīm* is actually the Egyptian *pr wr* 'a portable chapel containing a divine image'. The conclusion of the whole matter is this: we simply don't know the exact meaning of the word, and thus every translation remains uncertain.

1 CHRONICLES

2 : 18 (B) The word *'et* before the name Azubah cannot be the sign of the acc. since, according to v. 19, Azubah is not a daughter of Caleb but his wife. Thus *'et* must be understood here as a prep. to be translated 'by', i.e. 'Caleb begot children by Azubah'.

A second problem is presented by the MT 'a woman and Jerioth', Probably for *iššā(h)wᵉ* 'a woman and', one should read *ištō* 'his wife'. The DNV and RSV have translated in this way.

Still a third difficulty exists in the word *'et* before the name Jerioth. In the RSV this second *'et* of the verse has been taken as a prep., i.e. 'and by Jerioth'. It is preferable to understand it, however, as the sign of the accusative and thus translate the first part of the verse 'Caleb the son of Hezron begot Jerioth by his wife Azubah'. Cf. Rudolph, *op. cit.*, p. 23, and the critical notes of BH.

3 : 21 (B) The MT has literally 'the son of' (sing.). On the basis of a number of mss, the LXX, and the Pesh, the plur. construct form 'the sons of' should be read. Later in the verse the plur. construct 'sons of' occurs four times. In these occurrences the LXX and the Vg have translated in each place 'his son' (cf. the RSV). This translation, however, does not solve the problem as to whom the suff. refers. Are all the names mentioned here names of the sons of Hananiah, or are succeeding generations indicated, as the DNV implies? According to Rudolph (*op. cit.* p. 31) neither the RSV nor the DNV reflects the true reading. He believes the original to have been the simple connective *wᵉ* 'and' which would indicate that all of those mentioned in v. 21 are really sons of Hananiah.

4 : 3 (B) The MT reads 'and these the father of Etam'. The Greek codices Vat. and Alex. have alleviated the difficulty by translating 'sons of' in place of the MT 'father of'. This solution has been accepted by the DNV and the RSV. On the other hand it is possible that some words have disappeared from the beginning of the verse. It should be noticed that v. 4 is concerned with the sons of Hur, who has already been mentioned in 2 : 50-51 as the father of Sobal, Salma, and Hareph. Descendants of the first two sons are enumerated in 2 : 52, 54 but not those of Hareph. We should expect them to be mentioned here in

4 : 3. It is possible, then, that the text of this verse originally read 'these were the sons of Hareph, the father of Etam, etc'. If this addition is prefixed to the beginning of v. 3, the MT reading 'father of' is maintained (cf. Rudolph, *op. cit.* p. 30).

17 (B) Adopting the witness of many mss, the LXX, and the Vg, the plur. word 'sons of' is to be read at the beginning of this verse instead of the MT sing. form.

17,
(B) Both the DNV and RSV transpose the words 'and these are the sons of Bithiah, daughter of Pharaoh, whom Mered took (i.e. married)', and place them in v. 17 after the name Jalon. The word *wattahar* 'and she conceived' has, then, some meaning, although even then one must still add the words 'and she gave birth' (RSV). Rudolph rejects this transposition but finds himself compelled to alter and supplement the text still more drastically.

28 (B)
T 6 : 13) Translations have added the name *Joel*. In the DNV it is placed between round brackets to indicate that it is added. Since *Joel* is mentioned later on in this chapter (cf. 6 : 33 = MT 6 : 18) and since 1 Sam 8 : 2 states clearly that he was the first-born of Samuel, his name should be supplied in translation here.

7 (C) The RSV translates 'Gera, that is, Heglam'. It is questionable, however, whether the Hebr *heglām* is a proper name. If it is a verbal form (cf. the RSV footnote), the text could read 'Naaman, Ahia, and Gera-he led them away'. According to Rudolph (*op. cit.*, p. 76), the pers. pron. *hū'* would then refer to Gera, which would be very strange, since it raises another question as to the antecedent of the 3rd pers. masc. plur. suff. of the verb *heglām*. It is possible, however, to translate 'as far as Naaman, Ahia, and Gera are concerned, they were led into captivity'. In this case, the pron. *hū'* would indicate the subject in general. It would seem that the text in verses 1-7 has been damaged, and thus the correct connection throughout escapes our grasp.

26 (B) The words 'they the Levites' or 'they (were) the Levites' are difficult to understand. The simple omission of the article, i.e. 'they were Levites' gives meaning to the phrase in this context.

11 : 22 (C) Cf. the notes on 2 Sam 23 : 20. According to Rudolph (*op. cit.*, pp. 98 f.), Ariel is not a proper name here, but rather it means 'warrior'. The vocalization of the word is not known. The pointing *'ărî'ēl* 'lion of God', is probably a case of popular etymology. The word is found in the Egyptian papyrus *Anastasi* I, 23, 9, and it could be a Canaanite loan-word having the meaning that is noted above (cf. Albright, *Archaeology and the Religion of Israel*, 1946, p. 218, n. 86).

12 : 21 (C) The prep. *'al* here can be understood in two different ways. First,
(MT v. 22) it can have the meaning 'over', making the translation 'they stood by David in leading the troop', i.e. David's troop (cf. RSV margin). Or, *'al* can have the sense of 'against', in which case the translation would be 'they helped David against the band of raiders', i.e. the band or troop of the Amalekites (RSV text, cf. 1 Sam 30). Either translation is possible.

15 : 13 (C) The translation of *lᵉmabbārī'šōnā(h)* as 'the first time', is not certain. Rudolph (*op. cit.*, p. 116) reads *lᵉmibbārī'šōnā(h)*, believing that the word is made up of *lᵉmin* 'because', and *bārī'šōnā(h)*. The resulting translation is the same.

15 : 27 (C) The Hebr words for 'leader' and 'singers' are quite clear, but the meaning of the word *maśśā'* is not so clear. The word comes from the verb *nāśā'* 'to lift up'. It could mean in this verse 'carrying', and thus refer to the carrying of the ark. In that case, though, one would expect it to be in a construct relation with the preceding word *śar*. But *śar* has the article and thus cannot be a construct. Actually, the literal Hebr reads 'the leader, the carrying, the singers', for which the DNV has 'who had the leading of the transport and of the singers'. In this case, the words 'transport' and 'singers' might each be explained as an acc. of reference. The RSV, on the other hand, has understood the word *maśśā'* as referring not to the lifting up of the ark, but to the lifting up of the voice, i.e. music. Thus, it translates 'the leader of the music of the singers'. Either translation is possible. The BSG has simply 'who was in charge of the transport', thus omitting the word 'singers', presumably because the word is already found in the verse.

3 (C) See the note on 2 Sam 6 : 19.

17, Both verses contain knotty textual problems. First of all, at the close
C) of v. 17, a literal translation would seem to be ‘thou hast seen me as a row of ascending people’. The DNV has tried to adhere closely to the MT by rendering ‘therefore thou hast seen in me a row of people in an ascending line’. This would mean that God has not only blessed David, but He has committed Himself to bless his dynasty as well. The ‘ascending line’ is rather vague. The RSV has translated much more freely ‘and hast shown me future generations’, but this implies that the verb is causative, whereas it is the simple *qal* form. The conjectures of various commentaries are far from being satisfactory; ancient versions present no solution, nor does the parallel passage in 2 Sam 7 : 19. We can conclude one thing from a comparison of the two passages, i.e. the consonants *t w r*, found in both references, belong to the original text. The passage in Samuel reads *tōrat hāʾādām* and the verse here in Chron *k^{e}tōr hāʾādām*. In Chron, the word can be either *tōr* ‘row’, or *tūr*, inf. of the verb ‘to fathom, search out’. It is this last reading that Rudolph (*op. cit.*, p. 131) prefers, but he believes that two textual changes are necessary. He alters the prep. *k^e* to *min* and reads *tarʾēnī*, the causative form of the verb in place of the MT *qal* form. In this way he secures the translation, *und hast mich mehr als die Menschen ergründen können, die Zukunft schauen lassen*. A corresponding change could then be proposed for the traditional reading *tōrā(h)* of 2 Sam 7 : 19. This would mean that the Samuel verse could be rendered ‘and that goes beyond human understanding’, and not as it is in the MT, i.e. ‘this is the law of the people’. Though Rudolph’s reading is conjectural, it does make good sense.

In v. 18, the Hebr reads literally ‘what more (can) David (say) to thee because of the honor (shown to) thy servant’. The brackets indicate how much apparently has to be added in translation to give meaning to the sentence. The word ‘say’ can be supplied on the basis of 2 Sam 7 : 20, though the DNV translation ‘what could David add further to the honor which thou showest to thy servant‘ has dispensed with the addition of the verb ‘to say’. Both the RSV translation ‘and what more can David say to thee for honoring thy servant’, and the DNV, are attempts to show due regard for the Hebr text. Still a further difficulty in the sentence is contained in the noun in the acc. ‘thy servant'. According to the above-mentioned translations, an inf. *kabbēd* should actually precede it instead of the noun *kābōd*. Many interpreters prefer to read the inf. form.

20 : 3 (B) The MT reads the word 'saw' twice, the sing. form followed by the plur. Instead of the plur. *mᵉgērōt* 'saws' the DNV and RSV understand *magzērōt* 'axes'. This alteration is based on one Hebr ms and the parallel passage in 2 Sam 12 : 31.

21 : 12 (B) The MT reads *nispe(h)* a *niph.* part. which means literally 'torn away'. But a part. does not fit well into the context of the sentence. We should rather expect a substantive or at least a verbal form used as a substantive. The parallel passage in 2 Sam 24 : 13 has the word *nuskā* 'your flight', which would definitely fit better into the context here. The LXX and Vg have read *nuskā* in both passages. The RSV has followed the MT here in Chronicles 'three months of devastation', but it is worthy of note that in 2 Sam 24 : 13 where the MT has 'seven years of famine' the RSV translates 'three years of famine' to harmonize with the phrase in 1 Chron 21 : 12. The DNV has accepted the MT reading in the Samuel passage. We are probably to conclude that two slightly different accounts were handed down separately, and that the early versional evidence of the LXX and Vg represents various attempts to make the accounts agree.

26 : 20 (B) The MT has 'the Levites, Ahijah, over the treasuries'. The reading is admittedly difficult. The RSV has retained the proper name *Ahijah* and translated 'and of the Levites, Ahijah had charge of the treasuries'. This rendering seems incomplete while actually the equivalent of the word 'of' before 'the Levites' is not found in the Hebr. Another possible solution to the difficulty of the MT is seen in the DNV which translates on the basis of the LXX 'the Levites, their brothers, had the supervision of the treasuries. The proper name *Ahijah* then disappears and this verse becomes a kind of heading to the personalities enumerated in v. 21 (cf. Rudolph, *op. cit.* p. 174). The LXX has probably suggested the true reading.

26 : 21 (B) The DNV has omitted two words, i.e. the second *bᵉnē(y)* and the second *lᵉlaʿdān*. The RSV retains these words but has a footnote to the effect that the Hebr text is confused.

2 CHRONICLES

10 (B) Instead of the MT *makkōt* 'blows' the DNV reads *makkōlet*
T 2 : 9) (= *maʾ^{a}kōlet*) 'food'. The text then agrees with 1 Kings 5 : 11 (MT 5 : 25) and has the external testimony of the Vg, the Pesh, and the Tg. The RSV does not alter the text since 'crushed wheat' reflects the MT *ḥiṭṭīm makkōt*. The question remains, however, as to whether *makkōt*, considered as a *hiph.* fem. plur. part., can have a passive sense. No explanation is given in the RSV of its translation. Or, should we vocalize *mukkōt*, part. *hoph.*, i.e. passive?

16 (A) The word *badd^{e}bīr* 'in the sanctuary', i.e. 'holy of holies', is strange in this context, since in verses 15-17, the writer is describing the two pillars that stand before the temple *outside* of the sanctuary. It is conjectured that the form *badd^{e}bīr* originated in the transmission of the text by metathesis (the *daleth* and *resh* exchanging places), and thus, that the original word was *bārābīd* 'like a necklace' (RSV). The DNV has translated 'round the edge', thus picturing molded decorative chains encircling the column.

9 (B) The difficulty of the MT lies in the word *ʾăšer*. Rudolph (*op. cit.* p. 218) believes that the verse means that there were many Israelites who were not compelled to do forced labor. However, since 1 Kings 9 : 22 (MT 9 : 21) says definitely that no Israelite did compulsory labor, it is better to omit the word *ʾăšer* here in Chron to make it accord with Kings. External witness favors this omission since seven mss, the LXX, the Vg, and the Pesh have omitted *ʾăšer*.

15 (B) The Hebr *miṣwat* is an example of haplography. The word *mimmiṣwat* 'from the commandment' is undoubtedly the true text as revealed in three mss, the LXX, and the Vg.

16 (B) The MT has the word *ʿad* 'unto' twice here. In its first occurrence, the prep. *min* 'from' should probably be read in its place. The context favors this change, as do the LXX, Pesh, and Tg. Furthermore the article with the word 'day' should probably be omitted, thus placing the word in a construct relation with the following words. The phrase then would read 'from the day of the laying of the foundation'.

9 : 4 (B) The MT has 'his upper room', which has no meaning in this connection. Rudolph asks, *Warum sollte an dem Obergemach etwas so besonderes sein?* (*op. cit.* p. 222). The DNV and RSV, on the basis of the ancient versions, have translated 'his burnt offering(s)' thereby understanding the sing. form *'ōlātō* collectively interpreted (cf. 1 Kings 10 : 5), or the plur. form *'ōlātā(y)w*. This would mean that the verb following *'ăšer* would be taken as a *hiph.* 'to offer up' rather than a *qal* 'to go up'. No change in vocalization is involved since the forms are identical.

9 : 11 (C) The word 'steps' in the RSV is an attempt to render the word *mᵉsillōt*. The parallel word in 1 Kings 10 : 12, *mis'ād*, is unknown (cf. the notes in 1 Kings). The noun *mᵉsillā(h)* means a 'beaten road', but 'a beaten road of algum wood' can hardly be the meaning. Rudolph translates 'banister, parapet', but he feels that the translation is dubious. Some believe it means a *parquet*, i.e. an inlaid floor or wood flooring. The translation 'steps' is related to the word *ma'ălōt*, which the LXX evidently read, not to the MT *mᵉsillōt*.

10 : 14 (B) As BH notes, the cod. L has at the beginning *'akbīd*, impf. *hiph.* 1st pers. sing. 'I shall make heavy'. The context makes it clear, however, that the form here cannot be in the first pers. The pron. *'ănī* that follows gives the sense 'someone else has made your yoke heavy; but I shall make it still heavier'. Undoubtedly the word *'akbīd* is to be understood as a mutilationof *'ābī hikbīd* 'my father has made it heavy', which is the reading of 1 Kings 12 : 14. The change is supported by the so-called Bombergiana (text by Jacob B. Chajim).

10 : 16 (B) The structure of the text, a comparison with 1 Kings 12 : 16, and the witness of the versions, all justify the insertion of a verb 'to see' after the words 'all Israel'. Thus the translation 'when all Israel saw'.

11 : 18 (B) Instead of the *Kethib* reading *ben* 'son' one should, of course, adopt the *Qere* reading *bat* 'daughter', i.e. 'daughter of Jerimoth'. The *n* of the consonantal text is a slip of the pen.

15 : 8 (B) The DNV translates 'the prophecy which Azariah, the son of Oded, had spoken', essentially the same as the RSV rendering. This means an alteration of the Hebr. The MT has 'the prophecy, Oded the prophet'

which is difficult. Since the context refers to a prophecy of Azariah, the son of Oded (2 Chron 15 : 1-7), one expects the name Azariah in v. 8. If the name Azariah is inserted in v. 8, the words 'the prophet' after Oded can be omitted. Following the word *n*^{e}*bū'ā(h)* 'prophecy', which is in the absolute state, it is necessary to add *'ăšer dibbēr* 'which he spoke', or *'ăšer nibbā'* 'which he prophesied', in order to complete the relative sentence. Another solution to the problem would be to omit the words 'Oded the prophet' viewing them as a note that appeared in the wrong place (cf. Rudolph, *op. cit.* p. 244, who proposes this view but not in a convincing manner).

: 8 (B) The MT reads 'and to decide disputed cases, and they returned to Jerusalem' (cf. BSG). Since, however, it has just been stated that this Levitical tribunal was set up in Jerusalem, the word 'return' in this context can hardly be correct. The problem is met by a change of vocalization. Read the form *yēš*^{e}*bū* from the verb *yāšab* 'to sit' instead of *yāšubū* from the verb *šūb* 'to return'. The DNV and RSV have accepted this change and rendered 'they had their seat in Jerusalem'. Yet. against this interpretation is the fact that the phrase says nothing new. The LXX offers a different solution, understanding the form as *yōš*^{e}*bē(y)*, i.e. 'inhabitants of Jerusalem'. This is the basis of Rudolph's translation *in Jerusalem setzte Josafat . . . Männer ein für das Gericht Jahwes und für 'die Streitsachen der Bewohner' Jerusalems* (*op. cit.*, p. 256).

: 1 (B) The MT 'Ammonites' is difficult because of the mention of them earlier in the verse. Probably 'Meünites' is to be read as in the LXX. Presumably they should be counted among the Edomites (1 Chron 4 : 41; 2 Chron 26 : 7). Cf. Rudolph, *op. cit.* p. 259, and Montgomery, *Arabia and the Bible*, 1934, p. 183.

: 2 (B) One ms reads 'Edom' instead of the MT 'Aram'. The RSV has 'Edom'. The DNV has 'Aram' but must of necessity attach a wide significance to the name. Cf. above 2 Sam 8 : 13.

: 25 (B) Two changes from the MT have been suggested for this verse. First, the word *b*^{e}*hēmā(h)* 'cattle' should be read for *bāhem* 'among them'. The change involves the addition of one consonant and is witnessed by the LXX, which is followed by the RSV. In the second place, the word *b^e^gādīm* 'clothes' (cf. the DNV and RSV) should be read for the MT *p^e^gārīm* 'dead bodies'. The word 'clothes' is actually found in seven mss though the RSV makes no mention of this nor of their deviation from the MT.

22 : 6 (B) The MT has Azariah, which is clearly a scribal error for Ahaziah. The word *kī* following the first occurrence of 'Jezreel' should be changed to *min*, thus 'to be healed in Jezreel *from* his wounds' (cf. the parallel in 2 Kings 8 : 29). This altered reading is found in various Hebr mss as well as in the LXX.

25 : 19 (B) One should compare 2 Kings 14 : 10 where the 2nd pers. masc. sing. is correct, i.e. *hikkītā* ('you have indeed smitten Edom'). Here in 2 Chron, however, the text begins with 'you say', or, possibly 'you are thinking'. Then follows the gist of their thought and this calls for the 1st pers. sing. form *hikkītī*. Thus the text should probably read 'you say, behold I have smitten'. Support for the 1st pers. sing. form is found in some of the old versions.

25 : 20 (B) The Hebr reads 'to give them in the hand'. The question naturally arises, in the hand of whom? The RSV, like the AV, adds 'their enemies', but this is rather arbitrary. Another possibility is to read *b^e^yādō* 'in his hand', i.e. of Joash. This is the understanding of the old Jewish tradition.

25 : 23 (B) The Hebr reads 'to the gateway of the one turning'. A very slight change in vocalization introduces the reading *happinnā(h)*. The translation thus becomes 'corner gate' (cf. the DNV and RSV), the reading that is found in the parallel passage of 2 Kings 14 : 13. 'Corner gate' has the support of several mss as well as ancient versional evidence.

25 : 24 (B) The Hebr lacks a verbal form at the beginning of the verse. The parallel in 2 Kings 14 : 14 suggests supplying the form 'and he took' (cf. the DNV and RSV). Rudolph (*op. cit.* p. 280) has a different solution to the problem. Leaving the beginning of the verse unchanged, he changes the impf. *waw consecutive* form 'and he returned' to a perf. *hiph.* of the same verb 'made (it) return'. Thus, everything in the

verse up to the last two words of the MT becomes the object of this altered verb form 'he brought back to Samaria . . .'.

: 5 (B) The MT reads *hammēbīn bir'ōt hā'ĕlōhīm* 'who made (him) understand visions of God', which would imply that Zechariah gave Uzziah lessons in 'seeing God'—hardly the fruit of training! The phrase may also have the meaning 'who had some insight in seeing God', the word *mēbīn* thus losing its causative meaning. But it is preferable to regard *bir'ōt* as a form of the verb *yārē'* 'to fear', than of *rā'ā(h)* 'to see'. The form would then be an unusual type of the inf. On the other hand, the Talmud (b. Sota 48b) and the ancient versions (cod. Vat., cod. Alex., and the Pesh) support a noun formation of *yārē'* in the construct state. This is the basis of the RSV translation 'who instructed him in the fear of God'.

: 5 (B) The MT reads *waya'al 'al hammigdālōt* 'and he raised up on the towers'. The reading is clumsy, to say the least, but the sense becomes clear when a different word division from the MT is adopted. The phrase should read *waya'al 'āle(y)hā migdālōt* 'and he raised up upon it (i.e. the wall) towers'. This preferred word division has the support of ancient tradition and has been adopted by recent translations (cf. the RSV).

: 22 (B) The MT reads at the close of the verse 'and he (i.e. the Lord) led them on every side'. It is preferable, however, to read a different verb and a different word division, i.e. *wayyānaḥ lāhem missābīb* 'and he gave them rest on every side'. In the first place, this change is suggested by 2 Chron 15 : 15, which lies in a similar context. Also the LXX and Vg clearly favor this rendering (cf. the DNV and RSV).

: 28 (B) Two slight changes are necessary to give the verse its proper meaning: first, the word *'urāwōt* 'shelters' must be read for *'ăwērōt*, and second, the last two words need to be transposed to give the sense 'shelters for the flocks' (cf. the RSV). This transposition is in agreement with the LXX.

: 4 (B) Since the word *haqqᵉbārīm* 'graves' is in the absolute state, the MT reads literally at the close of the verse 'over the graves, those who were sacrificing to them'. The DNV, RSV, and AV translate as though there were a construct state, i.e. *qibrē(y)* 'the graves of'. If the absolute state is retained, it is necessary to insert within brackets a few words to give a smooth translation, i.e. 'the graves (where there were buried) those who were sacrificing to them'.

34 : 6 (B) Neither the consonantal text 'he chose their houses' nor the *Qere* reading 'by their swords' gives a satisfactory meaning in this context. The RSV 'in their ruins' and the DNV 'which everywhere lay in ruins' reflect an attempt to give meaning to the verse. Another suggestion is to read *birḥobōtē(y)hem* 'on their squares', or 'on their open places'.

34 : 13 (B) Read *ʿal* at the beginning instead of *weʿal* to obtain a satisfactory connection between v. 12 and v. 13.

36 : 9 (B) According to the MT, Jehoiachin was eight years old when he became king (cf. the RSV). It is preferable to read 'eighteen' years on the basis of the ancient versions. Furthermore, the parallel passage in 2 Kings 24 : 8, 15 states not only that he was eighteen when he began to reign but also that he was married.

EZRA

3 : 3 (B) By a very slight change, the MT phrase 'upon its foundations'' becomes clearer 'upon its (old) place' (cf. the RSV).

The next five words read 'for in fear on them for the peoples of the lands' (i.e. non-Israelites). A slight change in vocalization allows the word *beʾē(y)mā(h)* 'in fear' to become *bāʾ ʾē(y)mā(h)* 'fear had come', and thus introduces a smoother rendering 'for fear of the peoples of the land had come over them' (cf. the DNV and RSV).

4 : 7 (C) The Hebr word *bišlām* is generally taken as a proper name (AV, RSV, etc.). Another possibility is to understand it as a noun with a prep. meaning 'with the approval of'. In Hebr this would be vocalized as *bešālōm*, but, when translated into Aram, it would become *bišlām*, the word that we find in this text. It is possible that an Aram word could be here. However, it would be in strange company with the

other words of the verse which are Hebr. Thus, the safe way is to understand *bišlām* as a proper name. Rudolph (*Ezra und Nehemia* HAT, 1949, Erste Reihe 20, p. 34) conjectures the reading *bīrūšālēm* 'against Jerusalem', but this is unlikely.

18 (C) This verse reveals that the letter that was written in Aram was read aloud to the Persian king. But what is the meaning of the word *m^e^pāraš*? According to Schaeder, it is a technical term from the Persian official language. But the word is more generally explained as a pass. part. form of the Aram verb *p^e^raš* which means to 'separate, distinguish, make clear, explain'. Thus the verb form here is rendered 'clear' by the DNV, and 'plainly' in the AV and RSV. Rudolph, however, renders the word *in Übersetzung* (*op. cit.*, p. 44) which raises a question of interpretation. Was the letter in Aram read to the Persian king by sections, each section made clear to him by being translated into Persian? If this is true, it is evident from their renderings that the ancient versions missed this meaning. Rudolph's translation has many supporters. It has been noted that there is a possible connection of the use of the Aram word *m^e^pāraš* here, with its Hebr equivalent *m^e^pōrāš* in Neh 8 : 8. There the RSV has translated the word 'clearly', but it has a marginal note giving an alternative meaning 'with interpretation'. But, more precisely, and on the basis of Rudolph's reading in Ez 4 : 18, the word in the Neh reference might be rendered 'with translation'. This would mean, that following Ezra's arrival, the Hebr law was read aloud and then followed up by a translation into Aram, so that all who heard could understand clearly. If this explanation is correct, it would lend support to the rabbinical opinion that this bi-lingual practice was carried out at this time. While the explanation is not entirely certain, either in the Neh passage or in Ezra, yet, it does deserve serious consideration.

: 4 (B) The Aram reads 'we said'. If this form is retained, the 'we' must be taken to refer to the Jews, the translation being 'after that we told them what were the names of the men who . . .'. The difficulty is that this statement does not meet the question that the governor of the province and his associates direct to the Jews according to v. 3. Verse 4 is more likely to be a second question of the governor to the Jews. Thus, not only does he ask 'who gave you permission to build'

(v. 3), but also 'what are the names of the builders' (v. 4). This sense is given in the LXX and Pesh and is found in the DNV and RSV. It requires a slight change in the verb form, i.e. from the MT *'ămarnā'* 'we said' to *'ămarū* 'they said'.

6 : 3 (A) The words *'uššōhī m^esōb^elīn* have frequently had a rather free translation, i.e. 'its foundations must be laid'. But, in reality, *m^esōb^elīn* is a *po'el* or *po'al* pass. part. of the Aram verb *s^ebal* meaning 'to bear', or, possibly 'to take care of'. The meaning then would be, 'its foundations must be preserved', i.e. must receive special care. Some, however, vocalize *'uššōhī* as *'eššōhī* derived from *'eššā'* 'fire', thus making the reference in this context to the fire of the burnt offerings. In this case, the part. *m^esōb^elīn* is to be identified as a *safel* form of the verb *y^ebal* 'to bring'. Thus, the RSV among others, translates 'and burnt offerings are brought'. Other suggestions have been made concerning the verse, but they involve changes in the Hebr text. From the point of view of the consonantal text, the RSV translation 'burnt offerings' is, grammatically, just as feasible as the rendering 'foundations'.

10 : 6 (B) The MT reads 'and he went to the room of Jehohanan, the son of Eliashib, and he went there'. This can hardly be correct. On the basis of the LXX (ed. Lagardiana) the second verb form *wayyēlek* should be changed to *wayyālen* 'and he spent the night'. The change is found in the DNV and RSV.

10 : 16 (B) The MT reads 'there were selected (or separated) Ezra the priest, men . . .'. The reading is doubtful since it is obvious in the context that Ezra must be the subject. Accordingly, the plur. *niph.* impf. verb form *wayyibbād^elū* 'and there were separated' should be changed to the *hiph.* impf. sing. *wayyabdēl* 'and he selected' with the possible addition of the word *lō* 'for himself' (cf. BH apparatus). The change has ancient versional support and is found in the DNV and RSV.

10 : 19 (B) By a slight change in vocalization the MT reading 'and the guilty a ram of the flock' can be changed to read with greater sense 'and their guilt offering (was) a ram of the flock' (cf. the DNV and RSV).

10 : 44 (A) Several difficulties meet the translator here. First, it should be noted

that, beginning with the word *wyēš*, the MT contains two independent sentences, side by side. A further problem is the use of masc. forms of the suff. and verb with a fem. subject 'women'. This is unusual, yet, grammatically, it is possible. But still a third problem is the meaning of the verb *śîm* in this context. Can it have the meaning 'to bring forth'?

The DNV has attempted to render the MT as it is, 'among them were women who had brought forth sons'. It is believed, however, that the Hebr text has suffered corruption and that the verse originally told of the sending away of women and children. Thus, the RSV has altered the text and translated 'and they put them away with their children'. This agrees with the reading of 1 Esdras 9 : 36. Cf. Rudolph, *op. cit.*, p. 100.

NEHEMIAH

5 (C) The RSV (cf. the AV) has translated the last two words as 'the work of their Lord', noting in the margin the translation 'lords'. It is more likely that the translation should be 'their lord', i.e. Nehemiah.

8 (C) The RSV has 'and they restored Jerusalem as far as the Broad Wall'. The translation 'restored', however, is uncertain. The Hebr verbal form is derived from *'āzab* which means to 'leave, abandon'. A literal but unlikely translation, then, would be 'they could leave Jerusalem at the broad wall', i.e. they did not need to make any repairs there. Some have felt that here the verb *'āzab* means 'to plaster', a meaning that KBL suggests—but, with a question mark. On the basis of the same stem in a South-Arabic inscription, Margoliouth (*Relations Between Arabs and Israelites*, 1924, p. 25) believes that *'āzab* here in Neh 3 : 8, means 'to repair'. Similarly, in Grossman-Segal, *Compendious Hebrew-English Dictionary*, 1951, one meaning that is given to *'āzab* is 'to strengthen' or 'to fortify'. Thus, some support is found for the RSV 'restored', and for the AV 'fortified'.

2 (C)
3: 34) For the word *'āzab* in this verse, cf. the notes on 3 : 8. The translation 'restore' in 4: 2 is a possibility (cf. also 'to fortify' and 'to plaster'). Against the translation 'shall we leave them alone' are varied objections, including the question on the required change

in the text in order to secure this reading. Cf. Rudolph, *op. cit.* p. 122.

4 : 12 (C) (MT 3 : 34) The sequence of events here, and in the context, is briefly, as follows: the enemies of the Jews plot secretly to frustrate the wall-building operations, through a fifth column infiltration (v. 11); Nehemiah gets wind of the plan through reports from certain Jews living among the enemies (v. 12); Nehemiah takes defensive measures to defeat the plot (v. 13). In the light of this train of thought, one approaches the textual difficulties found in the direct speech at the close of v. 12. First of all, the prep. *ʿal* should probably be translated here simply 'to'. Thus, the MT literally reads 'the Jews who lived with them said at least ten times to us, from all places (= from all sides): *you must return to us*' (the word *ʾăšer* can introduce direct speech). The direct speech thus refers to fellow Jews in Jerusalem. The meaning would be that the Jews who lived in the country, heard of the plot of the enemies (v. 11). By repeated warnings ('ten times') they summoned their fellow countrymen who lived near them but commuted to Jerusalem, to quit their jobs, and come back to the country and stay there, because of the imminent danger. This explanation of the text makes some sense, but at the same time, it labors under numerous objections.

The RSV has 'they said to us ten times, *From all the places where they live they will come up against us*'. This translation involves two textual changes. First, it understands the form *yēšebū* in place of the MT *tāšūbū*, and, further, it supplies the form *yaʿălū* that is not found in the MT. This means that the direct speech refers to the action of the adversaries. At best, this translation is most uncertain. The DNV has 'when the Jews who lived with them came ten times to tell it to us from all the places which chose our side'. One thing seems clear in this difficult verse, and that is, that the 2nd pers. plur. form ought to be changed to a 3rd pers. plur. to secure some kind of sense.

4 : 23 (A) (MT 4 : 17) The last three words of the MT are puzzling. Translated literally, they read 'each one, his weapon, the water'. Even translations that try to keep to the text diverge sharply from one another. The AV has 'saving that everyone put them off (i.e. they stripped off their clothes) for washing' (i.e. either to wash their clothes, or/and, to

wash themselves). This translation is nothing more than a guess, similar to Luther's translation, *ein jeglicher liess das Baden anstehen.* The consonants *šlḥw* can be vocalized as the Masoretes did, i.e. *šilḥō* 'his javelin', or, the pointing can be changed to read a verbal form from *šālaḥ* 'to send'. On the basis of v. 17 (MT v. 11), the vocalization 'his javelin' is better. But in that case, it is preferable to change the perplexing *hammayim* 'water', into the word *bīmīnō* 'in his right hand', or into the word *bᵉyādō* 'in his hand', or into *hēmīnū* 'to hold on the right side'. The RSV has 'each kept his weapon in his hand', which, though it has meaning, remains a conjectural reading.

15 (C) The Hebr word *ʾaḥar* 'after', is difficult in this context. It is generally rendered 'besides', or, 'moreover' (cf. the AV and RSV), but it is doubtful if the word has ever had this meaning. Some have followed the Vg and translated 'daily'. In the Hebr text, this means the difference between the *daleth* and the *resh*, i.e. *ʾeḥād* 'one' (with *yōm* 'day' understood), in place of the MT *ʾaḥar*.

11 (C) Two translations are possible; either 'what man such as I could go into the temple and live' (RSV), or, 'what man such as I would go into the temple to save his life' (RSV margin).

3 (C) The RSV has 'while they are still standing guard', which is a most uncertain rendering. Can *ʿāmad* mean 'to stand guard', and who are the 'they'? Some are of the opinion that instead of the MT plur. part., a sing. form of the part. should be read, thus referring to the sun. Hence, the translation 'and while it (i.e. the sun) is in the sky' (literally 'standing'). Since this is nothing more than a conjecture, it is probably best to follow the RSV, uncertain though it is.

67 (C) On the basis of some Hebr mss, cod. Alex. of the LXX, and Ez 2 : 66, the AV and RSV have inserted an additional verse at the end of v. 67. The insertion begins with 'their horses', and ends with 'two hundred and forty-five'. In the best mss, however, the verse is lacking, and, accordingly, the DNV has omitted it.

: 8 (C) See the notes on Ez 4 : 18.

9 : 38 (C) (MT 10 : 1) The MT reads literally 'and upon the sealed our princes, our Levites, our priests'. The reference must be to a sealed document, a scroll provided with seal impressions, similar to the deed of purchase complete with such a seal as is mentioned in Jer 32 : 11. Thus the BSG renders' . . . our priests are enrolled upon the sealed document', i.e. their names were included in the sealed document. This is a correct translation, but essentially so also are the DNV and RSV translations. The RSV has '. . . our priests set their seal to it'.

JOB

1 : 5 (C) The Hebr text contains the verb 'to bless', but actually the opposite, i.e. 'to curse', is meant (cf. also 1 : 11; 2 : 5, 9). Either the writer or a later reviser is responsible for the euphemism.

1 : 22 (C) The first two words are generally rendered 'in all this', but the translation 'in spite of all this', is also possible. For the final phrase, the DNV has 'he did not accuse God of doing anything absurd', while the RSV translates 'charge God with wrong' (cf. the AV). The word *tiplā(h)* is used in Jer 23 : 13, where the RSV translates 'an unsavory thing' (AV 'folly'). It means something that annoys or offends, and here in Job 1 : 22 it could be translated 'something offensive'.

3 : 5 (C, B) The DNV, RSV, and other translations agree in the rendering 'let gloom and deep darkness claim it'. The verb *gā'al* means 'to redeem, claim as property', which justifies the above translation. Johnson (VT Supplement I, 1953, p. 73), however, believes the verb also has the meaning 'to cover', and suggests the translation 'let darkness, let utter blackness cover it'. For the sake of completeness, this interpretation is mentioned. At the close of the verse, the MT reading *kimrīrē(y) yōm* 'as the bitterness of the day' hardly fits the context. It is better to view *kimrīrē(y)* as derived from the stem *kmr* 'to be dark, black' (cf. Accad and Syr). Thus, with a slight vocalization change (*kimrīrē(y)* to *kamrīrē(y)*, the translation becomes 'blackness of the day' (AV and RSV), which the DNV has taken to mean 'eclipse of the sun'. Cf. *kamrīr* in KBL.

3 : 6 (C) The RSV renders 'let it not rejoice', thus understanding the verbal

form *yiḥad*, to be derived from *ḥādā(h)* 'to rejoice'. However, considering the parallel clause that follows 'let it not come into the number of the months' (RSV), one would expect a similar idea to be present in the clause containing the form *yiḥad*. Without consonantal change, this verbal form may be vocalized *yēḥad* from *yāḥad* 'to unite'. The translation would then be 'let it (i.e. the night) not unite with the days of the year', or 'let it not be counted with the days of the year'. This interpretation is founded on an old tradition and is worthy of consideration.

19 (C) The Hebr has 'small and great are there'. The DNV and others have rendered 'small and great are there the same', but this is uncertain.

21 (C) The Hebr has 'and they dig for it', which can also be rendered 'even if they dig for it'.

24 (C) The RSV renders the word *lipnē(y)* by the word 'as', i.e. 'for my sighing comes as my bread'. This translation of *lipnē(y)*, however, is not certain. Two other translations have 'before my bread', and 'in place of my bread'.

2 (B) On the basis of Aq and the LXX the DNV changes the vocalization of *dābār* 'a word, thing' to *dabbēr*, inf. *pi.* of the verb 'to say', thereby translating 'whenever one tries to speak a word to you'.

13 (C) The first word of the MT is translated 'reflections' in the DNV, and 'thoughts' in the RSV (KBL has 'disquieting thoughts'). Hölscher (*Das Buch Hiob* HAT, Erste Reihe 17, p. 18) has *Grübeleien*. One can translate 'after nocturnal visions', or better still 'as a result of nocturnal visions'.

17 (C) The twice-recurring prep. *min* can be translated in two ways; either 'before God', and 'before his Maker' (RSV text), or 'more than God', and 'more than his Maker' (RSV margin).

19 (B) In agreement with the MT, the RSV (cf. the AV) translates at the end of the verse 'who are crushed before the moth'. It is possible, however,

that a different word division should be adopted, i.e. *yiddakᵉʾū millip-nē(y)* 'they were crushed (dead) more than (or 'rather than') moths' (cf. the DNV).

4 : 20 (C) Translate either 'between morning and evening', or 'from morning till night'.

5 : 3 (C) The RSV renders 'I cursed his dwelling'. The verb *nāqab*, however, is not the usual word meaning 'to curse'. It means more definitely to 'bore through, define, indicate, state precisely'. It also means, in an unfavorable sense, 'to identify as wicked and evil', and this may be what is meant here.

5 : 5 (B) The word *ṣammīm* at the end of the verse is found also in Job 18 : 9, where, according to the context, it must mean a snare or net ('snare' in the RSV and *Schlinge* in German). Here in 5 : 5, however, the translation 'the snare pants after their wealth' gives no adequate meaning. The LXX, Aq and Symm have understood the word *ṣᵉmēʾīm* 'the thirsty', which is the basis of the preferred renderings of the DNV and RSV. Whether the final word should be translated 'their wealth' or 'his wealth' is not so important.

5 : 7 (C) The translations usually read 'as the sparks fly upward', but the word 'as' is not in the Hebr, and the rendering 'sparks' for *bᵉnē(y) rešep* remains doubtful, though in Ps 78 : 48, the word *rešep* means 'lightning' or 'fiery flashes'. However, some feel that the expression here in Job may mean birds (eagles, or birds of prey). Perhaps one should see here the god *Reshef* of whom Albright writes, "Reshef was the lord of the underworld, the god of war and pestilence" (ARI, p. 79). *Reshef* could then be taken as the god of death, and the expression *bᵉnē(y) rešep* would indicate people, mortals, those who belong to *Reshef*. Thus the translation here might be 'man is born to trouble, but mortals try to fly high'. Since, obviously, mortals cannot do this (cf. the stories of Phaëton and Icarus in classical antiquity), the verse is saying that calamity is man's portion in this life. A. Weiser (*Das Buch Hiob*, ATD 13, 1951, p. 50) rejects this interpretation and retains the traditional translation 'sparks'.

8 (C) The Hebr words *'ūlām 'ănī* have been translated variously as follows:
'On the contrary, I'
'I, on the other hand'
'Nevertheless, I'
'As for me, I'.
One can choose his translation here, the one provision being that the translation express a contrast with what precedes.

9-13 (C) Except for v. 11, the Hebr has participles throughout, 'who does great things', 'who gives rain', etc. One might, therefore, render these participles as dependent clauses as the BSG does. The DNV, however, translates them as independent sentences, i.e. 'he does great things', 'he gives rain', etc. The RSV is not consistent, but renders v. 9 as a dependent clause, and verses 10-13 as independent sentences (cf. also the AV). As far as the Hebr is concerned, there is no reason for any change in sequence.

6 (C) The meaning of the final word *ḥallāmūt* is not certain. The AV has 'white of an egg', but others think of a definite vegetable such as the 'purslane' (RSV). Another suggestion is that it means a plant, i.e. 'marsh mallow'.

7 (C) Literally, the MT reads 'they are as the impurity of my bread'. One needs to translate somewhat freely, since we do not have here the special term for impure food. Thus the DNV has rendered 'they are food that is nauseous to me', and the RSV 'they are as food that is loathsome to me'.

10 (A) The last word of the verse is generally taken to be a name for God, i.e. 'the Holy One'. Though the name is not a usual one in this book, this is an acceptable explanation. The verb *sālad* earlier in the verse occurs only here in the OT and may have the meaning 'to skip with joy'. The prep. *bᵉ* before *ḥīlā(h)* can mean either 'in spite of', or 'in'. Translations vary on this point. The two words *lō' yaḥmōl* are rendered in the DNV as a relative sentence with God as the subject (cf. also the AV 'let him not spare'). On the other hand, they can be taken together to mean simply 'merciless' (RSV 'unsparing'). The chief difficulty in

translating this verse lies in the uncertainty as to how to combine the words and phrases together.

6 : 11 (C) The MT has had a fairly literal translation in the RSV, which is as follows:

> 'What is my strength, that I should wait?
> And what is my end, that I should be patient?'

The text could also be interpreted as follows:

> 'How could I stand it any longer,
> And how could I remain patient to the end?'

The word *qēṣ* 'end' can be taken as 'that which is the measure of the days', 'that which lies before one' (cf. Ps 39 : 5, v. 4 in the RSV).

6 : 14 (A) According to KBL, the word *lammās* has no explanation. On the basis of the ancient translations and Mic 2 : 3, one may understand *mās* to mean *māš*, which, when joined with the prep. *min* that follows, would mean 'to remove from someone, keep something from someone'. The prep. *lᵉ* can thus mean here 'as far as concerns', or it can strengthen the subject (cf. the DNV and the RSV 'he who withholds kindness from a friend'). Another solution is to read with many Hebr mss the form *lᵉmō'ēs* or *lammō'ēs* from the verb *mā'as* 'to reject'. The translation would then be 'to the one who throws (his) sympathy away from his friend'—'who has no sympathy with his friend'. The thought of the verse would then be that the friends of Job fail to comfort him in his sorrow. To Job this means that they have not only denied sympathy to him, but they have forsaken the fear of the Almighty as well. Still a third interpretation worthy of study comes from the pen of Artur Weiser (*op. cit.*,) pp. 54, 58). A free rendering of Weiser's thought would be 'to him who is despondent and ready to succumb to his sufferings, love is due from his friend, even if the despondent one should renounce the fear of the Almighty'. The first part only of this rendering is found in the AV 'to him that is afflicted, pity should be showed from his friend'.

6 : 21 (B) The AV has attempted to reproduce the MT by translating 'for now ye are nothing'. Two slight changes in the text, however, fill the

verse with meaning. The word *kēn* 'thus' should be read for *kī* 'because, for', and the word *lī* 'to me' should be read in place of *lō* 'not' (*Qere* has *lō* 'to him'). The resulting translation is 'such you have now become to me'. Job is describing his deep disappointment in his friends. They have become to him like the dry torrent beds, full of water in the rainy season, but a source of disappointment to the thirsty desert caravan in the hot summer time (cf. verses 15-17).

25 (C) The translation 'to be forceful' for the verb *māraṣ*, is based on ancient Jewish tradition. Another translation is 'to be sweet, pleasant'. Elsewhere, however, the OT indicates that the verb means 'to be painful' (cf. 1 Kings 2 : 8). KBL prefers this translation here, but he must then translate as follows, 'what? Are sincere words grieving', or 'what is there that grieves in sincere words'.

15 (B) The AV has translated the second part of this verse 'and death rather than my life'. This is not a literal translation since the MT reads 'and death rather than my bones' (cf. the RSV). By changing one letter—*m* into *b* (*'aṣṣᵉbōt* for *'aṣmōt*) the DNV has obtained a reading giving the following translation appropriate in this context 'death rather than my griefs' (cf. BH).

8 (B) The MT *kōnēn* is generally interpreted as *kōnēn lēb* 'to fix one's attention on'. A very slight change, however, makes possible the preferable *bōnēn* 'to pay attention to'. No additional word is then required.

17 (C) The MT 'he sees a stone house' does not make sense. The RSV rendering (cf. the LXX) 'he lives among the rocks' means that it has read *bē(y)n* 'among' instead of the MT *bē(y)t*, and the verbal form *yiḥye(h)* from *ḥāyā(h)* 'to live', instead of the MT *yeḥĕze(h)* from *ḥāzā(h)* 'to see'. For other emendations, cf. BH.

3 (C) Who is the subject of the verb 'to wish', and to whom does the 3rd masc. suff. in the word *'immō* refer? There are two possible answers to these questions. One translation is 'if one (i.e. man) wished to contend with him (i.e. God)'. This is the preferable sense. The other

possible meaning is 'if He (i.e. God) wished to contend with him (i.e. man)'.

9 : 5-10 (C) The DNV has rendered these verses as independent sentences. The RSV, however, has translated the Hebr participles consistently as dependent clauses (cf. 5 : 9-13).

9 : 8 (C) The MT has 'and treads upon the waves of the seas' (cf. the AV and RSV). The word 'waves' is a translation of the plur. form of *bāmā(h)* 'high place'. The DNV has rendered 'high places' which would seem clearly to indicate 'high waves'. The RSV margin, however, has 'trampled the back of the sea-dragon', a translation that understands *bāmā(h)* here to be the equivalent of the Ugaritic *bmt* meaning 'back'. Albright (ARI, p. 149) writes, "all these cosmic sources of water were conceived in mythological imagery to be dragons, as we know from . . . Canaanite where . . . [it] is true of *yammu* 'sea'." The word *yammu* is identical with Hebr *yām*. The question remains, however, as to whether "mythological imagery" is present here in Job 9 : 8.

9 : 9 (C) Instead of 'the Bear' (cf. the RSV), some have translated 'the Lion' (cf. Job 38 : 32 and KBL, p. 702). Hölscher (*op. cit.* p. 30 f., on 9 : 9) mentions additional literature.

9 : 15 (C) The DNV renders 'my judge' (RSV 'my accuser') which is supported by the vocalization of the MT form, an unusual *po.* part. of *šāpaṭ* 'to judge'. In its marginal reading, the RSV indicates that another vocalization is possible, i.e. *mišpāṭī* 'my right'.

9 : 23 (C) The meaning of the word *lᵉmassat* from *massā(h)* is not certain. It has generally been translated 'fear, doubt, despair, calamity (RSV), trial (AV)'. The translation 'trial' is apparently based upon the use of this word in Deut 4 : 34. In Job 9 : 23, however, it is better to view *massā(h)* as a derived form from the verb *māsas* 'to melt', or, in a metaphorical sense 'to lose courage', and *not* from *nissā(h)* 'to put to the test'.

9 : 27 (B) In the MT this verse begins with the conj. *ʾim* followed by the inf. of *ʾāmar* 'to say' with the 1st pers. sing. suff. The usual construction in

this chapter, however, is *'im* with a finite verb (cf. verses 3, 16, 20, 30). So here it is better to vocalize the inf. as a perf. *'āmartī* or an impf. *'ōmar* to be translated 'if I say' (AV and RSV) or 'when I think' (DNV).

33 (B) The MT vocalization *lō' yēš* is to be translated 'there is no (umpire)'. Though this method of negation in a nominal sentence is unusual, it is not impossible (cf. the RSV and Weiser, *op. cit.* p. 70). The DNV, in agreement with numerous Hebr mss as well as the LXX and Pesh, has understood the vocalization *lū yēš* which gives the sense 'if only there were an umpire but there is not'. This then would have to be understood as an *irrealer Vordersatz, der das Gegenteil eines vorhandenen Tatbestandes annimmt* (cf. Beer-Meyer, *Hebräische Grammatik II*, 1955, p. 158).

35 (C) The RSV has rendered literally 'for I am not so in my self'. It can also be translated 'because in this way I cannot on my own'. In this case, Job would mean that the possibility of speaking to God without fear is not in man's capacity: it can only be given by God.

: 9 (C) The second strophe is taken as interrogative in sense by the AV and RSV and others. It need not be so. It can be rendered 'remember that thou hast formed me out of clay (literally 'like clay') and that thou wilt turn me to dust'.

: 17 (C) At the end of the verse the Hebr has 'release and service with me'. If the word *ṣābā'* means 'service', it must indicate a burdensome and difficult service. The two words together 'release and heavy service' (KBL 'hardship after hardship') point to a continuous hard service without permanent relief. On the other hand, the word *ṣābā'* might mean 'armed force'. The RSV has understood this meaning, and through a change in text it has rendered 'thou dost bring fresh hosts against me'.

: 20 (B) The vocalization of the MT suggests the translation 'are not my days few? Let him stop', or, 'are not my days few? And stop'. The LXX and Pesh suggest the vocalization *yᵉmē(y) ḥeldī* 'days of my life'. Thus the RSV and DNV have rendered 'are not the days of my life few?'

10 : 21 (C) The Hebrew has no equivalent of the word 'whence' that is found in the AV and the RSV. It is true that in antiquity one would say that the deceased went to a land whence he never returned, and that thought plays a part in this verse. The translation 'before I go, never to return, to the land of . . .', however, can also be defended.

11 : 6 (A) The Hebr is not clear. The word *tūšīyā(h)* is a technical term from the wisdom literature. The LXX has no consistent translation of this word, nor has the Vg which translates it by *prudentia*, *sapientia*, and *aequitas*. The word cannot mean 'salvation', but should be translated as 'wisdom' or 'insight'. It is difficult to see any connection between *kiplayim* 'double' and *tūšīyā(h)*. The DNV renders 'it doubles the insight', i.e. the wisdom God reveals to man doubles man's insight, but this interpretation is doubtful. The RSV connects both the words 'double' and 'insight' with God, and thus translates 'for he is manifold in understanding'. But this translation is only a guess. Weiser (*op. cit.* pp. 81, 83) translates *die doppelt schwer an Einsicht sind*. He thus understands that the depths or mysteries of wisdom are so difficult to understand *weil sie dem Menschen doppeldeutig erscheinen*. But this is not the meaning of the text. A translation here, whether it is from an unaltered or modified text, remains a surmise and nothing more. The same is true of the last part of the verse which the RSV renders 'know then that God exacts of you less than your guilt deserves'. The BSG is in basic agreement with the DNV which translates 'then you would acknowledge that God in your favor relegates into forgetfulness a part [partitive *min*] of your iniquities'.

11 : 8 (B) The MT reads *gobhē(y) šāmayim* 'heights of heaven'. The parallelism in the verse, however, suggests the vocalization *gᵉbōhā(h) miššāmayim* 'higher than heaven' (cf. the RSV). This corresponds exactly to the phrase 'deeper than Sheol' in the second half of the verse, which could possibly be rendered 'deep as the realm of death', as. e.g. Weiser, Hölscher.

11 : 18 (C) The RSV translation 'you will be protected', is based on a vocalization change of the MT to a pass. form, and upon the meaning of the Arabic *chafara*. KBL reads the pass. form also, but translates 'feel

abashed'. Others translate 'look around', leaving the MT unchanged. The translation remains uncertain.

: 5 (A) The first problem in the verse is the uncertainty of the word *'aštūt*, generally translated 'opinion'. A further difficulty lies in the word *nākōn*. If it is a verbal form of *kūn*, then i tmeans 'that which is prepared'. It could, however, be a substantive (not found elsewhere) derived from the verb *nākā(h)* 'to strike', and thus mean 'blow', or 'stroke'. In this case, the meaning of the verse would be that the 'carefree' or 'prosperous one' has no feeling toward the unfortunate and suffering one: he scorns grief and cruelly gives a blow to the one who is already tottering on his feet. It is difficult to decide which interpretation of *nākōn* is to be preferred.

: 6 (C) The RSV rendering 'who bring their god in their hand' is not certain. It is possible that the Hebr sing. verb could be interpreted as a plur. It is not likely that *'ĕlōăh* 'god' could be the subject. The text may mean that here are people who consider their hand or power as divine, comparable to the idea in Hab 1 : 11. Weiser (*op. cit.*, p. 90) rejects this view, believing that, according to this verse, God is degraded to an instrument of human power, i.e. religion is abused for evil ends. In the light of the uncertainty that is present in this part of the verse, it is best simply to translate as literally as possible.

: 8 (C) The word *śīăḥ* is either an impv. of the verb meaning 'to speak, mention' (Ps 69 : 13; 105 : 2), i.e. 'speak to the earth' (RSV margin), or it is a noun meaning 'bush', i.e. 'plants of the earth' (RSV text). The translation 'bush' or 'plants' seems to be required by the context (cf. 'beasts' and 'birds of the air'—v. 7, and 'plants of the earth' and 'fish of the sea'—v. 8).

: 15 (B) The RSV and others have followed the consonantal text reading *lō'* with an *aleph* and thus negative 'behold he will slay me; I have no hope'. The *Qere*, however, reads *lō*, prep. with 3rd masc. sing. suff. 'for him' or 'to him'. This Masoretic reading has the support of a considerable range of versional evidence including the LXX, and has been followed by the DNV and AV. The *hēn* at the beginning, then, is understood as a conj. Cf. the AV 'though he slay me, yet will I trust in him'.

14 : 6 (C) Most translations understand the verb *rāṣā(h)* here as meaning 'to find pleasure in, rejoice in' (cf. the RSV). The word, however, can also mean 'to pay, pay over' (cf. Lev 26 : 41). If this meaning is accepted here, the translation becomes.

> 'renounce him—then he will give it up,
> yes, as a workman, pay his day' (i.e. fulfil his task
> completely, and thus be ready).

This translation is somewhat unusual, but it is defended by Hölscher (*op. cit.*, p. 37). If *rāṣā(h)* means 'to rejoice in', the text is usually interpreted to mean that an afflicted person is more than happy with a little bit of rest, just as the hard laborer is glad to have a short rest at the end of his daily task. Another interpretation is given in the AV 'turn from him, that he may rest, till he shall accomplish, as an hireling, his day'. *Ḥādal*, however, does not mean, 'to rest', but, 'to desist'.

14 : 14 (C) The translation 'I could wait till' connects the second part of the verse closely to the first part. It is possible, however, to regard the two sections as independent sentences. The translation of the second sentence would then be 'then I should nourish hope all the days of heavy service; until my release comes'.

15 : 20 (C) The RSV renders the second part of the verse 'through all the years that are laid up for the ruthless'. The BSG, however, gives another possible translation 'and but few years are in store for the tyrant'. The words *mispar šānīm* indicate years that can be counted. Cf. *šᵉnōt mispār* 'few years' in Job 16 : 22. The verb *ṣāpan* means here 'to be hidden', or 'to be kept in store'.

15 : 22 (C) The word *ṣāpū(y)* can be taken as the pass. part. of *ṣāpā(h)* which means 'to spy, select, destine'. Thus the form here can mean 'he is destined (for the sword)'. The form has also been understood to be an abbreviation of *ṣāpūn*, pass. part. of *ṣāpan* meaning 'to cover, keep', i.e. 'he is kept for the sword'. The meaning of the two translations is practically the same.

: 23 (C) Usually translations reflect the MT literally; as a whole however, the text is not certain. For example, the MT has the word 'where' standing by itself with no predicate.

: 29 (C) The meaning of the last word *minlām* is not known for certain. The LXX has *skian* 'shadow' and the Vg *radicem* 'root' (cf. the RSV 'nor will he strike root in the earth'). Others translate 'his possessions do not spread out over the earth'.

: 11 (C) The final word *yirṭēnī* by its vocalization, would point to a verb *rāṭā(h)*, but such a verb is unknown. The DNV translation 'he surrenders me', and the RSV 'casts me' understand a vocalization *yirᵉṭēnī* from *yāraṭ* 'to throw'. These translations are not certain.

: 13 (C) The meaning of *rabbā(y)w* here is not clear. Usually the word is related to the verb *rābab* 'to shoot', i.e. arrows (cf. Gen 49 : 23). The noun, then, could mean 'arrow' or 'dart' (LXX 'lance'). Is the meaning then a 'fire-arm' or a 'weapon to be thrown'? Both the AV and the RSV translate *rabbā(y)w* as 'his archers'. The word could also mean 'his many', but what the meaning would then be is not clear. Cf. note on Jer. 50 : 29.

: 21 (B) The MT *ūben 'ādām* 'and a person' is understood by the Tg and Vg as *ūkᵉben 'ādām* 'like that of a man' (cf. the RSV). A still different reading in some mss is *ūbē(y)n 'ādām* 'and between the person' (and his neighbor). This is the reading accepted by the DNV. The context must play an important part in the decision here.

: 4 (B) In translating, the object, 'them', must be understood. The MT has only *lō' tᵉrōmēm* 'thou shalt not make to triumph'.

: 6 (B) The form in the MT *limšōl* is a prep. with the inf. construct and could be translated in either one of two ways: 1. 'to rule over', thus understood to be derived from *māšal* 'to rule', or 2. 'to utter a proverb', understood to be from *māšal* 'to speak in proverbs'. Neither of these two meanings fits the context here. It is better to vocalize the word as *limšal*, prep. with a noun construct formation of *māšāl* meaning 'for a proverb' or 'byword'. This translation has the external witness of the ancient versions (LXX, Aq, Symm, Th, and Vg) and has been accepted by the DNV and the RSV.

17 : 10 (B) Instead of the MT *kullām* 'all of them', the form *kullekem* 'all of you' should be read on the basis of a number of mss as well as in keeping with the context.

17 : 12 (C) The verse as a whole is a translation problem. It would appear that the friends of Job have wanted to show him an easy way out of his trouble. In their eyes Job's basic need is repentance. Job remarks that his friends are those who would, as it were, turn night into day (v. 12a). But now comes the textual problem of 12b. Do the words mean '(they think) the light is closer than the darkness', or 'the light (they say) is close by, away from the darkness' (i.e. the darkness is far away)? The DNV has 'the light would be nearer than the darkness', thus taking the prep. as the comparative *min*.

17 : 13-15 (C) With respect to the conditional sentence introduced by the word *'im* 'if', translations reflect considerable variation. The RSV and others have made the protasis or conditional sense continue to the end of v. 14. They then proceed to make the apodosis or conclusion of the conditional sentence begin with v. 15, i.e. 'where then is my hope' (RSV). Another possibility is to make the conditional part of the sentence end with the first part of v. 13 and thus translate 'if I should look for Sheol as my house, then I should have spread my bed in darkness; have said to the pit . . . but where then would be my hope'. Still another possible sense is to take the particle *'im* as introducing a question 'should I cherish hope' (the verb *qāwā(h)* pi. means 'to wait for, to expect'). Job would then proceed to answer his question in saying 'Sheol is my house, I have spread my bed in darkness'.

17 : 16 (A) The MT as it stands is a problem. Should the first word *baddē(y)*, plur. construct form, be rendered 'depths' or 'bolts' or something else? The BSG suggests that the text should be altered to read *'immādī* 'with me'. Another problem is the verb *tēradnā(h)*. The form is 3rd pers. fem. plur. Its subject is apparently the word 'hope' twice-mentioned in v. 15. But, in that case, why should the subject be sing.

and the verb plur.? One vocalization change in the verse seems fairly certain. The last word *nāḥat* 'rest', should be pointed to read *nēḥāt*, impf. 1st pers. plur. of the stem *nḥt* 'to go down'. In general the DNV has translated the verse in a positive sense. On the other hand, the RSV understands the verse as containing a double interrogative sentence 'will it go down . . . shall we descend . . .'? This means that the RSV has understood that the interrogative *ha* was originally prefixed to the first word *baddē(y)*, and that the word *'im* in the middle of the verse is an interrogative particle introducing the second query. Both the DNV and the RSV are possible translations.

: 2 If in the first part of the verse Bildad is addressing his friends, the
C) plur. form *tᵉśīmūn* is entirely in place.

The RSV translation, 'how long will you hunt for words', and the DNV rendering, 'how long will you set traps with words', are both very uncertain. By virtue of its form, the word *qinṣē(y)* is clearly a plur. noun in the construct state, from *qeneṣ* 'fetter, bond'. Literally, then, the text reads 'how long will you put fetters for words', which possibly means 'how long will you put the words in fetters' (= 'when are you going to learn to control your words'). Some have viewed *qinṣē(y)* as derived from *qēṣ* 'end', plur. *qiṣṣē(y)*, the *ṣṣ* being replaced by *nṣ*. At a later time, this replacement should be considered a possibility. In this case the translation would be 'when will you set a limit to your words'. A further difficulty in the verse lies in the 2nd pers. plur. verb form. Apparently Bildad is speaking to more than one person, but, who are they—Job and his friends, or the devout in general of whom Job has just spoken (17 : 8)?

12 (B) The MT is capable of two different renderings; 1. 'his destruction is hungry' which could mean 'disaster hungered for him'. The word *'ōnō*, in this case, could be explained as a construct form with suff. from *'āwen*. This is approximately the translation of the DNV. One can also read a slightly different text, i.e. *yirʿab 'āwen lō*, disaster hungered for him'. 2. 'His strength is (shall be) hunger-bitten' (AV and RSV). This translation takes *'ōn* as a substantive meaning 'power, strength'.

18 : 15 (C) The RSV translation 'that which is none of his' is uncertain. The phrase may imply 'things strange to him', or 'terrifying things' such as are mentioned in Is 13 : 20 ff.

19 : 25 (C) Cf. the commentaries for the necessary information on this verse. For the word *gō'ēl*, the RSV suggests the renderings 'redeemer' and 'vindicator'. More recently, the translation 'protector' has been suggested by Johnson (Supplements to VT, I, 1953 pp. 67-77).

19 : 28 (B) From the standpoint of the context and on the basis of many mss and ancient versions, the last word of the verse, *bī* 'in me', should be changed to read *bō* 'in him'.

19 : 29 (B) The last word of the verse can be understood either as *šāddīn* 'that there is a judgment' (Aq, Symm, Th, followed by the DNV and RSV), or as *šeddayyān* 'that there is a judge'. The word contains the relative *ša*, *še*.

20 : 2 (C) The RSV translation 'because of my haste within me', is not certain. Nor is the DNV rendering 'because of the tumult within me'. The word *ḥūš* can mean either 'to make haste' or 'be agitated' (cf. BSG 'because of the agitation within me'). Some believe that the verb here means 'to consider', i.e. 'because of the consideration within me'.

20 : 3 (B) There are two possible translations of the second half of the verse: 1. the RSV, translating the MT *mibbīnātī*, has 'and out of my understanding a spirit answers me'; 2. the DNV following the example of the LXX renders 'but spirit without understanding answers me', i.e. *mibbīnā(h)*. It is clear that here the interpretation of the text and the choice of textual reading, influence each other.

20 : 22 (B) The MT reads *'āmēl* 'laborer, sufferer' (AV incorrectly 'wicked') which has little if any meaning in this setting. It is better to change the vocalization slightly and read the word *'āmāl* 'misery' (cf. the DNV and RSV).

20 : 23 (B, C) The word *yᵉhī* is omitted in translation. Some have felt that the tetragrammaton (the name Yahweh) is here, but this is unlikely.

The translation 'food' for *l*^{e}*ḥūm* is uncertain. The word *leḥem* is a possible parallel. Another suggestion is that the word means 'meat' or 'bowels', but these translations do not fit here as they do in Zeph 1 : 17. Still others translate 'anger'.

25 (B) The MT has *gēwā(h)* which should be vocalized as *gēwō* 'his back' or 'his body'.

26 (C) The RSV has 'what is left in his tent will be consumed' (DNV 'a fire consumes what is left in his tent'). The verb *yēra'* can be viewed as a form of *rā'ā(h)* 'to browse, graze', and then, with reference to fire, as here, 'to devour, consume'. However, instead of the neuter 'what is left', one can translate 'who is left' or 'survivor'. Thus the translation would be 'it consumes also the last survivor in the tent'.

28 (B) The word *niggārōt*, *niph.* plur. part. of the verb 'to flow away', is rather surprising. One would expect a sing. form to parallel the first half of the verse. In view of other problems here it is perhaps better for the present to follow the translations of the DNV and RSV.

12 (B) The word *b*^{e}*tōp* 'to (or 'with') the tambourine' should be read instead of the awkward MT *k*^{e}*tōp*.

13 (B) It is difficult to fit the MT *yēḥāttū* into the context since the word is from *ḥātat* 'to be dismayed'. It is preferable to read *yēḥātū* from *nāḥat* 'to go down'. The translation then becomes 'they go down to Sheol', and this fits the context perfectly. The change has the support of the ancient versions.

19 (C) The RSV at the beginning adds the explanatory words 'you say'. This addition may serve to make the first part of the verse understandable. For it is true that Job's friends have clearly expressed the conviction that God keeps calamity for the children of the godless, and that he may punish children for the sins of their parents who were left unpunished during their lifetime. The second part of the verse, however, sets forth Job's own idea: the sinner himself should receive the punishment for his deeds. In this situation, then, for the sake of clarity, it would have been better for the RSV to introduce this section

with the additional words 'but I say' to balance its additional words 'you say' at the opening of the verse. It is preferable to use brackets in making additions. One should, of course, be very sparing in introducing any explanatory additions into the text, for in doing so he thereby chooses one interpretation and excludes all others, some of which may deserve consideration.

21 : 24 (C, B) The meaning of the word *'āṭīn* is not certain. The DNV has 'loins' and the RSV 'body' (cf. 'bowels' in the LXX and Vg). The AV 'breasts' can hardly be right. Some believe the form here should really be *'ăṭāmā(y)w* from Aram. *'āṭām* 'flank, side'.

On the basis of the LXX the word *ḥēleb* 'fat' should be read instead of the MT *ḥālāb* 'milk'.

22 : 2 (B) Instead of *'ālē(y)mō*, an apparent plur. form, the word *'ālā(y)w* 'to himself' should be understood.

22 : 17 (B) On the basis of the context and the ancient versional evidence the last word *lāmō* 'to them' should be read as *lānū* 'to us'.

22 : 21 (B) The MT *tᵉbō'ātᵉkā* is a mixed form from *tᵉbū'ātᵉkā* 'your profit, your produce' (cf. the DNV), and from *tᵉbō'ăkā* 'shall come to you'. Thus the RSV renders 'good will come to you' (cf. also the AV).

22 : 25 (C) This verse can be rendered 'and the Almighty shall be your precious gold and your best silver'. The word *beṣer* (plur. *bᵉṣārīm*) is related to *bāṣar* 'to refine, purify'. The meaning here, then, is purified or refined gold. The word *tō'āpōt* really means 'horns, tops', thus 'the best'. Another translation is 'shining silver'. Cf. Hölscher, *op. cit.*, p. 56, and Weiser, *op. cit.*, p. 169.

22 : 30 (B) At the beginning of the verse the RSV has understood *'et nāqī* 'the innocent man', but the DNV has kept to the MT *'ī nāqī* and translated 'him that is not innocent'. In the second part of the verse the Hebr consonants *nmlṭ* should be vocalized as *nimlaṭṭā*, *niph.* perf. 2nd masc. sing. of *mālaṭ*, meaning here 'you will be delivered'.

23 : 2 (C) The Hebr has literally 'also now, rebellion is my complaint'. Thus,

m^erī comes from *mārā(h)* 'to rebel'. But in place of the MT *m^erī*, the RSV has followed the Pesh, Tg, and Vg in reading *mar*, i.e. 'my complaint is bitter' (cf. also the AV). A textual change, however, is unnecessary. In the second part of the verse, some believe that the reading *yādō* 'his hand', supported by the LXX and Pesh, is correct. The MT, however, can be explained. Its reading 'my hand lies heavy on my groan' may indicate that the groan can be suppressed, at least to some extent. Thus the DNV has 'although my hand controls my groan'. It is possible that the final phrase 'on my groaning' actually means 'on me the one who groans'.

3 (C) The RSV translation 'that I might come even to his seat' implies a dependence upon the words *mī yittēn*. But it is also possible to translate 'then I should go to his seat'.

7 (C) The RSV translation 'and I should be acquitted forever by my judge' (cf. also the DNV) follows the MT pointing. Literally the Hebr reads 'and I should make myself safe for my judge'. It is preferable to adopt a slight change in vocalization. Following a number of Hebr mss and the ancient versions, read the last word as *mišpāṭī* 'my right'. The translation of the verse will then become 'there a righteous man can plead with Him, and I should make my right safe for ever'. (Cf. KBL s.v. *pālaṭ*), The word *lāneṣaḥ* can mean not only 'for ever', but also 'glorious' (cf. the lexica), which would give a note of triumph to the phrase. This alternative translation of the verse is worthy of definite consideration.

12 (B) In the second strophe the MT reads *mēḥuqqī* 'away from my commandment'. It is clear that this reading does not tie in with the context in which Job is citing his close adherence to the commandments and words of God. Rather than the word *mēḥuqqī*, one should read *b^eḥēqī* 'in my bosom', a reading that has the support of the LXX and the Vg. Thus the RSV (cf. the DNV) renders 'I have treasured in my bosom the words of his mouth'. The AV translation 'more than my necessary food' for the MT 'away from my commandment', illustrates how far it has strayed from the MT meaning while attempting to give a literal sense.

23 : 17 (C) The DNV has retained the negative *lō'* 'not', and translated 'therefore I do not perish because of the darkness, nor because darkness covers my face'. This rendering is dubious. On the basis of one Hebr ms, the RSV and others omit the *lō'* and read *pānay* instead of *mippānay*, i.e. 'for I am hemmed in by darkness, and thick darkness covers my face' (RSV). Still another possibility is to retain *lō'* and understand it in a positive sense, like the Accad. *lu*. Thus the translation might be 'for I perish as a result of darkness, because darkness covers (me)'. This means, however, that one reads *mippᵉnē(y)* 'because', instead of the MT *mippānay*, thereby paralleling the *mippᵉnē(y)* in the first half of the verse.

24 : 1 (C) This verse can be taken as a direct continuation of chap. 23. Thus a possible translation is 'why are times hidden from the Almighty, while those who know him do not see his days'. The 'times' are 'times of judgment'.

24 : 5 (C) The DNV has followed the MT punctuation and, accordingly, connected the word *'ărābā(h)* with the second part of the verse. This makes the translation 'seeking food, the wilderness must give them the food for the children'. Others connect *'ărābā(h)* with the first part of the verse and read 'as food' instead of 'food to him', omitting *lō*. Thus the RSV renders 'seeking prey in the wilderness as food for their children'. Another possibility is to interpret the word *lō* 'to him' as though it were *lō'* 'not'. This makes possible the rendering 'seeking prey in the wilderness, because they have no bread for the children'.

24 : 9 (C) The RSV has 'and take in pledge the infant of the poor'. This means that it has adopted the reading *'ul* 'infant' instead of the MT *'al* 'upon'. With regard to the verb *ḥābal*, it can mean 'to accept as a pledge'. But a verb *ḥābal* also exists meaning 'to act in anger'. Thus, the DNV has 'and act violently against the poor'.

24 : 11 (B) The Hebr reads *šūrōtām*, a plur. noun from *šūrā(h)* with the 3rd pers. masc. plur. suff. From the evidence of late Hebr, the word probably means 'row' (i.e. 'row of trees', cf. Dalman, *Aramäisch-Neuhebr. Handwörterbuch*). Specifically here the *šūrōt* are 'rows' or 'terraces' of the vine and olive orchards. Cf. KBL 'supporting wall' (of terraces).

The RSV has rendered 'among the olive rows of the wicked'. The words 'of the wicked' are a helpful clarification of the 3rd masc. plur. suff. of *šūrōtām*. The DNV, on the other hand, has read a dual form *šūrōtayim* 'two terraces'.

12 (B) Instead of the MT *mᵉtīm* 'men', the word *mētīm* 'dying' should be read.

17 (B) Instead of the Hebr sing. form *yakkīr*, read the plur. *yakkīrū* 'they are friends with'.

18 (A) The two words of the MT *qal hū'* 'quick is he' are better read as one, *qallū* 'swiftly they float on'. The RSV has made this change and clarified the text further by the introductory phrase 'you say'.

The third strophe apparently reads 'the way of the vineyards does not turn'. Does this mean that the vineyards produce no fruit? In comparison with the first two sentences of the verse as well as the context of the next verse, it is certain that some misfortune is implied. Should the verb be made a plur., i.e. 'they do not turn down the roads to the vineyards', the meaning still is not clear. The RSV has vocalized the MT *derek* 'way, road' as *dōrēk* 'a treader', and thus translated 'no treader turns toward their vineyards'.

19 (A) The last two words read literally 'realm of the dead, they sin'. The problem has been solved in most translations by relating closely 19a, which has subject, verb, and object, to 19b. Thus the subject of 19b is 'realm of the dead', the missing verb is supplied from 19a, and the object in 19b becomes the perf. verb form *ḥāṭā'ū*, possibly to be taken in a relative sense, i.e. 'they who sin'. The resulting translation, however, is very hypothetical. The RSV (cf. also the AV) has 'so does Sheol those who have sinned'.

20 (C) Like the DNV, the BSG (cf. also the AV) has kept to the traditional text, and rendered as faithfully as possible 'the womb forgets him; the worm sucks him; he is no longer remembered'. The form *mᵉtāqō* from *mātaq* means here 'to suck with pleasure'. The RSV, however, has followed an altered text, reading *rᵉḥōb mᵉqōmō* 'the squares of the

town' instead of the MT *reḥem m^etāqō*, and *š^emō* 'his name' in place of the MT *rimmā(h)*. In addition, the RSV has changed the sing. suff. attached to the first word into a plur. 'them'. Thus it renders 'the squares of the town forget them, their name is no longer remembered'.

24 : 24 (B) The translation of the RSV and DNV 'and they are no more' (RSV 'and then are gone'), is actually a faithful rendering of the MT *'ē(y)-nennū*, *'ē(y)n* with 3rd pers. masc. sing. suff. It is true that in order to obtain this translation, one would expect the form *'ē(y)nām* which contains the 3rd pers. masc. plur. suff. On the other hand the sing. can be understood as a collective which allows for the use of the plur. in translation.

26 : 7-9 (C) It is possible to translate these sentences as dependent instead of independent. They would then be linked to the main idea in v. 6, i.e. 'Sheol is naked before him (v. 6) . . . who stretches out the north' (v. 7). In this way, the Hebr participles in verses 7-9 can be viewed as being in apposition to the word *negdō* 'before him' of v. 6. Both possible meanings, the independent and dependent, are reflected in various translations. Cf the notes on 5 : 9-13 and 9 : 5-10.

26 : 10 (B, C) The cognate phrase in the MT *ḥōq ḥāg* 'he enclosed a boundary' has been read in some versions as *ḥāqaq ḥug* 'he marked out a circle' (cf. the RSV). The DNV renders 'he drew a circle over the surface of the water'. The prep. *'al* can mean 'above' or 'over' as well as 'upon'. The word *ḥōq* can be taken as an inf. (cf. the inf. in 9b). Thus, one can translate,

> 'he covers the sight of his throne
> by spreading out his clouds over it,
> by drawing a circle above the surface of the water'.

This 'circle' then, must mean the firmament (cf. 22 : 14 where the RSV has 'vault of heaven'). Instead of 'throne', some propose to read, with a different pointing, 'full moon', but this emendation is unnecessary.

26 : 12 (C) The verb *rāga'* here should mean 'to terrify' and not 'to still'. The 'sea', here personified, becomes terrified by God's great power. Even

Rahab, a primeval monster, is overpowered. Cf. KBL, Hölscher (*op. cit.*, p. 62), and Weiser (*op. cit.*, p. 190). In this section of Job, one finds many mythological characteristics.

8 (B) The MT *yēšel* is derived from *šālā(h)* 'to pull out'. Its vocalization is that of a shortened impf., an unusual form in this place. But even if the vocalization is changed, the meaning remains essentially the same. Cf. the RSV 'when God takes away his life'. The DNV rendering 'if he demands' springs from a conjectured form *yiš'al*, impf. verb from *šā'al* 'to ask, demand'.

19 (B) The Hebr has 'he goes to bed rich and does not perish' (literally 'and is not gathered', cf. Gen 49 : 33). The context makes this meaning dubious. Rather the sense is that he goes to sleep a rich man which he cannot do again, for, before the next night comes, his riches will have vanished. Accordingly, one needs to change the vocalization from the MT *niph.* form *yē'āsēp*, derived from the verb *'āsap* 'to gather', and form the word *yōsīp* 'he will do again', derived from *yāsap* 'to increase'. The LXX and Pesh read this altered form and it has been accepted by the DNV and RSV. The RSV reads 'he goes to bed rich, but will do so no more'.

23 (B) On the word *'ālē(y)mō*, cf. 22 : 2.

The word *kappē(y)mō* 'their hands' or 'his hands' can hardly be correct in this place. One obtains a satisfactory reading, however, by dropping the *waw* at the end of the word 'thus reading *kappayim* 'hands'.

5 (C) Both the DNV and RSV translate the last two words 'as by fire'. The literal Hebr, however, reads 'as fire'. A faithful translation of the whole verse follows:

> 'the earth out of it comes bread,
> and beneath it there is turned over as fire'.

Evidently the meaning is that under the earth there is a turning and churning similar to the action of fire as its flames turn up, or curl under. Thus, the translation should apparently be, 'but underneath it, it is turned up like fire (turns up)'.

28 : 11 (B) The MT followed by the RSV reads 'he binds up the streams so that they do not weep', i.e. 'trickle'. The reference is to running streams in the mines (KBL s.v. *ḥbš*). Instead of the MT *mibbᵉkī* 'from trickling', however, the DNV (Cf. KBL, Supplementum, p. 141) has read *mabbᵉkē(y)* or *nibkē(y)* 'sources of'. On the other hand, an alteration of the text may be unnecessary since KBL mentions another substantive *mibkī* with the meaning 'place of trickling'. Since the word *mibkī* however, is unknown elsewhere, one cannot be sure that it exists.

29 : 3 (B) The RSV translates 'when his lamp shone upon my head' (cf. also the AV), but the DNV has 'when he (i.e. God) made his lamp shine above my head'. The difference between the translations is tied up with the first word of the MT *bᵉhillō*. The DNV has read this as a causative verb form *bahăhillō* (= *bahillō*), and has, accordingly, taken the suff. as referring to God and the following word *nērō* 'his light' as the direct object. On the other hand, the RSV has read the MT *bᵉhillō* as it stands and thus taken the suff. as referring to the word 'lamp' and the suff. of the word 'lamp', i.e. *nērō*, as referring to God. The RSV, then, reflects the literal rendering of the Hebr 'in its shining (that is) his lamp upon my head.'

29 : 10 (B) The difficulty of the MT is that the sing. subject 'voice' has a plur. verb *neḥbā'ū* 'they were hidden', perhaps by influence from the plur. of the preceding noun, *nᵉgīdīm* 'nobles'. Since the verb *neḥbā'ū* is found shortly before in v. 8, it is possible that here in v. 10 it may be a scribal error for *ne'ĕlām* 'was silent, stilled'. Thus the RSV renders 'the voice of the nobles was hushed' (cf. also the DNV and AV).

29 : 16 (C) The Hebr reads literally 'and a cause, I did not know, I searched it out'. This can be rendered either 'the cause which I knew not' (AV), or, 'the cause of him whom I did not know' (RSV). The Hebr gives no hint of preference here so that one should regard both possibilities as being of equal value.

29 : 18 (A) Cf. the extensive critical notes in BH. The phrase *'im qinnī* 'with my nest', or 'along with my nest' cannot be translated 'in my nest' (AV and RSV), or 'with my nestlings' (BSG). The expression is apparently

literal, possibly referring to the story of the phoenix that burned in its nest to rise rejuvenated from the ashes (Ovid, *Metamorph.* XV 396). The phoenix does seem to be mentioned here in 18b. It is true that the word *ḥōl* means 'sand', and that the RSV translation 'and I shall multiply my days as the sand' gives an understandable sense. The difficulty, however, is fitting this idea with the *'im qinnī* of the first half of the verse. It is, therefore, entirely possible that by *ḥōl* (possibly *ḥūl*) the phoenix bird is meant. This agrees with the ancient Jewish tradition (cf. also the LXX) and has been accepted by the DNV. Cf. G. Hölscher (*op. cit.*, p. 72, 73, 75) and A. Weiser (*op. cit.*, p. 205). This understanding of the verse is open to objections. The basic question, of course, is whether by the use of 'phoenix' one is interpreting the text instead of translating it.

13 (C) The last three words of the MT read 'no helper for them', i.e. 'without anybody helping them'. It is possible that instead of the verb *'āzar* in the MT, the verb *'āṣar* 'to restrain' should be read. Thus the RSV translates 'no one restrains them'.

15 (B) In place of the MT *qal* form *tirdōp*, the *niph. tērādēp* should be read. Thus the DNV renders 'my honor is swept away', but the RSV more literally 'my honor is pursued'.

18 (C) In the first half of the verse the DNV has kept the traditional text 'my garment is disfigured', whereas the RSV has followed the LXX and rendered 'it seizes my garment'. In the last part of the verse, the RSV takes the word *pī* in *keपī* as a noun meaning 'collar' (cf. KBL and Ps 133 : 2). The verb *'āzar* is then translated 'to tie' or 'to encircle narrowly'. The word *kepī*, however, can mean 'as', 'like', in which case the noun 'collar' would cease to exist. The word *'āzar* does not necessarily mean 'to encircle narrowly', but regularly means 'to gird, surround as a girdle'. Thus, the DNV has 'it hangs around me as my tunic', which can also mean 'it hangs on to me to the size of my tunic', i.e. as far as my tunic reaches.

20 (B) The parallelism of the verse calls for the repetition of the word 'not' in the second strophe.

30 : 22 (B) The DNV has understood the last word of the verse as *tᵉšūʾā(h)* 'heavy weather' (RSV 'the roar of the storm'). There is no connection with the word *tušīyyā(h)* of the Wisdom literature meaning 'effectual working' (cf. the commentaries).

30 : 24 (B) The MT has the word *bᵉʿī* translated 'in a heap of ruins' by the RSV. The translation is difficult in this context. The DNV has understood an additional consonant and thus read *tōbēăʿ* 'drowning person', or, 'someone falling down'. Further on in the verse, the DNV has read *lō yᵉšuʿā(h)* and has translated these words 'if he is helpless in his misery'. The MT *lāhen šūăʿ* cannot be understood. The RSV has translated the verb form *yᵉšawwēăʿ* 'cry for help'.

31 : 32 (B) The DNV and RSV have adopted a widely-accepted vocalization change and read *ʾōrēăḥ* 'traveller', instead of *ʾōraḥ* 'path'.

31 : 33 (C) The word *kᵉʾādām* can be translated 'like Adam' (cf. Gen 3), or 'in a human way', or 'as people are accustomed to do'. Usually, however, the word is changed to read *mēʾādām* 'from men'. While the change provides an excellent meaning, it is not necessary.

31 : 36 (B) In agreement with the LXX, the RSV and DNV understand a sing. form 'as a crown' or 'diadem' in place of the Hebr plur. On the other hand it is possible to view the plur. as intensive ('magnificent crown') rather than numerical.

32 : 9 (B) The word *zᵉqēnīm* 'aged', in the second half of the verse, leads one to translate the parallel *rabbīm* in the first half as 'old men', which is actually done in the LXX (cf. also the DNV and RSV). The AV, on the other hand, by adding the word 'always', has given a meaning to the verse that is foreign to the Hebr.

32 : 16 (C) The word *kī* can mean here either 'because' or 'although'. The way in which one translates the word depends on his interpretation of the text as a whole.

33 : 17 (B, C) On the basis of the Tg and Vg, the DNV and RSV have read *mimmaʿăśēhū* 'from his deed', instead of the MT *maʿăśe(h)*.

The last word in the verse is the verb 'to cover'. By changing only one letter, the translation becomes 'to cut off' (RSV 'and cut off pride from man'). Nevertheless it is not necessary to alter the text. The MT means 'to cover up pride away from man', i.e. so that pride cannot reach man. The prep. *min* before the noun *geber* fits this interpretation. Thus a translation of the MT is 'to keep pride away from man'.

18 (C) The last word *šālaḥ* is rendered 'sword' in the RSV and 'javelin' in the DNV. KBL translates the two words *ʿābar baššelaḥ* as 'rush into a javelin'. The parallelism of the verse, however, requires some word that will correspond to the word *šaḥat* 'the pit' in 18a. Dhorme (JPOS, 1920, p. 45) believes that *šelaḥ* here means a shaft to the nether-world or Sheol.

27 (B) Read the first word as *yāšir* 'he sings'.

30 (C) Translations here tend to read *lirʾōt* and render 'that he may see the light of life' (cf. the RSV). But again, the MT as it stands, though unusual, can be translated. The form *lēʾōr* can be the same as *lᵉhēʾōr* 'to be lighted with'. Thus, the MT reads 'so that he may be lighted with the light of life'.

3 (B) It is possible to read the MT *leʾĕkōl* and translate the latter part of the verse 'as the palate tastes while eating'. For two reasons, however, the noun form *ʾōkel* 'food' should be read: first, the parallelism of the verse favors the word 'food' which fits the noun 'words' in the first strophe, and, second, Elihu is here quoting Job's words in 12 : 11. Therefore the phrase 'as the palate tastes food' that occurs in 12 : 11 should be adopted as the reading in 34 : 3 as well. The change involved is one of vocalization only.

6 (C) Most translations have 'my wound' (AV, RSV, etc.). The MT reads literally 'my arrow'. The meaning is possibly a wound caused by an arrow, or possibly 'illness' (cf. Job 6 : 4 'the arrows of the Almighty stick in me').

13 The prep. *ʿal* with the 3rd masc. sing. suff. offers two possible trans-

(C, B) lations. First, it is possible that the influence or force of the prep. extends into the second strophe without being actually repeated. Thus the RSV renders the second part 'and who laid on him the whole world'. The second possibility is that *'al* belongs only to the first strophe. The verb *śīm* in 13b, then, would mean 'to found'. Accordingly, the DNV renders 'who has founded the entire world'.

The MT vocalization *'ārṣā(h)* 'earthward' should be read either as *'arṣō* 'his earth' or as *'ereṣ* 'earth'.

34 : 16 (B) The MT *weʾim bīnā(h)* 'and if insight' should be understood with the old Greek versions as *weʾim bīnōtā(h)* 'and if you have insight'.

34 : 18 (B) The first word of the MT is an interrogative particle with the inf., which is difficult to translate smoothly. The AV has tried, i.e. 'is it fit to say to a king', but in doing so it has added to the text. The awkwardness vanishes if the Hebr pointing is changed to form *hā'ōmēr* 'he who says' (cf. the LXX). The change sheds light on the verse. Elihu has been illustrating his conviction that with God, might and right go hand in hand. God does not need to regard even the king, for (v. 18) he can call a king a 'worthless person' and nobles 'wicked ones'.

34 : 20 (C) Apparently the Hebr reads 'the people are made to waver'. The translation 'to be startled' is, therefore, uncertain. The sequel at the close of the verse is, thus, 'and they make the mighty (Hebr sing. noun) to yield, not by a hand'. The RSV rendering 'and the mighty are taken away by no human hand' understands the sing. noun *'abbīr* as a collective. Job 24 : 22 might be compared: there, however the plur. *'abbīrīm* is employed! It may be, then, that *'abbīr* in this place (34 : 20), means 'the Mighty One', i.e. God. The preceding plur. verbal form *yāsīrū* could be read *yesīrō*, a sing. form with the suff. referring back to the word *'ām* found two words before. One Hebr ms actually has the form *yāsīr*. This evidence points to the DNV rendering as a definite possibility, 'and the Mighty One makes it disappear, not by human hand'.

34 : 23 (B) The word *mō'ēd* 'appointed time' should be read instead of *'ōd* 'yet' (cf. the RSV 'for he has not appointed a time for any man'). The MT

as it stands can only be rendered 'he did not take any more notice of man': it does not support the AV with its addition 'for he will not lay upon man more than right'.

29 ff. Out of an obscure Hebr text that has been frequently altered, one must try to produce an understandable translation in these verses. Ancient versions do not provide much help. To weigh translations does not aid us materially, since they are all uncertain. An illustration is v. 29c. It reads literally 'both one nation and one man together'. Does this mean 'whether it be a nation or a man' (RSV)? Other translations believe there is a verbal form here.

3 (C) In agreement with the DNV, the RSV translates 'how am I better off than if I had sinned'. A different translation, however, is perhaps preferable. The MT reads literally 'what does it avail me away from my sin', which apparently means 'what does it avail me that I do not sin'. Cf. the translation of Hölscher (*op. cit.*, p. 84), *wenn ich von Sünde rein*. Weiser (*op. cit.*, p. 227) has a translation that deserves serious consideration. It reads *was frommt mir's, ohne Schuld zu sein*.

15 (B) The word *paš* in the Hebr text is unknown. On the basis of Th and Symm one should read *peša'* 'transgression'.

14 (C) The last word in Hebr reads 'among the cult prostitutes,' but translations generally avoid the literal sense. The RSV has 'their life ends in shame', since cult prostitution was a shameful thing to Israel. The BSG has 'their life ends prematurely', which agrees with the idea that those who are dedicated to such a low existence will not live long. This idea parallels the preceding phrase 'they die in youth'. The AV has 'their life is among the unclean'.

29 (B) Near the beginning of the verse, the DNV has understood the word *mī* 'who' instead of the Hebr *'im* 'if'. The change, however, seems unnecessary in view of the fact that *'im* can have either a hypothetical sense 'if', or an interrogative sense. The RSV has accepted the interrogative idea with an indefinite subject 'can any one understand'.

33 (B) The MT 'cattle' appears to be unrelated to the context. It is better

to alter the vocalization of the second strophe and read *mᵉqanne(h) 'ap ʿal ʿawlā(h)* 'he is jealous with anger against iniquity'.

37 : 4 (C) The MT has 'and he does not restrain them'. Since flashes of lightning are apparently meant, the RSV has spelled the object out, i.e. 'and he does not restrain the lightnings'.

37 : 6 (B) The last word of the verse is *ʿuzzō* 'his power'. Since the parallelism of the verse favors an imperative, it is better to read *ʿōzzū* 'be strong'.

37 : 7 (C) The second half of the MT reads 'that all the people of his work (or, 'the people whom He has made') may know' (cf. the RSV margin). Thus the last two words are in a construct relation. On the other hand, it is possible that here is a case of haplography, the final *m* of *'ănāšîm* 'men' in the absolute state having dropped out before the *m* at the beginning of the next word. If the original text had the absolute form *'ănāšîm*, the translation should be 'that all men may know his work' (AV, RSV).

37 : 9 (C) The DNV translates *mᵉzārîm* as 'sheds' (= storehouses). But this is actually a translation of *mᵉzāwîm*. Both Ges-Buhl and KBL explain *mᵉzārîm* as a *pi.* part. plur. from *zārā(h)* meaning here 'the scatterers'. In accord with an old Jewish tradition, the meaning would evidently be the cold north winds (cf. Hölscher, *op. cit.*, p. 87, and 'scattering winds' of the RSV). Thus the word *ḥeder* 'storeroom' in the first half of the verse, must mean 'the south' (cf. 9 : 9 where mention is made of 'the rooms of the south'). This means, then, that the text actually refers to both the northern and southern regions of the sky. The AV and BSG are brief and to the point here. The AV has 'out of the south cometh the whirlwind: and cold out of the north', while the BSG reads 'from the South comes the whirlwind; and from the North the ice'.

37 : 11 (C) Since the verb *ṭāraḥ* means 'to be burdened with', the translation of the *hiph.* causative form with the first part of the verse, would be 'He also burdens the clouds with water' (or 'moisture'). The thought is that the water is the load which the clouds have to carry, and thus it is

possible to translate 'he also loads the clouds with masses of water' (cf. the RSV).

12 (B) On the word *'ārṣā(h)*, cf. the note on 34 : 13.

13 (B) The Hebr word *šēbeṭ* is rendered by the AV and RSV as 'correction', though in 9 : 34 and 21 : 9 both versions translate the same word by 'rod'. Here in 37 : 13 both have interpreted the 'rod' as the instrument of punishment or correction ('whether for correction or for his land' = the RSV). The DNV has omitted the second *'im* and thereby joined this part of the sentence to the beginning 'to a rod for his land'.

8 (B) The initial Hebr *waw consecutive* connects this verse with the preceding one, i.e. 'and all the sons of God shouted for joy and he shut in the sea with doors'. This can hardly be the original sense since a new section, dealing with the origin of the sea, begins with v. 8. Therefore, instead of the MT *wayyāsek* 'and he shut in', one should read *mī sak* 'who has shut in'.

11 (B) The form *yāšīt* with the prep. *bᵉ* is unusual. It is better to read *yišbōt gᵉ'ōn* and translate the second part of the verse 'here the pride of your waves (= 'your proud waves') shall remain' (cf. the AV and RSV).

36 (C) A problem is present in the words *ṭuḥōt* and *śekwī* which have been rendered respectively in the DNV as 'dark clouds' and 'fantastic masses of clouds'. But this translation is just as uncertain as the AV 'inward parts' and 'heart', and the RSV 'clouds' and 'mists'. According to KBL, *śekwī* means 'a cock'. Hölscher (*op. cit.*, pp. 95, 97), after considering in detail many translations, concludes that *ṭuḥōt* also probably means a bird, i.e. the ibis. The translation would then be,

'who has given wisdom to the ibis,
and insight to the cock'.

Some objection to this translation might be offered since the series of wonders taken from the animal world does not begin until v. 39. While this is true, it may be that the context and sequence of verses here have been jumbled in transmission. Cf. the commentaries for further discussion.

39 : 13 (C) (DNV, 16) The RSV (cf. also the DNV and BSG) has translated 'but are they the pinions and plumage of love', but this is very dubious. The early versions have the names of birds, in which case the text must be altered. The word *ḥăsīdā(h)* can be a fem. adj. from *ḥāsīd* 'devout', but it can also be a noun ('stork'? or 'heron'?). The Hebr text simply is not clear.

39 : 16 (B) (DNV, 19) In agreement with two mss the form *taqšīăḥ*, impf. 3rd pers. fem. sing., should be read instead of the MT *hiqšīăḥ*, perf. 3rd pers. masc. sing.

39 : 18 (C) (DNV, 21) The RSV rendering 'when she rouses herself to flee' is very uncertain. Hölscher (*op. cit.*, p. 92) has *Aber schnellt sie in die Höhe*, while others have 'when she claps proudly with her wings'.

39 : 19 (C) (DNV, 22) The RSV follows the Tg in rendering 'do you clothe his neck with strength'? It is usually thought that the horse's mane is meant. Cf. KBL on *raʿmā(h)*. There is also a word *raʿmā(h)*, similar to *raʿam* meaning 'thunder'. Hence the AV has 'hast thou clothed his neck with thunder', but this is definitely not the meaning. There is no reason why the translation 'mane' should not be used.

39 : 21 (B) (DNV, 24) In agreement with the LXX, the Pesh and the Vg, one should read the first word as sing. This will make it fit in with the other two sing. verbs in the verse.

39 : 30 (B) (DNV, 33) For the word *yeʿalʿū* one should understand *yelaʿleʿū* from *lāʿaʿ* 'to gulp'.

40 : 5 (B) (DNV, 39 : 38) The RSV has followed the MT reading 'I have spoken once but I do not reply'. The DNV renders 'I have spoken once but I shall not do so again' (i.e. repeat it), thereby accepting a slight alteration to the text. The old versions, however, do not support this change and it is not necessary.

: 13 (C) The MT has literally 'hidden place'. Even if it should be demon-
NV, 8) strated to mean 'the world below' (RSV), there is no need to translate it thus. For the word translated 'their faces', some suggest the rendering 'in person'.

: 19 The Hebr 'ways of God' can readily be understood as 'works of
B) God' (cf. Job 26 : 14; Prov 8 : 22). The second half of the verse is
NV, 14) admittedly difficult. In the first place, the form *hāʿōśō*, *qal* active part., has both article and a suff. The RSV has rendered 'let him who made him bring near his sword'. On the basis of the LXX the DNV has read *heʿāśū(y)* 'the creature' instead of *hāʿōśō*. Then again, the meaning of this part of the verse is not clear (cf. the RSV). A rather drastic alteration of the text produces the following translation 'made to rule over his fellows'.

: 24 (C) The RSV translation 'hooks' in place of the MT 'eyes', means a
NV, 19) textual change. It is better, however, to take the MT as it is. 'In his eyes', however, can hardly mean 'if he sees it, and is therefore on his guard', or 'in front'.

: 9 (B) The MT reads 'his hope' which probably means the hope of him
NV, who is trying to attack the crocodile (cf. the RSV). The translation
: 28, remains uncertain. In the second part of the verse *gam* should be read
Γ, 41 :1) instead of the MT *hăgam*.

: 11 (C) The translation of the first two words *mī hiqdīmanī* is very uncer-
NV, 2, tain. The DNV has 'who would come towards Me (apparently
Γ, 3) 'God') whom I should leave unharmed', which is a possible rendering. The RSV has 'who has given to me, that I should repay him', but this is not certain. It is a free translation, based perhaps on Mic 6 : 6 where the *pi*. form of *qādam* occurs in the sense of approaching another with a gift. The LXX renders Job 41 : 3 as 'who came against me (as an enemy, cf. Amos 9 : 10) and continues to stand firm'. This translation means that the verb form from *šālēm* was understood to be in the 3rd. pers. and not the 1st pers. as in the MT.

: 12 (C) The meaning of the word *ḥīn* is uncertain. Various translations

(DNV, 3, MT, 4) for the final phrase are ‘goodly frame’, ‘grace of this structure’, ‘beautiful stature’.

41 : 13 (B) (DNV, 4, MT, 5) On the basis of parallelism in the verse as well as the LXX (cf. the RSV) the word *siryōnō* ‘his armor’ should be read for *risnō* ‘his bridle’. The word ‘armor’ is clearly more applicable to the crocodile.

41 : 15 (B) (DNV, 6, MT, 7) The context as well as ancient versions (LXX and Aq) support the reading *gēwō* ‘his back’. The MT *gaʾăwā(h)* is probably a scribal error.

41 : 20 (B) (DNV, 11, MT, 12) The DNV has understood the last word to be *ʾōgēm*, part. of *ʾāgam* ‘to be hot’, thus translating ‘steaming pot’. The MT *ʾagmōn*, however, is found in 41 : 2 (DNV 40 : 21, MT 40 : 26) where it means ‘rush’ (RSV ‘rope’). It corresponds to *ʾăgam* ‘pool’, a loan-word in Hebr. The RSV evidently had this word in mind translating it in 41 : 20 as ‘burning rushes’. Understood in this way, a textual change is unnecessary.

41 : 29 (B) (DNV, 20, MT, 21) The Hebr plur. verb form in 20a implies that the substantive should be understood in a collective sense (cf. the RSV ‘clubs are counted as stubble’). If, however, it is understood that both halves of the verse have the same subject, the verb in 20a must be read in the sing. (cf. the DNV ‘he regards clubs as stubble’).

PSALMS

1 : 2 (C) The word *hāgā(h)* ‘to meditate’ may also mean ‘to read half aloud’ or ‘to mutter’ (cf. KBL).

2 : 12 (C) In the RSV translation ‘kiss his feet’, the translators have accepted a well-known suggested textual change, i.e. *raglā(y)w* ‘his feet’ in place of the MT *bar*. The word *bar* has various meanings:

1. *bar* — ‘son’ in Aram. The rendering then is ‘kiss the son’ (DNV, AV).
2. *bar* — ‘ground’ in Hebr. Thus, ‘kiss the ground’, a sign of complete subjection and homage. This translation deserves careful consideration.

3. *bar* — 'pure' in Hebr. This is clearly the sense of the Vg translation, *adorate pure*.

Consult the commentaries.

4 (C)
T, 5)
The *pi.* form of *ḥālaṣ* can mean either 'to rescue', or 'to shake out', 'to plunder'. Part of the difficulty in translation is due to the word *rē(y)qām* 'without a cause'. If the word is related to the noun 'enemy', then the phrase means 'the one who has no reason to be my enemy' (cf. the AV and Ps 25 : 3). If the word is connected with the verb, it means the writer has no excuse or reason for doing what he has done to his enemy (RSV). Another question is whether the second part of the sentence clearly continues the contrary-to-fact condition, in which case the verb would have the meaning 'to plunder'. Thus, the RSV has interpreted verses 4-5 as 'if I have requited my friend evil or plundered my enemy without cause, let the enemy pursue me . . .' On the other hand, the writer may be illustrating how far from the truth the 'if' clause, or supposed condition of 5a, actually is. In this case the verb would have the meaning 'to rescue'. The AV has 'if I have rewarded evil unto him that was at peace with me; (yea, I have delivered him that without cause is mine enemy); let the enemy persecute my soul . . .' This would mean that the writer is so far removed from the position of recompensing evil to the peaceful man, that he can actually say that he has personally rescued (from danger) the one who has been without cause his enemy.

6 (C)
T, 7)
The DNV has followed the MT vocalization *'ēlay* and translated 'awake to me', i.e. 'awake to my help'. The RSV has accepted an altered pointing *'ēlī*, i.e. 'awake, O my God'.

7(C)
T, 8)
The MT has the impv. form *šūbā(h)* from *šūb* 'to return'. The translation, then, is 'return on high', i.e. after God has come to the writer's help. The phrase is a fitting complement to the imperatives of v. 7, 'rise up' and 'awake to my help'. That is, God has answered the writer's cry of v. 7 and has come down to his rescue. Now (v. 8), since God has delivered, he prays again 'return on high'. Notwithstanding the fitting sense of the MT, the RSV has read an altered text, *š^{e}bā(h)*, impv. of *yāšab* 'to sit down', and translated 'and over it take thy seat on high'. This gives the sense of Yahweh presiding

over an assembly of heavenly beings, if such an assembly is indicated by the phrase 'the assembly of the nations'!

8 : 2 (B) The word *tᵉnā(h)* in the MT, as it stands, is the *qal* impv. 2nd masc. sing. of the verb 'to give'. Translations reflect the difficulty of the form in this place. The DNV reads 'thou hast put thy glory over the heavens', thus understanding the form *nātattā* 'thou hast put, given' instead of the form *tᵉnā(h)*. On the other hand, the RSV has evidently read the word *tunnā(h)*, *pu.* perf. of *tānā(h)* 'to recount, rehearse', understanding 'thy glory' as the subject, i.e. 'thou whose glory above the heavens is chanted'. This change is one of vocalization only. Eerdmans *The Hebrew Book of Psalms*, 1947, pp. 113 ff.) vocalizes the word as *tinnā(h)*, *pi.* perf. of *tānā(h)*, with its subject as 'thy name'. His translation reads '(thy name) which relates thy dignity along the heavens'.

11 : 1 (C) The MT reads literally 'flee, your mountain, bird'. The *Qere* reading of the verb as a 2nd pers. fem. sing. impv. is undoubtedly correct. It is natural to understand the subject of the impv. as the fem. word *napšī* 'my soul' which immediately precedes. As to the word *harkem* 'your mountain', the 2nd pers. masc. plur. suff. seems very strange. It is possible that 'your mountain' or 'your mountain range' means the mountains of Judah to which one fled in danger (cf. Mark 13 : 14). The plur. suff. might be explained as a reference to the inhabitants of Judah: the mountains do not belong to the psalmist alone. Although the final word of the verse *ṣippōr* does not have the prep. *kᵉ* 'as' before it, it can still be translated 'as a bird'. The comparison of the soul to a bird is well known. Thus, the AV translation is surely worthy of consideration, 'flee as a bird to your mountain'. Some, however, have divided the three words of the MT into four, i.e. *nūdī har kᵉmō ṣippōr* 'flee like a bird (to) the mountains' (RSV). It does not seem likely that the word *ṣippōr* can be taken as a vocative as the RSV note implies.

13 : 2 (C) (MT, 3) The word *'ēṣōt* here must mean 'counsels' (Sirach 30 : 21). Thus the translation is 'how long shall I hold counsels in my soul'. The RSV rendering 'how long must I bear pain in my soul', implies a change in text, from the MT *'ēṣōt* 'counsels' to *'ăṣṣābōt* 'pains'.

2-4 (A) The last two words of v. 2 *bal ʿāle(y)kā* 'not above you', are difficult as to sense in this context. It seems that they should be connected with the preceding word *ṭōbātī* 'my good'. The writer is apparently saying that he cannot imagine any good or any happiness that surpasses God. For him God is the greatest happiness. The RSV reflects what most translations have, i.e. 'I have no good apart from thee'. Eerdmans (*op. cit.*, p. 146) says, "the preposition *ʿal*, with, plus, expresses that his *ṭōbā(h)* is confined to Jahu." (i.e. Yaweh). Thus, he identifies God with the good, which is a possible interpretation (cf. v. 5), but which does not differ very much from Symm, the Vg and Tg. The translation in v. 3 'they are noble', assumes that the copula 'and' before *ʾaddīrē(y)* is to be omitted, which is the case in some Hebr mss. In v. 4, while the word *ʾaḥēr* is generally taken as an adj. 'other', Eerdmans suggests that it is a *pi.* inf. of *ʾāḥar* 'to postpone', or, more precisely here 'to place a substitute'. The form *māhārū* can either come from *māhar* (*qal* form) 'to obtain', 'to compete for the favor of', 'to choose', or, as Eerdmans believes, from *mahēr* 'to hasten' (*pi.* form). All of this discussion serves to point out the textual uncertainty that is present in this passage.

14 (A) The translation 'from men' occurring twice, is dubious, the reason being that there is no *daghesh forte*. This makes the presence of the prep. *min* doubtful. The word *ḥeled* means 'duration of life' or 'world', but the connection of the word *mēḥeled* in this verse with the preceding word is linguistically weak. The translations 'worldly men', or 'men whose portion in life is of the world' (RSV), are doubtful. Translation here involves guesswork, for the text is corrupt. Cf. H. J. Kraus, Psalmen (Bibl. Komm.) p. 129.

35 (C) The word *ʿanwā(h)* 'humility' is generally taken in the sense of
T, 36) 'condescending goodness', which, in reality, means 'help' (cf. the RSV).

4 (A) Neither the DNV 'their preaching', nor the RSV 'their voice' are at
T, 5) all certain as translations for the word *qawwām*. The parallelism of the verse calls for some phrase answering to 'their words'. The ancient versions interpreted *qaw* as meaning here a certain sound. Generally *qaw* means 'measuring line'. Possibly here, then, it means 'tenacity

of purpose, fixed rule, fixed course' or something of this kind. However, in view of the fact that the exact meaning is not definitely established, it is better to hold to an existing conception. Cf. Kraus, *op. cit.* p. 153: *qaw* means here „Schall", in agreement with the traditional translation 'sound'.

20 : 9 (C) (MT, 10) The RSV in agreement with the DNV has rendered 'give victory to the king, O Lord'. It is debatable, however, whether the word *hammelek* should be taken as the object of the verb. In the MT it is found after the accent which indicates a separation. It is possible to translate by two vocatives here, i.e. 'give victory, O Lord; O King, answer us when we call'. In this sense, the King is God Himself (cf. the RSV margin). Whether this interpretation is accepted or not, depends largely on the question as to how regular and common is the use of *melek* 'king' to designate God.

22 : 16 (B) (MT, 17) The MT reading 'as a lion' is strange since one would expect a verbal form. However, a verbal form based on the consonants *k'r* is not to be found in Hebr. The LXX has translated the perf. form of *kārā(h)* 'to bore, pierce, dig', and this translation is reflected in the DNV and RSV (RSV—'they have pierced'). This translation is widely accepted because it connects the psalm in a fitting way with the suffering of Christ. But the question remains as to whether 'dogs' and 'evildoers' that are mentioned just before, 'pierce' hands and feet. The KBL, p. 454, understands here another verb *kārā(h)* 'to bind together', which verb fits the context well. Evildoers work in this way. H. Schmidt, *Die Psalmen* (HAT), Erste Reihe 15, p. 36, translates *zerfleischten* which fits the connection with dogs well.

22 : 21 (C) (MT, 22) The DNV has translated 'save me from the mouth of the lion, and from the horns of the wild oxen. Thou hast answered me'. This is an attempt to avoid the unlikely connection of the 'horns of the wild oxen' with answered prayer as is evident in the AV. A different solution through textual change is often adopted, a change suggested by ancient versions (cf. also the RSV 'save me . . . my afflicted soul from the horns of the wild oxen'). The consonantal text, however, appears to have a verbal form. Possibly one should take this last word of v. 22 (RSV, v. 21) and make it the first word of the following

verse where it actually fits better. This is perhaps the best solution to the difficulty (cf. DNV; Kraus, *op. cit.* p. 176).

27 (C) There is not sufficient reason to change the MT 'before thee' to
', 28) read 'before him' (RSV).

29 (C) The MT has *ʾākᵉlū* 'they ate', the subject coming later, i.e. 'all the
', 30) proud (or 'fat ones') of the earth shall eat and worship'. The RSV has divided *ʾākᵉlū* into two words *ʾak* and *lō*, and translated 'yea, to him shall all the proud of the earth bow down.'

30 (B) If one translates with the LXX 'the following generation', it means
', 31) only that the first word of v. 32 becomes the last word of v. 31. Eerdmans (*op. cit.* p. 178) retains the verse division as it is, but interprets the word *laddōr* in a distributive sense, i.e. 'generation after generation'. On the whole it is better to follow the LXX.

4 (C) The vocalization of *ṣalmāwet* indicates the translation 'shadow of death'. But it is preferable to read the word as *ṣalmūt*, a word derived from *ṣālam* 'to be dark'. The translation, then, would be 'deep darkness' (cf. KBL).

6 (B) On the basis of the ancient versions the second half of the verse is usually translated 'I shall dwell in the house of the Lord'. Though the word *šabtī* in the MT might be taken as an unusual form of *yāšab* 'to dwell', yet it is the normal form of the perf. 1st pers. sing. with *waw consecutive* of *šūb* 'to return'. Schmidt (*op. cit.* p. 40) actually states his preference for the translation 'I shall return'.

6 (C) On the basis of the LXX and the Pesh, the RSV has translated 'who seek the face of the God of Jacob', whereas the MT has simply 'who seek thy face, Jacob'. The MT has also been translated 'who seek thy face; (this is) Jacob'. Still another possibility is that the word 'generation' in the first strophe corresponds to the name 'Jacob' in the second. The translation would then be:

> 'such is the generation of those who seek him,
> Jacob, who seeks thy face'.

Although the word order in the Hebr text of v. 6b is not the same as it is in 6a, this translation is entirely possible.

25 : 11 (C) The words *kī rab hū'* 'for it is great', can also be rendered 'how great it may be'.

29 : 9 (C) The translation 'makes the hinds to calve' (RSV margin), is just as possible as 'makes the oaks to whirl' (RSV text).

30 : 3 (C) (MT, 4) The *Kethib* reading, supported by the LXX, Th, and the Vg, has 'from among those who go down to the pit'. This means that the text contains the form *yōrᵉdē(y)*, a plur. part. in the construct state. The *Qere* reading of the Masoretes, supported by Aq, Symm, and the Tg, has *yordī* 'my descent', i.e. inf. plus the 1st pers. sing. suff. In this case the translation becomes 'that I should not go down to the Pit' (RSV margin). The writer would like to suggest a somewhat different translation. It will be noted that the psalmist has employed a strong figure of speech in the first part of the verse, i.e. 'thou hast brought up my soul from Sheol'. Thus, in the second part of the verse, we may have a similar strong metaphor, i.e. 'restored me to life after (or 'out of') my descent to the Pit'. The prep. *min* can be understood in more than one sense!

30 : 7 (C) (MT, 8) The MT reads 'O Lord, by thy favor, thou hast established to my mountain strength' (cf. the AV and the DNV). Eerdmans (*op. cit.*, p. 200) reads 'thy favor . . . made my mountain to stand strong'. This may have a literal or figurative meaning. Cf. the RSV 'thou hast established me as a strong mountain'.

31 : 10 (C) (MT, 11) The MT word 'iniquity' seems quite in place. Because of injustice, the psalmist felt that he was in a miserable state. On the basis of the LXX the RSV has adopted the reading 'misery'.

31 : 11 (C) (MT, 12) Without change in the MT, the beginning of the verse can easily be rendered 'because of all my adversaries, I have become a scorn to my neighbors exceedingly'. The prep. *min* with a causal sense is well known. Thus it is not necessary to alter the text as the RSV does in its translation 'I am the scorn of all my adversaries, a horror to my neighbors'.

4 (C) The word *lāšād* occurs also in Num 11 : 8 where it means a kind of cake or dainty (cf. KBL). Here, the word apparently means ‘sap, marrow, juice’. Thus , *l^{e}šaddī* means ‘my juice’ (= ‘my life-moisture’), if the text has been handed down correctly. The verb *hāpak* means ‘to be changed, turn’, and is probably best rendered here ‘to dry up’. The translation, however, is not certain.

5 (C) The first word is a 3rd pers. plur. perf. form, i.e. ‘they look to him’;
, 6) likewise, the second verb, ‘they are radiant’. These forms agree with the 3rd pers. plur. suff. in the word ‘their faces’. However, the RSV, on the basis of ancient versions, has changed the verb forms to imperatives of the 2nd pers. plur., and similarly read ‘your faces’ instead of ‘their faces’.

7 (B) The word *šaḥat* appears to be in the wrong place, for two reasons: first, ‘pit of their net’ has no meaning (the AV has to add the word ‘in’ to obtain the translation ‘they hid for me their net in a pit’), and, second, the word ‘dig’ in the second strophe has no object. The problems are resolved by transferring the word *šaḥat* to the last half of the verse, and to read with the RSV ‘for without cause they hid their net for me; without cause they dug a pit for my life’. This gives meaning to the verse as well as a better metrical division.

15 (C) The translation ‘cripples’ for the word *nēkīm* is very uncertain. Apparently it is derived from the verb *nākā(h)* ‘to strike’, but the form here could just as well mean ‘strikers, smiters’. One cannot be certain.

16 (C) The first part of the verse is difficult. The DNV has ‘a circle of godless mockers’, and the RSV ‘they impiously mocked more and more’. Both translations are uncertain. According to KBL, the first word *b^{e}ḥanpē(y)* should be rendered ‘alienated from God’, but in that case one would expect the absolute state, not the construct. The verb *lāʿag* means ‘to mock’, or ‘to speak indistinctly’. The noun *māʿōg* could mean ‘cake’, but, according to KBL, it indicates a place to go for food. Thus its translation is not certain. If one reads *lāʿăgū lāʿōg*, the text becomes somewhat clearer. The translations noted above

represent attempts to give a plausible meaning to the passage as a whole, with a minimum of textual changes.

36 : 1 (B, C) (MT, 2) Instead of the MT 'deep in my heart', read 'deep in his heart'. The suff. 'his' fits the context and has the support of the ancient versions as well as a few Hebr mss. Thus, generally, the sentence is rendered 'transgression speaks to the wicked deep in his heart'. But another translation is entirely possible, i.e. 'an oracle about the sin for the sinner (or 'an oracle about the sin of the sinner') is deep in his heart'. A question also surrounds the meaning of the suff. of the final word 'his eyes'. If the suff. refers to the godless, then the translation should be 'there is no fear of God before his eyes' (RSV, DNV, AV). If, however, the suff. refers to God, then the end of the verse would picture the whisperings of sin as saying that one need not take the fear of God seriously (the fear of God before Him just does not exist).

37 : 35 (C) The RSV following the LXX renders 'and towering like a cedar of Lebanon'. (LXX has the plur. 'the cedars'). The MT is difficult. The final word clearly means 'green', but what is the word *'ezrāḥ*? The translation 'native plant' may be the best to be found. Nevertheless the translation is dubious.

38 : 19 (C) (MT, 20) The MT reads 'my enemies live, mighty are they' (cf. the DNV). This rendering is capable of being understood. The RSV, however, in place of the MT *ḥayyīm* 'live, living', has adopted the reading *ḥinnām* 'without cause', translating 'those who are my foes without cause are mighty'.

40 : 2 (C) (MT, 3) The word *šā'ōn* which usually means 'tumult', appears in this context to mean 'wild, deserted place) (RSV 'desolate pit'). The DNV has 'ruin'. Cf. KBL.

40 : 7 (C) (MT, 8) The final word 'of me' can also be rendered 'for me'. The meaning, then, would be 'in the scroll it is written what rests on me', i.e. what is intended for me. The phrase *kātab 'al* can definitely mean 'prescribe' (cf. 2 Kings 22 : 13). In this scroll in Ps 40 : 8, then, there is written 'what is prescribed for me'.

: 3 (C) The MT has 'all his bed'. The RSV translation 'all his infirmities'
T, 4) rests on a changed text.

: 5 (B) At the end of the verse, *pānay* 'my face' should be read for *pānā(y)w* 'his
T, 6) face', and the first word of v. 7 should become the last word of v. 6. In this way the text reads the same as 42 : 12 and 43 : 5. The change is present in a few mss and is seen in the ancient versions. The DNV translates 'my deliverer and my God' while the RSV has 'my help and my God'. Either rendering is possible for the word 'deliverance'.

: 4 (C) The DNV follows the MT closely in translating 'thou surely art my
T, 5) King, O God; ordain . . .' A slight change in word division by adding the final *m* of *'ĕlōhīm* to the next word produces the following translation, 'thou art my King and my God, who ordainest . . .' (RSV).

: 4 (C) The MT reads literally 'for the cause of truth, meekness, and right'.
T, 5) This has a clear meaning and is supported by the ancient versions. Instead of the MT *'anwā(h)*, however, some read *'anē(h)*, a form of the verb *'ānā(h)* 'answer for, testify', or 'defend'. Cf. the RSV 'for the cause of truth and to defend the right'.

: 12 (C) One can translate 'as for the daughter of Tyre (or, 'O daughter of
T, 13) Tyre'), the richest of the people shall seek your favor with presents'. The translation continues in the next verse 'sheer splendor is the king's daughter there within'. The RSV has understood 'there within' as meaning 'in her chamber'. That is a possibility. The variation is due to the fact that the words of verses 13 and 14 (RSV, verses 12, 13) can be grouped differently.

: 7 (C) Instead of *berūăḥ*, i.e. 'by the east (wind thou didst shatter'), a few
T, 8) mss read *kerūăḥ*, i.e. 'as the east wind (which shatters . . . so art thou)'.

: 14 (C) The last two words mean 'about death'. Some believe that this
T, 15) phrase should be added to the words of the heading of Ps 49 that immediately follows, feeling that there is some connection between the words and the contents of Ps 49. The DNV has retained the phrase in Ps 48 and renders 'he shall lead us till death', but the

translation of *'al* as 'up to' or 'till' is uncertain. Perhaps it means 'beyond death'. The RSV has 'for ever'.

49 : 11 (C) (MT, 12) The first word of the MT reads *qirbām* 'their innermost', i.e. 'their deepest thoughts' (cf. the DNV). The meaning is that they think that their houses will exist for ever. This sense fits in with the remainder of the verse. The RSV, however, on the basis of the LXX, reads *qibrām* (metathesis of the *r* and *b*) 'their grave', and translates 'their graves are their homes for ever'. This translation calls for the addition of the word 'though' before 'they named'. The Hebr gives no indication that this addition should be made.

49 : 14 (A) (MT, 15) The RSV translation 'straight to the grave they descend' is based on three main modifications of the MT. It has read *wᵉyērᵉdū* instead of the MT *wayyirdū*, and has combined the words *bām* and *yᵉšārīm* to form *bᵉmē(y)šārīm*, and finally, in place of the MT *bōqer* 'morning', it has read *qeber* 'grave'. Without change, the MT reads 'the upright shall have dominion over them in the morning', the meaning of which is not at all clear in this context. It is a question as to whether *labbōqer* connects with what precedes or with what follows. Still another problem lies in the word *mizzᵉbul* (i.e. *min zᵉbul*) at the end of the verse. This apparently means 'from a dwelling'. However, the vocalization *mizbūl* (without *daghesh* and thus without the prep. *min*) is found in many mss. This is thought to be another form of *zᵉbūl* meaning 'dwelling-place'. The RSV reads 'Sheol shall be their home'. The real problem of translation in the verse is that of relating suffixes to their proper antecedents.

49 : 19 (B) (MT, 20) The MT reading 'you shall come to the generation of his fathers' is difficult in this context. The DNV has altered the suff. of the last word to read 'your fathers'. The RSV and AV have altered the first word from *tābō'* 'you shall come', to *yābō'* 'he shall come' (cf. the LXX). The difficulty goes back to v. 19 where the text begins with the 3rd pers. and ends with the 2nd. The RSV translates by the use of the 3rd pers. throughout the two verses.

50 : 11 (C) The MT 'all the birds of the mountains' has meaning. However,

on the basis of the LXX and Tg, the RSV renders 'all the birds of the air' (LXX = 'all the birds of the heaven').

: 1 (C) The MT, without change in text or word order, reads 'why do you
T, 3) boast, o mighty man, of mischief? The kindness of God is all the day. You are plotting destruction'. The RSV, however, has read *ʾel ḥāsid* 'against the godly', in place of the MT *ḥesed ʾēl* 'the kindness of God'. This translation proceeds to add the words 'all the day' to the next verse, i.e. 'all the day you are plotting destruction'.

: 7 (C) The last word is literally 'in his passion, anger', or 'in what is
IT, 9) his destruction'. The RSV has read *bᵉhōnō* 'in his wealth'.

: 9 (C) In place of the MT 'I will wait for thy name', the RSV translates
IT, 11) 'I will proclaim thy name', which involves a slightly altered text.

: 5 (C) Since the verse diverges sharply from the parallel in 14 : 6, it is best
IT, 6) to retain the MT as it is, and translate 'the bones of him who encamps against you' (the form *ḥōnāk* is from *ḥānā(h)* 'to encamp'). The 2nd pers. sing. suff. 'you', helps to prepare us for the verb in the 2nd pers. sing. that follows 'you have put them to shame'. The RSV accepts an altered reading *ḥānēp*, translating 'the bones of the ungodly', and then changes the 2nd pers. of the verb into the 3rd pers. to read 'they will be put to shame'.

: 3 (C) Two different readings have been handed down: *ẓārīm* 'strangers',
IT, 5) and *ẓēdīm* 'insolent persons'. Cf. Ps 86 : 14.

: 3 (B) The MT *yāmīṭū* 'they cause to totter' should be read *yāʿīṭū* 'they
IT, 4) pour out'. Cf. the RSV 'they bring' and the AV 'they cast'.

: 15 (C) The first word in the *Kethib* reading is 'desolations'. It is better to
IT, 16) follow the Masoretic vocalization which divides the word into two words *yaššī māwet* 'let death come' or 'let death overcome (them)', cf. Ps. 89 : 22 (MT, 23). At the close of the verse, the MT reads 'for evil is in their dwelling, in their midst'. This fits the context well. Nevertheless, the RSV has accepted a completely altered text and rendered 'let them go away in terror into their graves'.

55 : 18 (C) (MT, 19) The particle *kī* may have a causative sense here, i.e. 'because with many they are against me', or it may be concessive, i.e. 'even though many are against me'.

55 : 19 (B) (MT, 20) The verb should be vocalized as a *pi.* form and translated 'he shall humble them'.

56-superscription (B) (MT, 56 : 1) The MT literally reads 'a dove of dumbness from afar' (?). The LXX felt the difficulty of the sentence. Its reading 'for the people that is far removed from the sanctuary' is hardly a translation. Probably instead of *yōnat ʾēlem* 'dove of dumbness', one should read *yōnat ʾēlīm* 'dove of the terebinth', *ʾēlīm* being the plur. of *ʾēlā(h)*, cf. RSV, DNV.

56 : 7 (C) (MT, 8) The MT reads 'because of the crime, there is deliverance for them'. In the light of the context, this should be rendered as a question, 'could there be in such a crime an escape for them?' No textual change is then necessary. Eerdmans (*op. cit.*, pp. 291 f.) translates 'let them be free to calamity'. His reference to Mic 6 : 14 has little value as a comparison. His translation actually means 'that they may be a prey of calamity'.

57 : 4 (C) (MT, 5) The verb *lāhaṭ* should be rendered here 'to burn with desire for'. The phrase 'sons of men' would then be the object belonging to this verb (cf. the RSV). On the other hand, some believe the word *lōhăṭīm* is in apposition to 'sons of men,' i.e. 'people burning with desire' (cf. DNV). In this case one follows the lead of the AV which has had to supply a number of words for the sake of clarity. The AV renders 'my soul *is* among lions: *and* I lie *even among* them that are set on fire, *even* the sons of men'. The *underlined* words have all been inserted.

58 : 1 (B) (MT, 2) As in 56 : 1, the word *ʾēlem* 'dumbness' is found here. This has no meaning in this context. The supposition that *ʾēlem* means 'congregation' (cf. the AV) remains unproved. It is better to read *ʾēlīm*, plur. of *ʾēl* 'gods'. Thus the RSV renders 'do you indeed decree what is right, you gods' (cf. the commentaries).

7 (C) The translation of the second part of the verse is uncertain. Perhaps
, 8) one should take the verbal form *yidrōk* by itself and translate 'he aims'. It is clear that 'he' does not tread upon the arrows (in Ps 64 : 4 bitter words are the arrows that are aimed). Following *yidrōk*, the text continues 'his arrow (arrows) when they are cut'. The whole sentence, then, can be translated 'he aims, let his (i.e. 'the godless') arrows be as if they were blunt'. Eerdmans (*op. cit.*, p. 297) renders 'when he aimeth, let his arrows be like withered stalks'. Cf. the lexica for *mūl* and *mālal*. These translations are attempts to represent the Hebr text as it has been handed down. The RSV is based on a textual change which is no more than a guess.

15 (B) In the place of *yālīnū* from *līn* 'to spend the night', one should read
, 16) *yallīnū* from *lūn* or *lānan* 'to grumble, growl'. No alteration of the consonantal text is necessary.

6 (C) The MT reads 'they ponder over evil deeds', which is followed by
, 7) 'we are prepared, the plan has been carefully thought out'. This direct discourse is thus seen as the expression of the thoughts of the wicked. Textual change would seem to be unnecessary, yet the RSV has made a rather drastic alteration to arrive at the translation of the opening phrase, 'who can search out our crimes'.

8 (C) The MT reads 'they make him totter, their tongue against them, they
, 9) shake their head, all who look at them'. It is not clear who is the subject of the verb 'totter'. Perhaps it is 'all who look at them'. Do these persons, however, also put out their tongues at the evildoers whom God strikes down? The RSV has a dubious translation based on a change of text, i.e. *yakšīlēmō 'ālē(y)*.

1 (C) The MT is sometimes rendered 'stillness is due to thee, a song of
, 2) praise'. This means that the noun is pointed *dumīyyā(h)*. It is better, however, to read the form as *dōmīyyā(h)*, fem. act. part. of *dāmā(h)* 'to resemble, fit'. Thus the rendering is 'praise is due to thee'.

4 (C) The verb *sālal* means 'to prepare the way'. This translation fits the
, 5) verse well if one retains the translation 'deserts' for the word *'ărābōt*, i.e. 'prepare the way for the one who rides in the deserts'. On the

other hand, on the basis of the Ugaritic material, if one translates the last two words 'who rides upon the clouds', then the translation of *sālal* 'to make a way' does not fit as well. It could, however, be understood in a metaphorical sense, i.e. 'to make a way with a song' (RSV 'lift up a song').

68 : 8 (C) (MT, 9) Besides the translation 'yon Sinai', the rendering 'the lord of Sinai' also finds some support. The word *ze(h)*, then, would have the same meaning here as the Arabic *du* 'owner of'. However, there is considerable hesitation in accepting this interpretation, and it is probably better not to introduce it into a translation of the Bible. Cf. H. J. Kraus, *op. cit.* p. 467.

68 : 14 (A) (MT, 15) The little word *bāh* is a problem. Some believe it should be rendered simply 'in her', i.e. in the land, thus connecting it to the first part of the verse. The RSV has 'when the Almighty scattered kings there' (cf. also the AV). Another possibility, however, is to connect the word with the 'doves' in v. 14 (RSV, v. 13). In this case the *bāh* should be translated 'with them', i.e. with the doves. This would mean that the beating of the white wings of the doves, shining in the sunlight, is compared with the snow that falls on Salmon. Thus the DNV translates 'it was snowing by them on Salmon'. Eerdmans (*op. cit.*, p. 328) believes that the subject of *tašlēg* is the Lord (cf. v. 12). In that case, though, the verbal form *tašlēg* must be viewed as a 2nd masc. sing., i.e. 'you made it snow', whereas the more usual construction in describing weather is the 3rd pers. sing. fem.

68 : 17 (C, B) (MT, 18) The word *šin'ān* is usually interpreted as meaning 'repetition', thus 'thousands upon thousands' (RSV). KBL, however, cites the meaning 'highness', in which case the translation would be 'thousands high in rank'. This translation merits consideration. In the following clause, the MT reading *bām Sinai* 'among them Sinai' conveys no real sense. The LXX has translated this reading except that it introduces the prep. *bᵉ* 'among, in' a second time, i.e. before Sinai. The best solution is that offered in the DNV and RSV translations which understand the text to have read *bā' missīnay* 'he has come from Sinai'.

68 : 30 (C) (MT, 31) The DNV agrees closely with the RSV. It is best to keep close to the MT, but even then there is considerable uncertainty. For example, is

the first word an impv. 'rebuke', or is it a nominal form in construct with the following words, i.e. 'the threatening of the animals in the reed'? Again, is the rendering 'herd of bulls' correct, or should it be 'crowd of strong ones'? Furthermore, should one read 'with the calves (young bulls) of the nations', or 'among the calves of the nations'? In the final phrase of the verse, the MT has the *pi.* perf. form *bizzar* 'he scattered'. This has often been read as an impv. *bazzēr* 'scatter' (cf. the AV and RSV). Thus a possible translation for the verse is 'the rebuke of the beasts of the reed, of the herd of the very strong among the young bulls of the nations, trampling under foot those who lust after tribute, scatter the peoples who delight in war'. One thing is clear: every translation has its own difficulties.

: 22 (C) The MT has *š*^{e}*lōmīm*. It is not certain whether this is a plur. form
T, 23) of *šālōm* 'security', or of *šelem* 'sacrificial meals' (RSV).

: 26 (C) The MT reads 'they recount the afflictions of thy wounded ones'.
T, 27) This could mean 'they make the most of the afflictions (i.e. 'take pleasure in the afflictions') of thy wounded ones'. The RSV has accepted the LXX translation and rendered 'they afflict still more'.

: 3 (C) The MT reads 'be thou to me a rock, a dwelling-place to which I may continually come. Thou hast commanded to save me'. The RSV, however, has chosen to translate this verse in agreement with Ps 31 : 3 (RSV, 2), i.e. 'be thou to me a rock of refuge, a strong fortress, to save me'.

: 18 (C) The MT can easily be translated 'till I proclaim thy might to the generation, thy power to all that come, (v. 19) and thy righteousness . . .' The RSV, however, with a slight change in text and word order, has 'to all the generations to come'. Then, 'thy power' is taken to the following verse.

: 9 (C) According to the lexicon, the word *ṣī* means 'an inhabitant of a waterless district', or 'desert-dwellers'. If the meaning here is 'desert-dwellers', one is not certain whether animals or demons are meant. Another word *ṣī* means 'ship', which definitely does not fit here. Some have suggested a textual change to read *ṣārā(y)w* 'his adversaries'.

73 : 1 (C) By dividing the consonants of the word Israel, i.e. *y š r ʾl* into *y š r ʾē l*, one obtains the translation 'truly God is good to the upright' (RSV).

73 : 4 (B) The MT *lᵉmōtām* 'at their death', has in the past been translated as 'in' or 'until their death' which does not fit the context well. Both the DNV and RSV have taken *lᵉmōtām* as two words, i.e. *lāmō* (parallel form of *lāhem*) 'to them' which is read with the first half of the verse, and *tām* 'sound, whole' which is taken with the second strophe. The translation will then be 'for they have no pangs; their bodies are sound and sleek' (RSV).

73 : 10 (A) The DNV has attempted to translate literally and thus agrees with the RSV marginal reading 'abundant waters are drained by them'. This reading understands *yimmāṣū* as a form of the verb *māṣaṣ* 'to sip', and translates *lāmō* 'by them'. A different rendering 'and abundant waters are found for them' takes *yimmāṣū* as a form of *māṣāʾ* 'to find'. But in neither case does the verse take on meaning. The RSV translation 'and find no fault in them', rests upon a modified Hebr text in which consonants are rearranged to form other words. Another problem in the verse is the meaning of *hălōm* 'this way'. Eerdmans (*op. cit.* p. 349) views the word as an inf. of the verb *hālam* 'to strike'. From this point, he attempts to connect this verse with the action in Num 20 : 7, i.e. the striking of the rock and the flow of water from it. But if such a connection exists, it is hard to see how v. 10 has any relation to Ps 73 as a whole.

74 : 5 (C) The RSV translation 'at the upper entrance they hacked the wooden trellis with axes', is very uncertain. Admittedly, the MT is not easy. First of all, the subject of *yiwwādaʿ* is not clear. If its subject is *ʾōt* from the previous verse, the translation is 'it became known as', or 'it looked as if'. The verse goes on to mention the raising up of axes, but what is meant by 'in the undergrowth', or 'with the undergrowth'? Literally, the text can be translated 'it looked as if someone raised an axe on high in the undergrowth'. The meaning is not very clear. The rendering in the RSV 'they hacked' means a change in text at the beginning of the verse, i.e. a reading *yigdᵉʿū* in place of the MT *yiwwādaʿ*.

8 (B) The MT reads literally *nīnām* 'their descendants'. The word is difficult in this context and therefore a slight change in vocalization is suggested, producing a form of the verb *yānā(h)* with the meaning 'to suppress'. Cf. the RSV 'we will utterly subdue them'.

11 (C) The MT of the second half of the verse indicates a *contrast* (antithetical parallelism) to the first half. According to the Masoretic punctuation, the word 'and your right hand' belongs to v. 11a. The translation of the MT, then, is 'why dost thou hold back thy hand, thy right hand: out of thy bosom! destroy!' Another possibility is to take 'thy right hand' as part of the second strophe and read the last word with a final *aleph*, instead of a *he*, i.e. *tiklā'* 'you keep', instead of *kallē(h)* 'destroy'. In this case, the second half of the verse becomes a *synonymous* parallel with the first half. The translation would then be 'why dost thou hold back thy hand, why dost thou keep thy right hand in thy bosom?'

4 (C)
T, 5) The RSV has 'glorious art thou, more majestic than the everlasting mountains'. This means that, on the basis of the LXX, the RSV has read the word *qedem* 'ancient', instead of *ṭārep* 'prey', and understood the prep. *min* as showing comparative degree. It is possible, however, that *min* indicates here *source*, i.e. 'out of' or 'out from'. But, at the same time, it is difficult to understand the words 'mountains of prey'. Does the phrase indicate mountains on which wild beasts are found, or mountain ranges which have fallen as prey into the hands of enemies? Another translation is 'thou wast magnificent, glorious from off the mountains of prey', but this is not probable.

6 (C)
T, 7) The MT places the verb 'remember' at the beginning of v. 7. Thus, 'I remember in the night my music, I meditate in my heart and my spirit searches'. The RSV has made 'remember' the last word of v. 6, i.e. 'I remember the years long ago'; it reads *wᵉhāgītī* ('I commune') instead of *nᵉgīnātī* ('my music').

15 (C)
T, 16) The RSV omits the words 'and upon the son whom thou hast reared for thyself', probably because the same words appear at the end of v. 18. Undoubtedly they fit well into the context of v. 18.

13 (C) By the word *galgal* 'wheel' in this verse, KBL understands "the

(MT, 14) wheelshaped dryed calix of the thistle Gundelia Tournefortii which borne by the wind causes the shying of horses." In view of this, instead of the RSV 'whirling dust', one should translate 'whirling thistle'.

88 : 1 (C)
(MT, 2) The MT makes excellent sense and has the support of ancient versions. There is no reason, then, to change the text as the RSV has done.

88 : 15 (C)
(MT, 16) The word *ʾāpūnā(h)* is usually taken as a derived form of *pūn* 'to be helpless' (KBL 'to be embarrassed'). But the translation is uncertain.

89 : 19 (C)
(MT, 20) For the MT 'I have commanded help (*ʿēzer*) to a hero', the RSV has read *nēzer* 'a crown', translating 'I have set the crown upon one who is mighty'.

89 : 50 (C)
(MT, 51) The RSV has accepted a reading *k*^{e}*limmōt ʿammīm* 'the insults of the peoples', in place of the MT *kol rabbīm ʿammīm*. The Hebr could be rendered 'all great peoples', but the construction is somewhat strange. In any case, a fitting word such as 'insult' (AV 'reproach') needs to be supplied.

91 : 9 (C) If v. 9a is taken as the end of the previous verse, and v. 9b as the beginning of a new verse, it is possible to translate without textual change, 'for thou, Lord, art my refuge. (When) you have made the Most High your habitation, no evil . . .'

92 : 10 (C)
(MT, 11) The MT has 'I have poured over' which probably means 'I have been poured over'.

100 : 3 (B) Instead of the negative *lōʾ* (*Kethib* reading), read *lō* 'to him' with the *Qere*. Thus 'we are to him' = 'we are his'.

102 : 6 (C)
(MT, 7) The meaning of *q*^{e}*ʾat* is not certain. The RSV has rendered the word 'vulture' in this verse and in Zeph 2 : 14. But in Lev 11 : 18 and Deut 14 : 17, it has translated the same word as 'pelican' and in

Is 34 : 11 as 'hawk'. In all of these passages the DNV translates by the word 'pelican'. Cf. the doubt expressed in KBL.

5 (C) The word *ʿedyēk* comes from *ʿădī* 'ornament'. This might signify 'strength'. The 2nd pers. fem. suff. must refer to *nepeš* 'soul' (cf. v. 2). Thus the translation should be 'who satisfies your strength with good'. The RSV rendering 'as long as you live' is actually a translation of *ʿōdēkī*, not of the MT *ʿedyēk*.

17 (C) The MT reads 'fools because of their sinful ways and because of their iniquities suffered affliction'.

4 (C) Literally, the MT reads 'and I prayer'. This can mean that the psalmist under fire from enemies, asks God for mercy and pardon. It is not likely that intercession for his enemies is implied, since later in this psalm (v. 17) he calls down a curse upon them. It is doubtful if the text should be changed, cf. RSV "I make prayer for them".

28 (C) The MT can be rendered 'if they arise, let my assailants be put to shame'. A conditional sentence of this kind can quite readily be expressed by a perf. form of the verb without any addition.

3 (A) The first part of the verse reads quite smoothly. One can compare Judg 5 : 2. The difficulty begins with the words 'in holy festal attire'. The AV, DNV, and BSG, take these words with the following phrase, the RSV with what precedes. The textual change represented by the RSV translation 'upon the holy mountains' is unnecessary. A real problem is contained in the following phrase *mēreḥem mišḥār*. One can possibly translate 'from the mother's womb', thus meaning a statement of time. A word *mišḥar* 'early morning' is not known; it would have to be assumed here. Hence, the translation 'womb of the morning', or 'womb of dawn' is dubious. It is possible, however, to read the prep. *min* with the noun *šaḥar* 'dawn', i.e. *miššaḥar* 'from the dawn'. The final word of the verse *yaldut*, though an abstract, can still have the definite meaning 'young people'. It is a question, however, whether the preceding word 'dew' is to be connected with *yaldut*. Thus 'dew of your youth' (cf. the AV) is by no means a certain translation. The RSV has 'like dew your youth will come to

you'. It is possible that the words of v. 3b should be connected as 'mother's womb-youth' and 'dawn-dew', and to translate 'from the mother's womb your young people belong to you, like the dew from the dawn onwards'. Even if one adheres closely to the MT, he is nonetheless involved in conjecture, since in v. 3b there is apparently no verbal form present. Whatever verb is supplied to fill out the meaning, it is, in the nature of the case, a conjectured form.

119 : 128 (C) The MT has 'therefore I consider all precepts, about everything (or 'in everything'), to be right'. Though it is somewhat uncertain, yet this translation can be defended.

138 : 2 (C) The MT can be translated 'thou hast exalted thy word above all thy name', or 'thou hast exalted thy word (or 'promise'), for the sake of all thy name'. The RSV has chosen to take the words *ʿal kol* separately, i.e. 'above everything'.

138 : 3 (C) The MT has 'thou hast made me proud (with) strength in my soul', i.e. 'thou hast made me aware in my soul of my strength'. The RSV rendering 'thou didst increase' is based on the form *tarbe(h)* that is reflected in the LXX and Tg. This may be nothing more, however, than a free interpretation of the Hebr text.

139 : 14 (C) Following the clear opening word 'I praise thee', one can translate 'because I am made in a wonderful way which inspires awe'. This rendering is somewhat of a paraphrase, yet it can well be the meaning of the text. It is certainly a more difficult reading than the one found in the early versions (LXX, Vg, etc.) and adopted by the RSV, i.e. 'for thou art fearful and wonderful'. One can explain how the easier versional rendering originated out of the more difficult MT reading, but how could it be the other way around?

The next phrase 'wonderful are thy works' is clear. It is obvious from the context what those works are. The concluding three words of the verse *wᵉnapšī yōdaʿat mᵉʾōd*, are translated literally 'and my soul knows very well'. Apparently, the subject of the verb 'to know' is 'soul' (cf. the DNV 'my soul knows that very well'). Yet, with only a slight vocalization change, the subject could be understood as God (cf. the RSV 'thou knowest me right well'). Or, is there another possibility, i.e. that the words should be rendered 'my soul was well-known'? This last-named rendering accords well with the phrase in the following verse 'my frame was not hidden from thee'.

18 (C) The MT verbal form *hĕqīṣōtī* must be the *hiph.* of *qīṣ* 'to awake', thus 'when I awake, I am still with thee' (RSV). If the same consonants, however, are read, but pointed as *hăqiṣṣōtī*, the form is likewise *hiph.*, but derived from *qāṣaṣ* 'come to the end'. The translation would then be 'were I to come to the end I would still be with thee' (RSV margin).

: 20 (C) Difficulties exist in the second half of the verse. First of all, in agreement with two Hebr mss, one should probably read *nāśō'* 'a lifting up' instead of *nāśū'* which possibly means 'who lift themselves up'. The word *laššāw'* means 'for evil'. The word *ʿāre(y)kā* is uncertain. It might mean 'your enemies' (cf. 1 Sam 28 : 16). On the other hand, it is possible that it comes from a different stem *ʿūr* 'to arouse oneself'. The RSV 'against thee' suggests the conjecture *ʿāle(y)kā*, and still another conjecture is *š*^{e}*me(y)kā* 'your name', i.e. '(who) lift up your name for evil'. But a cloud of obscurity surrounds the text.

: 5-7 The Hebr text is obscure in places. The word *ṣaddīq* 'righteous one' leads us to expect in contrast, in the next part of the verse, the word *rāšāʿ* 'wicked one'. The reading 'wicked one' is actually found in the LXX and the Pesh in the place of the MT 'head'. What the Hebr 'head-oil may not refuse my head' means is a question. Both the DNV and BSG have tried to translate it literally. On the other hand, the RSV has accepted the altered text (cf. LXX), and rendered 'but let the oil of the wicked never anoint my head'. Although v. 6 reads literally 'and they shall hear that my words are sweet', many read 'the word of the Lord is true'. (RSV). This is not possible without changing the consonantal text. In this case the last word of v. 6 must be changed from *nāʿĕmū* to *neʾĕmān*. And *ʾēmer Yahweh* is read instead of *ʾămāra(y)*. A question of interpretation is present in the word translated 'their judges'. Is the meaning the people who judge them and administer justice (RSV, DNV), or does the word mean 'the judges among them'? In v. 7, on the basis of the Pesh and various mss of the LXX, many read 'their bones' instead of 'our bones' to secure a closer connection with v. 6.

143 : 9 (C) The last word of the MT *kissitī* means literally 'I have covered'. Perhaps the sense is 'I have provided with a cover, namely myself', but the object is left unexpressed. From this, then, would come the idea 'I have hidden myself towards you' = 'I flee to you'. Actually, instead of *kissitī*, one Hebr ms has *ḥāsītī* 'I have fled for refuge' (RSV). The Vg, which has *protectus sum*, evidently read *kussētī*, pass. form of *kissitī*, meaning 'I am safe'.

PROVERBS

1 : 21 (C) The MT has the form *hōmiyyōt*, part. of the verb *hāmā(h)* 'to make a noise'. The word probably indicates the busiest places in town, and thus the translation can be 'where the busiest (streets) begin' (DNV 'at the corner of the noisy streets'). Others render 'above the bustle', but this is an unlikely translation in view of the first word *beᵉrōʾš* 'at the beginning', or 'at the head', or 'on the top'. In place of the Hebr *hōmiyyōt*, the LXX read *ḥōmōt* 'walls'. The RSV has accepted this change and rendered 'on the top of the walls'.

2 : 22 (B) The form *yissᵉḥū* is capable of several different explanations. It can be taken as a *qal* impf. of *nāsaḥ* 'to pull out', to be translated here 'the faithless shall they tear away out of it'. If this is changed into the pass., the sense of the translation is almost the same, i.e. 'the treacherous will be rooted out of it' (RSV). KBL believes the form should be pointed *yissāḥū*, *niph.* impf. of *sāḥā(h)* 'to be scraped away'. The translation remains the same. It is clearly not necessary to read the form *yinnāsᵉḥū*, *niph.* of *nāsaḥ*, as the critical notes of BH suggest.

3 : 8 (B) The MT reads literally 'it will be healing for your navel'. The form *lᵉšārekā* 'for your navel', is generally altered slightly to read *lišʾērekā* 'for your flesh' (= 'for your body'). Cf. KBL.s.v. *šēr* This change is suggested by the LXX and Pesh, and it has been adopted by the DNV and the RSV.

3 : 24 (C) The MT is clear 'if you lie down'. There is, then, no reason to depart from this text even though the same verb *šākab* 'lie down' occurs in the second half of the verse. This repetition of the verb may well be the cause of the change the LXX has made from *tiškab* 'you lie down'

to *tēšēb* 'you sit down'. The RSV has adopted the LXX suggestion.

5 (C) If the Hebr word *mērīm* is interpreted as a part. sing., the meaning of v. 35b can be 'and, as for fools, (every one of them) exalts (i.e. 'carries away') his disgrace'. The translation could then be 'but the fools carry away disgrace', i.e. disgrace is their portion or share. It is possible, on the other hand, that God is the subject of *mērīm*, and that one should translate 'but as for fools, He makes the disgrace great', or 'but great makes He the disgrace of the fools'. The translation of the traditional text, without change, can be defended. The RSV, however, has adopted a conjectural reading *mōrīšīm* in place of the MT *mērīm*, and has translated 'but fools get disgrace'.

(C) The first word is capable of two different renderings. It can mean 'prize her highly' (i.e. wisdom), or 'embrace her'. Cf. the lexica. If the verb *sālal* means 'to plait', then, the translation 'embrace her' is clearly possible.

5 (C) In the intensive form, the verb *pālas* means 'to make smooth'. The translation, then, 'make smooth the path of your foot', can mean that one must choose carefully where he wants to go. This is the sense of the RSV rendering 'take heed to the path of your feet'. The intensive form of the same verb *pālas*, is found in 5 : 6 and 5 : 21, where it is usually accepted as meaning to 'investigate, get to know, pay attention to'. The question arises, then, as to whether it has this meaning in 4 : 26 At any rate, the sense of 4 : 26 seems clear. A man must take heed where he walks for danger lurks on every side.

(C) Cf. 4 : 26. The verb form *t^{e}pallēs* by itself can be either 2nd pers. masc. sing., or 3rd pers. fem. sing. The RSV has taken it as the fem. form and translated 'she does not take heed to'. This means that in verses 5 and 6 there is a four-fold description of the path of the loose woman. In this interpretation, the Hebr word *pen* is somewhat unusual and difficult. Some have suggested that the word *pen* should be replaced by the usual negation *bal* or *lōʼ*, but there is no reason to do this. If the verb form is understood to be a 2nd pers. masc. sing., the word *pen* can have its usual meaning. The translation would then be 'lest you should take heed to the path of life'. The meaning is clear. The woman, previously described, poses a genuine temptation to the righteous. Whoever keeps company with her loses his vision of the path of life.

5 : 10 (C) The RSV and DNV agree in viewing the verse as containing two independent parts of a sentence. This is a common phenomenon in Proverbs. Thus the RSV renders 'lest strangers take their fill of your strength, and [lest] your labors go to the house of an alien'. It is possible, however, to read the second half of the verse 'and of your labors in the house of an alien'. The translation 'in' is supported by the presence of the prep. *bᵉ*. Moreover, this translation has the advantage of rendering the MT as it is without the necessity of adding anything in the second part of the verse in order to fill out the meaning.

5 : 21 (C) Cf. 5 : 6 and 4 : 26.

6 : 2 (C) At the beginning of this verse, the RSV changes the text to read 'lips' instead of the MT 'mouth'. There is, however, no reason to depart from the MT.

6 : 3 (C) The Hebr word *hitrappēs* is not clear, though it is probably to be explained by the Accad *rapasu* 'to strike, stamp'. The reflexive form here, then, could be translated 'strike yourself'. This could mean 'humble thyself' (AV), or 'strike for yourself' (i.e. 'beat heavily'), or 'hasten' (RSV). There is some uncertainty in the translation here.

6 : 5 (C) The MT has merely *miyyād* 'out of a hand'. Some believe the word *ṣayyād* has dropped out of the text, and thus the translation should be 'from the hand of the fowler' (AV). Others have changed *miyyad* to read *miṣṣayyād* 'from the hunter'. Still others propose, without proof, that *yad* here means 'net' or 'snare'.

6 : 22 (C) The MT has the sing. subject 'it' throughout the verse. The RSV has translated 'they'. In any case, the reference is to the command of the father and the teaching of the mother. Either the sing. or plur. can be used in translation.

6 : 26 (C) The RSV sets forth a contrasting parallelism in this verse, rendering

'for a harlot may be hired for a loaf of bread, but an adulteress stalks a man's very life'. Another possible meaning, however, is that the verse contains the idea of synonymous parallelism. The Hebr actually reads 'for because of a harlot to a piece of bread', which evidently means 'for because of a harlot, one is reduced to a paltry piece of bread', i.e. he loses everything (cf. the AV). The second strophe, then, reads 'and the woman of (another) man hunts the costly life'. Both interpretations can be defended.

(B) The word *'îšōn* (diminutive of *'îš* 'man') occurs in v. 2, where, combined with *'ayin*, it means 'apple of the eye' or 'pupil'. Thus, in 7 : 9, the phrase 'in the pupil of the night' means 'in the dead of night'. In 20 : 20 the Masoretes vocalize the word as *'ĕšûn* 'time' or 'the breaking', which meaning seems to fit better in 7 : 9. Thus the DNV and RSV translate here 'at the time of'.

0 (C) The Hebr reads literally '(a woman) is guarded with respect to the heart'. Apparently this means that the harlot herein described keeps watch over her heart. She is on her guard and with all cunningness puts on a false front. Thus the translation may mean 'with cunning heart'. There is uncertainty here, and one can only try to establish the meaning from the context.

2 (A) Literally, the final phrase in Hebr reads 'and as a foot shackle to the chastisement of a fool'. The LXX has rendered this 'and as a dog to shackles, or as a deer', thereby relating the final words to v. 23. Other versions follow along with the LXX. Nevertheless, they all require a different Hebr text. With a few minor textual changes, G. R. Driver (ZAW, N.F., 1932, p. 143) arrives at the translation 'as a hart is tied to a cord', while still another suggestion is 'as a deer that runs to the snare' (cf. also the RSV 'or as a stag is caught fast'). It is implied, thus, that the deer is driven to a snare or to someone with a lasso, so that it is caught in it and afterwards killed with a bowshot (v. 23). This line of thought is in accord with the context, but we need more clear evidence as to ancient hunting technique. It is possible, of course, to modify but slightly the word order and arrive at the translation 'as a fool put in irons', or, as the AV has it, 'as a fool to the correction of the stocks'.

8 : 12 (C) The MT reads literally 'I, wisdom, dwell in prudence' (RSV). This might mean that wisdom and prudence always go together. On the basis that *šākēn* means 'to be a neighbor', one could also translate 'I, wisdom, am the neighbor of prudence'.

8 : 16 (B) For the final word, cod. L has *ṣedeq* which would make the translation 'all who judge in justice'. A great number of Hebr mss and editions read the word *'ereṣ* 'earth' as the last word (cf. also the AV, DNV and RSV). Following the example of the LXX, the RSV turns the noun 'judges' into a verb 'they rule', and thus translates 'and nobles govern the earth'. This probably provides for a smoother parallelism between the two halves of the verse.

8 : 22 (C) The RSV translates 'at the beginning of his work'. Since the prep. 'at' is not in the Hebr text, one can translate 'as the beginning of his way (= work)'.

8 : 26 (C) The RSV (cf. also the AV) has rendered the MT *ḥūṣōt* as 'fields'. Others translate 'that which is outside (the houses)', i.e. the streets. In the second part of the verse 'the first of the specks of dust' has been rendered 'the first specks of dust'. Some translate 'the sum total of dust', but this is unlikely.

8 : 28 (C) The second part of the verse reads literally 'by the being strong of the fountains of the deep', i.e. 'when the fountains of the deep bubbled up strongly'. It is not necessary to change the text to read *b^e'azz^ezō*, i.e. 'when he made strong the fountains of the deep'.

8 : 30 (C) The word *'āmōn* can be well translated as 'favorite', or 'foster-child'. This fits in with the context. The stem *'mn* means 'to be careful', or 'to educate' (cf. the part. *'ōmēn* in Num 11 : 12, etc.). KBL mentions two meanings for the word *'āmōn*, 'foreman' and 'fondling', but both are improbable here. Since God alone brings creation into being, He surely has no need of a foreman.

9 : 1 (C) The MT reads 'she has hewn out' which is certainly a possible translation if stone pillars are in view. The RSV, however, in agreement with the LXX, has rendered 'she has set up'. This

implies either a different text, or a very free translation of the MT.

13 (C) The RSV (cf. also the AV) renders 'a foolish woman'. The MT, however, has literally 'woman, folly', which can readily mean that the folly that brings man to destruction is comparable to the loose woman. We should, therefore, translate 'woman Folly'. In the second half of the verse, if the text is correct, the noun *p*^{e}*tayyūt* means 'lack of wisdom, inexperience, superficiality, frivolity'. Some prefer to read a part. in its place but this makes no difference to the translation. In the final phrase the Hebr has literally 'and she knows nothing'. In keeping with the context, the LXX has added the word 'shame' (cf. the RSV 'knows no shame'). This thought fits in well since the seductive woman symbolizes folly and frivolity.

: 10 (C) The Hebr of 10b is exactly the same as in 8b. If, then, the text is maintained, it should be translated in the same way in both places, as is done by the DNV. The RSV, however, has chosen to follow the LXX in which a completely different reading is found, i.e. 'but he who boldly reproves makes peace'.

: 22 (C) The RSV has 'and he adds no sorrow with it' (i.e. with the blessing). Here the subject 'he' clearly refers to 'the Lord'. It is questionable, however, whether 'the Lord' is the subject of the verb *yōsip*. The emphatic fem. pron. *hīʾ* 'it', in the first part of the verse, apparently stresses the fact that God's blessing and it alone can enrich man's life: even with all of his toil, man can add nothing to it. If this be the sense of the verse, the translation should be 'it is the blessing of the Lord which enriches, the toil adds nothing to it' (cf. the RSV margin).

: 28 (C) The Hebr text has *yippōl* 'shall fall'. The text is clear as it stands. The RSV, nevertheless, suggests the reading *yibbōl* 'will wither'.

: 30 (C) The Hebr reads 'and the one who takes souls is a wise (man)'. In order to keep this text, one has to try to understand the expression 'to take souls' in a favorable sense, i.e. to win and thus preserve the souls or hearts of people. On the other hand, the phrase 'to take souls' is probably to be taken in an unfavorable sense, meaning 'to take away lives'. Ps 31 : 14 (RSV, 13) bears out this thought, since the same expression is used there. Cf. the RSV 'takes away lives'. Since it is not the 'wise man' who takes away lives, it is advisable to replace the word *ḥākām* with *ḥāmās* 'lawlessness', or 'injustice' (cf. the RSV).

12 : 12 (C) This verse is generally considered to be corrupt. However, by translating as literally as possible, the first part may be rendered 'the wicked desires the hunting net of the evil things'. This could mean that the wicked person covets the means to effect greater wickedness. His aim is not only to do evil, but also to acquire new methods of doing it.In this translation, *mᵉṣōd* is interpreted as the construct state of *māṣōd* 'hunting net'. Other suggestions are that the word should be read as *mᵉṣād* or *mᵉṣudā(h)* meaning 'inaccessible place' or 'stronghold' (RSV 'strong tower'). The RSV rendering 'comes to ruin', represents a conjectured reading *yiššāmēd* or something like it, in place of the MT *ḥāmad*.

The second part of the verse reads 'and the root of the righteous gives'. No object for the verb is expressed. Some supply the word 'fruit' and translate 'the root of the righteous gives fruit'. Others suggest that instead of the MT *yittēn* 'gives', one should read *bᵉʾē(y)tān* 'in firmness', i.e. in firm ground (cf. Gen 49 : 24 for the meaning). Hence, the RSV renders 'the root of the righteous stands firm'.

12 : 26 (A) The first strophe does not make sense in the MT. Literally it reads 'the righteous man investigates concerning his friend (his neighbor)'. The form *yātēr* is derived from *tūr* 'to search out' (the DNV reads the form *yātūr*). The AV has 'the righteous is more excellent than his neighbor', thus understanding *yātēr* as related to the root consonants *y t r*(?).

The second word in the MT *mērēʿēhū* 'from his neighbor', or, 'more than his neighbor' has been taken by the DNV as a *hiph*. part. plus suff., from the root consonants *rʿʿ*, i.e. 'who wants to harm him', or 'what wants to harm him'. Thus, the DNV has 'the righteous man can tell who wants to harm him', which could also be rendered 'the righteous man considers what would cause him harm' (and thus avoids it). The RSV has expressed this thought more freely 'a righteous man turns away from evil'. A conjecture that has met with some favor is to read *mirʿēhū* 'his meadow'. This involves only a modified vocalization. The sense would be that the righteous man knows how to find the meadow that is suitable for him, i.e. what is good for him.

: 27 (B) In v. 27b, the order of the Hebr words is 'property, person, costly, industrious'. Obviously, the translation here can be varied. If the words 'person' and 'costly' change places, the translation can be 'but costly property is the part of the industrious', or, as in the RSV, 'the diligent man will get precious wealth'.

: 28 (B) It is difficult to hold to the MT in the second half of the verse. The italicized words in the AV indicate the difficulty it sensed here. The AV translation 'no death' for *'al māwet* is most unlikely, since for this translation one would expect the negative form *lō'* — not *'al*. If one tries to follow the MT no contrast is expressed between the two halves of the verse: the preceding verses however, indicate that a contrast is present. Thus, instead of *n^{e}tībā(h)* 'path', it is preferable to read *m^{e}šūbā(h)* 'backsliding, sin', and to vocalize *'al* 'not' as *'el* 'unto'. Hence the RSV reads 'but the way of error leads to death'. The reading, however, is a conjecture and by no means certain.

: 8 (C) The MT has 'but a poor man does not hear rebuke'. This is found also at the close of v. 1 where it refers to a scoffer who 'will not listen to rebuke and serious reprimands'. But, in v. 8, the subject is a poor man, and thus the meaning is 'a poor man does not come to hear rebuke', i.e. no one takes the trouble to seize a poor man, simply because there is nothing to be gained from him. This meaning should be recognized as a possible interpretation of v. 8. However, since 13 : 8a states that the rich man can pay a 'ransom' for his life, it has been thought that 8b expresses the thought that the poor man cannot pay. Thus the RSV renders 'but a poor man has no means of redemption'. But this means that the text must be emended to read *g^e'ullā(h)* in place of *g^e'ārā(h)*, and *māṣā'* 'to find' instead of *šāma'* 'to hear'.

11 (C) The MT reads 'wealth gotten by vanity' (AV), which apparently indicates riches that are obtained by idle dealings, or without effort. A slight change in text produces the translation 'wealth hastily gotten' (RSV, cf. 20 : 21). Still another proposed change is to read

the second word of the verse as *mᵉhubbāl*, and to translate 'riches acquired by deceit'. Neither change is advisable.

13 : 15 (C) The final word *'ē(y)tān* is difficult to render. It evidently means 'firm, lasting, enduring', but this can be interpreted in many different ways. A road which is *'ē(y)tān* can be viewed as one, which, from time immemorial, has not been changed, and which one cannot use any more without exposing himself to great unpleasantness. The DNV has 'impassable' but this is uncertain. The RSV has sought a solution through conjecture, reading *'ē(y)dām* 'their ruin' in place of *'ē(y)tān*.

14 : 1 (B) The Hebr reads *ḥakmōt nāšīm* 'the wise (or 'most wise') of women', which the DNV has read as *ḥokmōt nāšīm* 'the wisdom of the women'. The RSV has omitted *nāšīm* and translated 'wisdom builds her house'. This makes the text parallel to 9 : 1a, though there the RSV has used the English perf. 'has built', and here the present tense 'builds'.

14 : 3 (C) The MT has the word *ga'ăwā(h)* 'pride', and should be rendered here 'in the mouth of the fool (is) a rod for the pride'. This seems to mean that the foolish talk of the fool harms the fool himself. A change from *ga'ăwā(h)* to *gēwō(h)* 'his back', is the source of the RSV translation 'the talk of a fool is a rod for his back' (cf. Prov. 10 : 13).

14 : 4 (C) The translation of this verse is not certain. The word *'ēbūs* clearly means 'manger', but the word *bar* could mean 'corn', or it could be an adjective meaning 'pure' or 'clean'. It is possible that the word *bar* is used deliberately, that is, the writer may imply both meanings in the one word. Thus, he asks the question, 'where there are no cattle, does one expect to find there any corn (*bar*) in the manger?' The answer is 'of course not, for one expects to find in that case, a manger that is clean (*bar*)'. Hence, the translation may well be given 'where there are no cattle, the manger remains clean'. The RSV has evidently read *'epes* 'nothing' in place of the MT *'ēbūs*, and interprets *bar* as 'corn'. It renders 'where there are no oxen, there is no grain'.

14 : 9 (C) The MT can be translated 'the guilt offering mocks the fools'. The sense of the sentence is somewhat vague, though it seems to mean

that, because fools offer the guilt offering so often and so carelessly, it becomes a mockery to them. But *'āšām* also means 'guilt', and this may be its sense here. For, since v. 9b emphasizes that favor dwells in the midst of the righteous, one might expect v. 9a to state what is found among fools. Thus the BSG has translated the verse 'guilt harbors among fools, good will among the upright'. This translation follows the LXX quite closely and gives a well-balanced verse. It means, however, a change in a Hebr consonant, i.e. it reads *yālīn* 'pass the night' in place of the MT *yālīṣ* 'to mock'. The RSV has adopted a completely different reading eliminating any mention of 'guilt'. It renders, 'God scorns the wicked'.

: 14 (C) In the second part of the verse the MT reads *ūmē'ālā(y)w* 'and from upon him', or 'and with what is his'. However, the parallelism with 'ways' of 14a, leads one to expect in 14b a similar word. Thus the RSV has adopted a reading *ūmimma'ălālā(y)w*, translating the second strophe of the verse 'and a good man with the fruit of his deeds'.

: 17 (C) In Prov. 12 : 2 the word *meẓimmā(h)* is found with an unfavorable meaning. Therefore, it is quite possible to render the MT of 14 : 17 'and a man of evil devices is hated'. If, however, one explains *meẓimmā(h)* in a favorable sense, such as 'discretion', then, with a slight change in text he should translate 'is patient' instead of 'is hated'.

: 24 (C) The MT can be translated, but it is rather puzzling. Thus the RSV reads *'ŏrmātām* 'their wisdom', instead of the MT *'ošrām* 'their wealth'. It also reads *liwyā(h)* 'garland' instead of the first occurrence in the MT of the word *'iwwelet* 'folly'.

: 32 (C) The MT reads 'the wicked is overthrown in (or, 'through') his adversity (or, 'evil deeds'), but the righteous finds a refuge in death' (or, 'when he dies'). On the basis of the LXX and Pesh, the RSV has accepted a slight change in text and translated 'through his integrity' instead of 'when he dies'.

: 33 (C) No negation is present in v. 33b. Hence it is possible to translate 'wisdom abides in the mind of a man of understanding; even in the midst of fools it has shown itself'. Some believe that the negation should be inserted, in which case, v. 33b would read 'nowhere is any knowledge ascribed to fools'. Some feel that the verb *yāda'* in the pass. form here means 'to be submissive, oppress, humiliate' (cf. D. W. Thomas, JTS, 1934, pp. 298 ff.). No negation, then, is needed. But it is not certain that *yāda'* can have this meaning here.

15 : 2 (C) In place of the MT *tē(y)ṭīb* 'makes good', many accept the conjectured reading *taṭṭīp* 'drops' (RSV 'dispenses'). The parallelism with v. 2b is thereby better established.

15 : 26 (C) In the MT the words 'abomination' and 'pure' apparently stand in contrasting parallelism. The text would then be rendered 'the thoughts of the wicked are an abomination to the Lord, but pure are the lovely words'. Some believe, however, that the word 'pure' of 15b is opposed to the word 'wicked' of 15a. This necessitates a metathesis in the word order of the text, i.e. from *ṭᵉhōrīm 'imrē(y)* of the MT, to *'imrē(y) ṭᵉhōrīm* 'the words of the pure'. The phrase 'the words of the pure' would then mark a sharp contrast to 'thoughts of the wicked' (cf. the BSG, RSV, etc.).

18 : 1 (C) The MT of v. 1a can be rendered 'the solitary seeks his own desire'. The emphasis thus lies on the self-centered life of the solitary one. However, in place of the MT *ta'ăwā(h)* 'desire', it is probably best to read *tō'ănā(h)* 'opportunity, pretext' (cf. the RSV). If this change is accepted, it means that v. 1a and 1b are closely connected to each other. The RSV translation reads 'he who is estranged seeks pretexts to break out against all sound judgment'. Syntactically this rendering is quite possible, although the MT does not indicate that this is the meaning.

18 : 6 (B) Instead of the MT *qal* form *yābō'ū* 'they come', the DNV and RSV, on the basis of the LXX and Tg, have read the verb in the *hiph.* causative, i.e. *yābī'ū* 'they bring'. The translation, then, becomes 'the lips of the foolish lead to dispute' (DNV 'bring about dispute', RSV 'bring strife'). The MT could conceivably be rendered 'come with dispute', or 'bring dispute with them' (cf. the AV 'enter into contention').

: 19 (C) The Hebr word *nipšāʿ* is a *niph.* part. (not used elsewhere) of *pāšaʿ* 'to rebel'. Hence the form here means 'someone against whom one rebels', or 'someone against whom one turns', and thus 'someone who is disappointed and deceived and wronged'. The following phrase reads literally 'is more than a strong city', i.e. more inaccessible than a city. Thus the text describes pointedly and concisely how a man deeply wronged by his friends becomes embittered and so closes his heart to his friends as to resemble in himself a strong inaccessible city. This seems to be the clear meaning of the MT. The RSV, however, follows the ancient versions and reads *nōšāʿ* 'helped' in place of the MT *nipšāʿ*, and the prep. *k*^{e} 'like, as' instead of the MT *min* 'from, more than'. Hence, the RSV renders 'a brother helped is like a strong city.'

: 24 (C) The *hithpa.* inf. *hitrōʿēăʿ* from the stem *r*ʿʿ 'to break with', can be translated here 'to destroy one another' (cf. KBL on *r*ʿʿ II). Thus the MT can be rendered 'a man of friends' (= a man who has friends) can be destroyed' (= can go to his downfall). This translation remains uncertain. Often, in place of *ʾîš* 'man', the word *yēš* 'there is, there are' has been read. Moreover, instead of the *hithpa.* inf. of *r*ʿʿ, the ancient versions suggest the reading *hitrāʿōt* ('to feign friendship'), *hithpa.* inf. of *rāʿā(h)*. The text, then, would mean that there are 'so-called friends' who are not genuine, and to trust them can bring bitter disappointment. Thus the RSV renders 'there are friends who pretend to be friends'.

: 7 (C) The last two words of the MT read simply 'not they'. The DNV has rendered them 'they are gone', while the RSV translates 'but does not have them'. The translation here is dubious.

: 19 C) Instead of the *g r l* of the consonantal text, one should accept the *Qere* reading (Palestinean), *g*^{e}*dāl*. The translation, then, becomes 'a hotheaded one'. The AV and RSV render 'a man of great wrath', while the LXX has 'the evil-minded man'.

The last two words of the MT can be explained in two ways: the DNV has 'you add to it' (= you make it worse), but the RSV renders 'you will only have to do it again'.

20 : 28, 21 : 20, (C) 21 : 21 In these three texts it is entirely possible to adhere to the MT, thus making the RSV deviations based on the LXX unnecessary.

21 : 6 (B) The MT has *m^ebaqšē(y) māwet* 'the ones seeking death'. It is preferable to read with the LXX, as well as with some Hebr mss, *ūmōqšē(y) māwet* 'and snares of death', i.e. deadly snares. Both the DNV and RSV have accepted the LXX reading.

21 : 29 (C) The *Kethib—Qere* readings make possible the two translations 'establishes his ways' and 'considers his way'. If the translation is 'an upright man considers his way', one can still argue the question as to whether this means the way of the upright or the behavior of the wicked. If it is the behavior of the wicked, it means that they do not take note of their own behavior, but they are surely observed by the upright. The question, however, is one of exegesis, not of translation.

22 : 20 (B) The Hebr text is not certain. The *Kethib* reading *šilšōm* 'the day before yesterday' cannot be correct here. The DNV has accepted the *Qere* reading *šālišīm* 'adages, proverbs'(?). The vocalization *š^elōšīm* 'thirty' would be better (cf. the RSV 'thirty sayings'). Accordingly, in 22 : 17-24 : 22, an attempt has been made to distinguish thirty different admonitions. Some have compared this part of the book of Proverbs with the Egyptian text, *Wisdom of Amen-em-ope*, which consists of thirty chapters. Cf. the commentaries.

23 : 7 (C) The verb *šā'ar* seems here to mean 'to calculate, estimate, value', and thus the RSV renders 'one who is inwardly reckoning'. Another translation has 'someone who makes his own plans', but this is not certain. Textual emendation offers no solution.

23 : 34 (C) One can do no better than translate the second part literally as various translations have done. The verse clearly compares the drunkard with the sea traveller who is tossed about by the waves. But the meaning of the metaphor in the last part of the verse is difficult to grasp 'to lie on top of a mast'. Instead of 'mast', a different reading *ḥōbēl* 'skipper' has been proposed, and various other changes suggest-

ed to produce the translation 'skipper who is in a heavy storm'. The translation remains obscure.

5 (C) The RSV has 'mightier than a strong man' which means that it has accepted the reading *mē'āz* in place of the MT *ba'ōz* 'in strength', The MT indicates that true strength is manifested in wisdom and knowledge. Literally the MT reads 'a wise man possesses strength, and a man of knowledge makes the strength strong'. On the basis of ancient versions one can read here *mē'ammīṣ kōaḥ* '(is mightier) than he who has strength'. Thus, if the *min* is taken as comparative, wisdom and knowledge are set above power and strength (physical strength?).

21 (C) By rendering v. 21b literally, one obtains the translation 'with those who change you must not associate'. This may refer to people who strive after change in the existing state of affairs, i.e. rebels. On the basis of the LXX, however, another reading is often accepted, i.e. *'al šᵉnayim* (or *šᵉnē(y)hem*) *'al tit'abbār* 'do not disobey either of them' (RSV).

8 (C) The text reads literally 'do not go out hastily to a court room', i.e. do not rush to begin a law-suit. In the Hebr the word *pen* 'lest' follows. Some believe that this should be changed to read *kī* 'because', but the change is not necessary. The text means, do not be in a hurry to go to court lest it may happen that you do not know what you must do. This can be rendered 'because what will you do'.

20 (C) The *neter* of the MT can be correct thus obviating the necessity of changing the text to read *neteq* (RSV 'wound') which actually means 'itch' (Lev 13 : 30). Lye or natron used in the preparation of soap has oil added to it. But to add vinegar to natron is not only unnatural, but results in an unsatisfactory mixture and violent fermentation. It is likewise unnatural to discard a garment on a cold day, and to sing songs to an embittered heart.

27 (B) The latter part of the verse reads literally 'and investigation of their honor is honor'. The RSV has attempted to give sense to the phrase by reading *hōqar dibrē(y) kābōd* 'be sparing of complimentary words'. A different solution is to read *ḥōqēr kābōd mᵉkubbād* 'who scorns honor

is honored himself'. The advantage of this reading is that it retains the consonants of the Hebr text as they are and makes only a slight change in word division and vocalization. For *ḥāqar* meaning 'to scorn', cf. the Arabic *ḥaqara* 'to despise'. This reading and translation, however, are very uncertain. The DNV has suggested still a different solution involving only a vocalization change, i.e. *kebēdīm* in place of the MT *kebōdām*. The DNV translates 'but the investigation of difficult things is an honor'.

26 : 10 (A) The Hebr text contains numerous difficulties. The translation 'archer' (RSV) is somewhat uncertain, but it can be defended. The verb *ḥōlēl* means 'to stab', or 'to wound'. For the word *rab* cf. Jer 50 : 29; Job 16 : 13, and for *rābab*, cf. Gen 49 : 23. The AV has a remarkable insertion 'God', i.e. 'the great God'. Many transpose the word *'ōberīm* to follow *kōl*, and thus read 'all passers-by'. The RSV keeps the word where it is and translates 'a passing fool or drunkard'. It is questionable, however, if one should then have the plur. form *'ōberīm*. In the second part of the verse, the translation 'drunkard' in both the DNV and RSV is based on the reading *šikkōr* instead of the MT *śōkēr*. If one adheres to the MT, the following translation is possible 'like an archer, who shoots everybody, is one who hires a fool, or who hires passers-by'.

26 : 23 (C) For *kesep sīgīm*, the RSV has 'glaze'. One can also consider 'enamel' (cf. Albright, BASOR, 98, pp. 21 ff.), which covers the roughness of the earthenware vessel. In the second part of the verse the MT reads literally 'burning lips' (i.e. *dōleqīm*). It is preferable to read *ḥălāqīm* 'smooth'. Thus, smooth or flattering lips hide the true condition of the heart.

27 : 9 (C) The MT has 'sweetness of his friend', which could possibly denote 'warm friendship'. Then follows 'more than counsel of the soul', or 'because of hearty counsel'. The idea of the verse, then, may be that just as oil and incense please a person, so does warm friendship, because a man stands by this friend in word and deed. Instead of *'ēṣā(h)* 'counsel', some propose the reading *'eṣeb* 'trouble' and thus translate 'the sweetness of his friend is more than the trouble of the soul'. The RSV, however, reads quite a different text, i.e. *mitqāre'ā(h) mē'ăṣṣebet nāpeš* 'but the soul is torn by trouble' (cf. the LXX). It is

questionable, however, whether such a drastic emendation is warranted.

16 (C) The meaning of v. 16a undoubtedly is that one can no more apprehend and hide a contentious woman, than he can seize and hide the wind.

18 (C) The last two words are translated literally 'shall fall in one', which may mean 'in an instant', or 'unexpectedly'. But this translation is dubious, and thus many emend the last word to read *paḥat* 'pit', or *šaḥat* 'pit'.

10 (C) The first part of the verse is clear: bloodthirsty men hate the upright, i.e. they are out to ruin him. But the text continues 'but the upright seek his life'. The difficulty is that the expression *baqqēš nepeš* 'to seek someone's life' is always used in a hostile sense. Clearly this cannot be the meaning of 10b, for the upright are not after their own souls. The RSV has adopted a proposal to read *ūr^{e}šāʿīm* 'and the wicked' in place of the MT *wīšārīm* 'and the righteous'. The unfavorable sense of *baqqēš nepeš* can then be retained. The RSV translation has 'and the wicked seek his life'. Another solution is to retain the word 'upright' but, in place of *baqqēš*, to read a form of the verb *baqqēr*. Then, the translation becomes, 'but the upright seek his life', i.e. 'try to save it' or 'care for it' (cf. Ezek 34 : 11).

21 (C) The meaning of the Hebr word *mānōn* is unknown. The Vg renders *contumax* 'unmanageable'. This meaning fits the context, and it is perhaps best to accept it. Thus, those who pamper a slave when he is young cannot control him later.

1 (B) The word *l^{e}ʾītīʾēl* occurs twice in the verse and was apparently interpreted as a proper name by the Masoretes (cf. also the AV and RSV). The RSV footnote mentions that the Hebr is obscure. Generally, this puzzling word is split into two words, *lāʾītī* and *ʾēl*, translated 'I am worn out, O God', or 'I am tired, O God'. The DNV translates it in this way. This fits the immediate context, for *n^{e}ʾum haggeber* 'this man says', leads us to expect an object giving the content of his saying (cf. Num 24 : 3). It would appear certain, then, that no proper name

is meant here. Similarly *ʼukāl* is to be taken, *not* as a proper name, but is to be vocalized as *wāʼēkel* (cf. Ex 39 : 32) meaning 'I have done what I could' (cf. the DNV), or 'I am finished', or 'I am languishing'.

30 : 15 (C) Although the RSV comments on these verses that the exact meaning
30 : 16 is uncertain, it is best to follow its translation, which agrees with the DNV and others.

30 : 31 (A) The first word is rendered 'greyhound' in both the AV and the DNV, but other translations have 'cock' or 'horse'. The Hebr apparently implies 'the slenderwaisted', or 'the one tightened about the waist'. It is generally understood that the word describes an animal that walks in a stately manner.

31 : 4 (C) One cannot make sense either out of the *Kethib* *ʼō* 'or', or the *Qere* *ʼē(y)* 'where', and thus it is best to read the word *ʼawwē(h)* 'to desire'.

31 : 8 (C) The puzzling phrase *b*^{e}*nē(y) ḥălōp* is usually interpreted as meaning 'sons of loneliness', i.e. those who find themselves on the edge of the abyss. The RSV has 'who are left desolate'. This translation, however, is most uncertain. Nevertheless, it is probably the best that can be made out of the phrase, unless one arbitrarily alters the text. At any rate, the stem *ḥālap* that lies behind the form *ḥălōp* can mean 'to pass away' (cf. the lexica).

ECCLESIASTES

2 : 8 (A) The meaning of the last two words *sĭddā(h) w*^{e}*šiddōt* is not known. Ancient translations diverge sharply from each other. It was thought that a relation existed between these words and a verb 'to pour', but such a connection does not exist. The AV translation 'musical instruments' cannot be proven. A more acceptable translation is 'harem women' or 'concubines' (cf. the RSV). KBL refers to a Ugaritic word meaning 'lady'. The words, then, may mean 'many concubines' or 'various concubines'.

2 : 25 (B) The last word of the MT, *mimmennī* 'apart from me', is difficult. Even though it might conceivably be rendered with the AV 'more

than I', what meaning could this convey in the context here? It is necessary, then, to alter *mimmennī* to *mimmennū* 'apart from him', i.e. God. The change has the support of some Hebr mss, the LXX, and other versions, and has been accepted by the DNV and RSV.

17 (C) The last word is *šām* 'there', or 'at that place', i.e. 'because (there is) a time for every matter, and for every work there'. It is not clear what is meant by the final word 'there'. The RSV and other translations have 'for he has appointed a time for every matter, and for every work'. This means that they have read *śām* 'he has appointed' (from *śīm*) instead of the MT *šām*. No change in the consonantal text is involved. The translation is possible, but it is open to objection. For if the verb *śām* is intended, then it is construed in the same sentence with two different prepositions, *l*ᵉ and *'al*. While it is true that *śīm l*ᵉ means 'to appoint for', yet *śīm 'al* usually means 'to place on'. It is perhaps best, then, not to reproduce *šām* in translation, but to render simply 'for (there is) for every matter and for every work a set time'.

19 (B) As it stands the MT reads 'a fate the people, and a fate the animals'. It is clear that the word 'fate' should be a construct form and pointed accordingly. Both the DNV and RSV have accepted the slight change in vocalization. Cf. the RSV 'the fate of the sons of men and the fate of beasts'.

15 (C) The Hebr reads 'I saw everything living under the sun go with the young man, the second . . .' The RSV has omitted the word 'the second' from its translation, rendering 'that youth'. Others have considered it expedient to omit the word 'young man', and translate *haššēnī* 'the second' as 'the successor'. The DNV, however, has rendered 'I saw . . . go with the young man, the successor'. The RSV has translated *'im* by 'as well as' which does not give as good a sense as the ordinary translation 'with'.

7 (C) The MT has 'for through many dreams, there are also many vanities
(, 6) and words'. This probably means 'the result of dreams is only vain talk'. The RSV has rendered rather freely 'for when dreams increase, empty words grow many', which expresses the meaning quite well. More briefly and pointedly, one could translate 'many dreams many

empty words'. The alternative reading given in the RSV footnote does not agree entirely with the consonantal text.

5 : 9 (C) (MT, 8) The final word, the Hebr part. *neʿĕbād*, can mean 'to be served'. The difficulty, however, lies in the fact that a king is served by a people, and not by a field. The part., on the other hand, could belong to the word *śāde(h)* 'field', and thus the meaning could be 'a cultivated field'. But, in view of the fact that the word 'land' is already present in the verse, why should the word 'field' also be used? The RSV has 'but in all, a king is an advantage to a land with cultivated fields'. This translation is quite free, since various words are joined together which are considerably separated from each other in the MT. Grammatically, it is possible to translate the second half 'a cultivated field has a king', but what meaning can this have in this context? It is a question, then, as to whether or not 'cultivated fields' are mentioned in the verse. The DNV has rendered 'one advantage for the land is that besides all this, there is a king who encourages agriculture'. This is a possible rendering since the Hebr part. *neʿĕbād* could mean here 'to put himself at the service of, encourage, promote'. Nevertheless, every translation remains somewhat uncertain.

7 : 27 (B) The Hebr should undoubtedly read *'āmar haqqōhelet* 'the preacher says'. A comparison of 1 : 2 and 12 : 8 makes this quite certain. The change required is a different word division. Instead of the *h* being the final letter of the verb, which results in a peculiar 3rd pers. fem. perf., it should be taken as the article with the noun that follows. The verb would then become a 3rd pers. masc. perf., which is what would be expected.

9 : 2 (C) On the basis of some ancient versions, the RSV adds 'and the evil'. One might expect to find this opposite concept to 'the good' in this text. The MT, however, can easily be translated, thus making any textual change unnecessary.

9 : 4 (C) The MT has two readings. The *Kethib* reading or consonantal text has the verbal form *yibbāḥēr*, i.e. 'who is excepted from this? There is always hope in all the living'. The *Qere* reading, however, has the verbal form *yeḥubbar*, so that the translation becomes 'for all who

belong to the living'. At the end of the verse, one can translate either 'for a living dog is better than a dead lion', of 'for a living dog is in a better way than a dead lion'. On the question as to whether the prep. *l*ᵉ before *keleb* 'dog' is emphatic or not, cf. F. Nötscher (VT, III, 1953, p. 379), and R. Gordis (*Koheleth — The Man and His World*, 1951, pp. 294 f.).

1 (B) The MT reads at the beginning 'flies of death'. This could mean either 'dead flies' or 'flies which bring death'. Thilo, *Der Prediger Salomo*, 1923, p. 40, translates 'poisonous flies', and interprets *Aasfliegen, die faule Stoffe in die Salbe tragen*. This is possible. Cf. Ps 7 : 14 where 'the weapons of the dead' are undoubtedly 'deadly weapons' which bring on death. Later in the verse the word *mikkābōd* is a case of asyndeton. Probably the word 'and' should be added in translation.

15 (B) The Hebr reads literally 'the toil of the foolish ones wearies him'. The difficulty lies in the apparent lack of agreement in number between 'the foolish ones' and 'him'. One solution is offered by cod. Vat. which reads 'them' instead of 'him'; another by the DNV and RSV which read 'fool' instead of 'foolish ones'. It is doubtful, however, if any alteration is necessary since 'the toil of the foolish ones' can be interpreted as a general statement 'toiling as the foolish toil'. The sing. suff. of the verb 'wearies him' simply draws attention to the individual toiler (cf. the AV 'the labor of the foolish wearieth every one of them').

5 (C) The DNV renders 'as you do not know the way of the wind or how the bones grow in the womb of a woman with child'. The RSV places this translation in a footnote, but in its text it has 'as you do not know how the spirit comes to the bones in the womb of a woman with child'. The word *rūăḥ* can, of course, mean either 'wind' or 'spirit'. The RSV rendering, however, depends on the reading of a few mss, i.e. *bāʿăṣāmīm* 'in the bones' or 'to the bones', whereas the MT has *kaʿăṣāmīm*. The RSV reflects, then, an easier reading that is weakly attested, and it should thus remain secondary to the MT.

13 (C) At the close of the verse, the MT reads literally 'for this is all men', generally translated 'for this is the duty of all men'. The RSV and AV

have a less probable translation 'for this is the whole duty of man'.

12 : 14 (C) The RSV translates 'for God will bring every deed into judgment, with every secret thing, whether good or evil'. This rendering implies that there is a break or pause in the MT after the word *mišpāṭ* and that the prep. *ʿal* means here 'moreover' or 'with'. However, without a break after *mišpāṭ*, the translation becomes 'for God will bring every deed into the judgment on every secret thing, whether good or evil'. Either sense is possible.

SONG OF SOLOMON

1 : 7 (C) The MT has the form *keʿōṭeyā(h)* from *ʿāṭā(h)* 'to wrap oneself (in something)'. Accordingly, some translations have 'as one who is veiled' (cf. the DNV and BSG). On the basis of some of the ancient versions, the RSV and others translate the verb form *keṭōʿiyyā(h)* from *ṭāʿā(h)* 'to wander' (note the metathesis in the two Hebr words). The RSV translates 'like one who wanders' (cf. the AV 'as one that turneth aside').

1 : 17 (C) Many believe that the word *rāḥīṭ* means 'rafter', but this is not certain. Others render 'panels'. Some wooden object is meant.

2 : 1 (C) The word *ḥăbaṣṣelet* clearly is a flower. It has generally been translated 'rose', though 'meadow saffron' has been considered as well as 'narcissus'. It is probably best to choose the rendering 'daffodil' or 'narcissus'. The RSV note refers to the 'crocus'.

2 : 17 (C) The RSV renders the final phrase *hārē(y) bāter* 'upon rugged mountains', while the DNV has 'on the cloven mountains'. Very early the difficulty in translation of the phrase appeared. Both Aq and Symm transliterated *bāter* (cf. the AV 'upon the mountains of Bether'). It is possible, however, that the word *bāter* is to be viewed as coming from the verb *bātar* 'to share, divide in pieces'. Thus, the phrase could picture mountains which show holes or have clefts. It may be best to translate thus; the clause, however, remains uncertain.

3 : 10 (C) The RSV has 'it (i.e. the palanquin) was lovingly wrought within by the daughters of Jerusalem'. This is an acceptable translation. In

the MT 'its midst', one can think of the interior of the palanquin. The word *rāṣūp* is a pass. part. from *rāṣap* 'to fit closely together, to pave', the noun form *riṣpā(h)* meaning 'paving' or 'mosaic floor'. The part. form here, then, means 'covered'. The word 'love' that follows, can be interpreted in an adverbial sense 'with love' or 'lovingly'. The prep. *min* before 'daughters of Jerusalem' indicates the 'author' or 'cause'. In this way one may understand the RSV translation. The AV has 'the midst thereof being paved with love, for the daughters of Jerusalem'. Except for the word 'for', which is not correct here, this translation is acceptable. The BSG has 'its interior, inlaid with ebony', but this is founded on an alteration of the text, i.e. *hŏbnīm* instead of *'ahăbā(h) m*. The phrase 'daughters of Jerusalem' is then interpreted as a vocative and added to v. 11. This change, however, is unnecessary.

4 (C) The exact meaning of *talpiyyōt* is not known. The rendering 'arsenal' is questionable. Some believe that it represents a Grecism which is a possibility, but remains uncertain. The LXX has left the word untranslated and thus apparently saw no connection with any Greek word. According to Honeyman (JTS, 1949, pp. 51 f.), it must mean 'built of coursed masonry', which is an acceptable explanation. The Vg has *propugnacula*, thus a 'bulwark, front wall, entrenchment, battlement', or 'parapet'. Thus the DNV has 'which is built with battlements'. The translation remains uncertain.

11 (C) The RSV and DNV have 'his locks are wavy'. The word 'wavy' is a guess for the word *taltallīm*. Others have thought of 'palm branches' or 'a bunch of dates'. KBL has 'date-panicle' (i.e. cluster of dates), thereby connecting the word with the Accad *taltallu*.

12 (C) The word *millē't* is not clear. The verb *millē'* sometimes has the meaning 'to set something with (precious stones)'. From this explanation one understands the AV and RSV renderings 'fitly set' which thus describes 'his eyes', the first word of the verse. But *millē't* can also mean simply 'fulness', and this would suggest that the last three words should be translated 'sitting on fulness' or 'sitting on abundance'. The reference, then, would be not to 'his eyes' being 'fitly set', but to the 'doves' that stay by streams of water and bathe in

milk and that sit on abundance, perhaps meaning 'by an abundant spring' (BSG has 'sitting by a pool').

5 : 14 (C) For the RSV 'his body is ivory work', the DNV has 'work of art in ivory'. Others have 'his body is a plate of ivory'. The exact meaning of the word *ʿešet* is not certain.

6 : 12 (A) The Hebr text is completely incomprehensible. It reads literally 'I did not know my soul, she has placed me chariots my people noble (or 'prince')'. No one knows what this means. The RSV renders 'before I was aware, my fancy set me in a chariot beside my prince'. It is possible for one to regard *napšī* 'my soul' as the object of the verb 'to know', i.e. 'I did not know myself', or as the subject of *śāmatnī*, i.e. 'my soul has placed me' (= 'I have placed myself'), or 'I have sat down'. The RSV evidently follows this last suggestion since it translates 'my fancy set me'. There seems to be no possibility of securing a satisfactory translation on the grounds of the ancient versions. Little can be gained from a review of the various attempts at translation. The AV on the basis of the LXX and Vg takes the last two words as a proper name, Amminadib. The vocalization *ʿammī* 'my people' is puzzling. The DNV has simply omitted it, while the RSV has apparently read *ʿim* 'beside'. The word *markᵉbōt* is vocalized in the construct state, but one can break the connection with the word that follows by placing it in the absolute state. But whatever one may do with this verse, its translation remains very uncertain.

6 : 13 (C) The last two words can either be translated 'a dance before two ar-
(MT, 7 : 1) mies' (RSV text), or 'a dance of Mahanaim' (RSV margin). Since the word *maḥănāyim* means literally 'two armies', some have felt that the verse indicates a traditional wardance carried out between the two armies before the battle starts. On the other hand, Mahanaim may be a town or city, well-known for its dances.

7 : 5 (C) We do not know the meaning of *rᵉhāṭīm*. Since 'hair' has been
(MT, 6) mentioned in the preceding passage, it may be that the word means 'plaits', but this is not at all certain.

7 : 9 (C) A real translation problem exists here. The MT begins 'and your

Γ, 10) palate like the best wine'. The RSV has rendered 'kisses' instead of 'palate'. The bridegroom is here speaking to the bride. But in the next phrase 'which flows straight (others 'soft' or 'pleasant') to my loved one', the bride is speaking, since the 'beloved' or 'loved one' is the bridegroom. Finally, the last phrase has 'and in his sleep, flows to his lips'. Frequently the text is changed, but the danger is that the translation may become subjective and arbitrary. In such a case, it is best to keep to the text as it is and try to translate it as well as possible. The RSV has followed one or two changes here on the basis of the LXX, Aq, and the Pesh.

11 (C) The last word in the Hebr is *bakk*^{e}*pārīm* (plur. of *kāpār* 'village') 'in
Γ, 12) the villages' (cf. the AV and RSV). Some, however, suggest that the word is a plur. of *kōper* 'henna flower' (cf. the DNV and BSG).

2 (C) The MT has *t*^{e}*lamm*^{e}*dēnī* 'you taught me' (2nd pers. masc. sing.), or 'she taught me' (3rd pers. fem. sing.). In the MT the 3rd pers. fem. is more probable, the form being, then, a relative sentence without a relative particle. The translation should thus be 'I should bring you into the house of my mother who taught me' (= brought me up). The RSV has 'into the house of my mother, and into the chamber of her that conceived me'. This means that, on the basis of the LXX, the RSV has made the text of 8 : 2 conform to 3 : 4. This is unnecessary.

ISAIAH

10 (C) The Hebr word *tōrā(h)* can be rendered either 'law' or 'teaching'. Here, 'teaching' fits the context well. Cf. 2 : 3 and 8 : 16. In both 1 : 10 and 2 : 3, the BSG renders 'instruction'.

29 (B) The MT has the 3rd pers. plur. 'and they shall be ashamed', but the context calls for a 2nd pers. plur. 'and you shall be ashamed' (cf. the (RSV). The Tg and a few mss have the 2nd pers.

3 (C) Cf. the notes on 1 : 10.

6 (C) The Hebr has 'they are filled from (the) east'. The temporal sense 'from ancient times', does not make sense here. In the light of the

context, the RSV has added the word 'diviners'. The DNV has interpreted the words to mean 'to be completely under the influence of the east'. The general sense of the DNV and RSV is the same.

2 : 12 (C) The final word in this verse is *šāpēl*. Under the influence of the LXX, the RSV has rendered 'hiqh'; thereby placing v. 12c in harmony with 12b. This rendering, of course, accords with the larger context in 2 : 12-17. However, in view of the presence of *šāpēl* in v. 17 also, it is best to regard the word as original in v. 12. Thus, the translation in v. 12 can be 'against everything which exalts itself, so that it shall be humbled'.

2 : 16 (C) For the Hebr *ś*^{e}*kīyōt* the RSV has 'beautiful craft'. According to KBL, it is in Hebr a loan-word meaning 'ship' (cf. BSG 'barks').

3 : 13 (C) The DNV follows the MT in reading the final word as 'peoples'. The context favors the LXX rendering 'his people', which the RSV has adopted.

3 : 24 (C) The word *kī* near the end of the verse is generally regarded as a noun meaning 'brand' (BSG 'branding'). The RSV has 'shame'; in DSI^{a} we actually find *bōšet*, 'shame'. The word *kī* is not translated.

5 : 1 (C) The translation can be either 'for my beloved' or 'about my beloved'.

5 : 14 (C) The RSV has introduced the name of the city Jerusalem into this verse (i.e. 'the nobility of Jerusalem'), though the MT has merely 'her nobility'. The difficulty in the MT is that the 3rd pers. fem. suff. can hardly refer back to the masc. noun *ʿam* 'people' in v. 13. Thus, it may be that the prophet has Jerusalem and its inhabitants in mind when he refers to 'my people' in v. 13, which would then explain the fem. suff. in v. 14. Moreover, the writer may have used the fem. suff. by influence of the fem. noun *š*^{e}*ʾōl*. Undoubtedly he refers to the same group in both verses. The DNV has made the connection clear and definite by rendering the phrase of v. 14 as 'the splendor of this people'. This is a possible solution.

5 : 17 (C) The word *mēḥīm* as in Ps 66 : 15 means 'fatlings'. Instead of the MT

gārīm 'strangers', the RSV has read *g*^{e}*dāyim* 'kids' (a change from the *resh* to the *daleth*). But, without textual change, one can translate 'fatlings shall stay and feed between the ruins'. The word *gārīm* 'strangers', is thus interpreted as a plur. part. of *gūr* 'to stay as a guest'.

1 (B) Instead of the MT *š*^{e}*'ālā(h)*, read with Aq, Symm, and Th *š*^{e}*'ōlā(h)* 'realm of death' in the DNV, and 'Sheol' in the RSV. No change in the consonantal text is required.

4 (C) The RSV text has 'a young woman', but in its margin it notes the translation 'virgin'. It is indeed possible that by the word *'almā(h)*, a virgin is meant, since a young woman is called *'almā(h)* until the birth of her first child. Thus a 'virgin' is definitely an *'almā(h)*, but not every *'almā(h)* is necessarily a 'virgin' in the sense of the other Hebr noun *b*^{e}*tūlā(h)*, in which virginity is stressed. For a recent thorough treatment of this text, cf. *The Bible Translator*, vol. 9, no. 3, July 1958.

6 (C) Though somewhat uncertain, the MT without change can be translated 'and there is joy in Rezin'. The RSV has adopted an altered text, i.e. *ūmāsōs mipp*^{e}*nē(y) r*^{e}*ṣīn* 'and melt in fear before Rezin'.

21 (C) The MT reads 'and he (one) crosses over in it'. The RSV has evidently taken the fem. suff. as referring to *'ereṣ* 'land', since it has rendered 'through the land'.

3 (B)
Γ, 2) A decision must be made for either the *Kethib* reading *lō'* 'not' (cf. the AV), or the *Qere lō*, the prep. *l*^{e} with the 3rd pers. masc. suff. meaning 'to him' or 'for him' (cf. Ps 100 : 3). Externally, the *Qere* has the support of some twenty mss as well as the Tg. It is the reading accepted by the DNV and RSV. Internally, it suits the context better (cf. the RSV 'thou hast increased its joy [i.e. 'joy to him']; they rejoice before thee as with joy at the harvest').

11 (C)
Γ, 10) The MT reads *ṣārē(y) r*^{e}*ṣīn* 'adversaries of Rezin'. The difficulty is that the adversaries who are specified in v. 12 (Aramaeans and Philistines) can hardly be counted as enemies of Rezin of Damascus. The 'adversaries of Rezin' would be the Assyrians, who, according to 2

Kings 16, sack the city of Damascus, take the people captive, and liquidate Rezin. But here in Is 9 : 10-11 (RSV, verses 11-12), the Assyrians are not in view. So the problem is, who are 'the adversaries of Rezin'? Linguistically, the text is not obscure. The fact that a considerable number of Hebr mss have the reading *śārē(y) reṣīn* 'officers of Rezin', simply reveals that the difficulties of the text were realized very early, and that by only a slight phonetic shift the reading could be smoothed considerably. A different solution is suggested in the LXX, which has the translation 'mount Zion' in place of 'Rezin'. While this translation does not fit the context, yet it does indicate that the LXX considered 'Rezin' to be out of place here. Perhaps the best solution is to omit 'Rezin' and read simply 'adversaries' as the RSV does. In view of the context and the historical argument noted above, this translation may reproduce the original idea of the prophet.

9 : 20 (C) (MT, 19) The MT has 'the flesh of his (own) arm'. The Tg has interpreted this to mean 'the flesh of his neighbor' and this change has been accepted by the RSV and others. Such a change in interpretation, however, is not necessary since the MT has a clear sense as it stands.

10 : 5 (C) The RSV 'the staff of my fury' is quite a free translation with the more literal rendering found in a footnote. The phrase, however, can easily be translated 'a staff in their hand is my fury'. The 'hand' is Assyria. By the plur. suff. 'their', the prophet has in view the Assyrians themselves who together compose that 'hand'.

10 : 27 (B) The Hebr reads 'his burden shall fall from your shoulder and his yoke from your neck; a yoke shall be broken because of (or 'from before') the fatness'. The DNV has followed the MT up to the last word of the verse. However, instead of the word *šāmen* 'fatness', the DNV has read *šikmekā* 'your shoulder', translating the final phrase 'yes, the yoke shall be destroyed from your shoulder'. On the other hand, the RSV has taken the last three words of v. 27 as the first sentence of v. 28, reading by conjecture *'ālā(h) mippenē(y) Rimmon* 'he has gone up from Rimmon'. This phrase becomes, then, the first part of the description of the Assyrian advance on Jerusalem. Besides changes in vocalization, two consonantal alterations are required to produce this rendering; first, an additional *h* needs to be added to the

end of the consonants *'l* to make possible the translation 'he went up', and second, the letter *šīn* of *šāmen* has to be changed to a *resh* to obtain the place name Rimmon. Judg 20 : 45, 47 refer to a Rimmon in the vicinity of Bethel. 'Samaria' is another name that has been conjectured.

4 (B) The RSV translation 'with its majestic trees' is closely related to the LXX rendering 'with the lofty ones', whereas the MT has *b^{e}'addīr* 'with (or 'by means of') a mighty one'. The word *'addīr* occurs as an adjective qualifying trees (cf. Ezek 17 : 23; Zech 11 : 2), and, in this sense here, it fits perfectly with 'Lebanon'. But *'addīr* is also used to describe God. Thus, the DNV without deviating from the MT, has translated 'and Lebanon shall fall by means of the Mighty One', i.e. God.

5 (C) The *Kethib—Qere* readings allow for either the translation 'this is made known' (RSV margin—*hoph.* part.), or 'let this be known' (RSV text—*pu.* part.).

4 (C) In place of the word *madhēbā(h)* whose meaning is uncertain, the *marhēbā(h)* is generally read (*resh* instead of *daleth*). The word *marhēbā(h)* means 'assault' according to KBL. This reading known previously from ancient versions, has recently had confirmation in DSI[a] from *Qumran*. The DNV has translated 'oppression' and the RSV 'insolent fury'.

19 (C) The MT supported by DSI[a] has *nēṣer* 'shoot (of a plant)'. The RSV, however, on the basis of the Tg and Symm, has accepted the reading *nēpel* 'untimely birth'.

30 (C) The MT reads at the close 'he will slay', which can be readily translated in a pass. sense 'your remnant shall be slain'. Nevertheless the RSV has felt the weight of the preceding parallel phrase 'I will kill your root', and thus it has rendered the final phrase in the 1st pers., i.e. 'I will slay' (cf. DSI[a] which has the 1st pers.). There is, however, no reason to depart from the MT.

2 (C) The DNV has followed the MT closely and translated 'they go up to the temple (house), and Dibon (goes up) to the high places to weep'.

The word *bayit* is taken, thus, as the object of the verb *'ālā(h)*. The sense of the verse is that in their anxiety and doubt, the people go to the high places to pray to their gods. On the other hand, the RSV has accepted an altered reading at the beginning of the verse and translated 'the daughter of Dibon has gone up to the high places to weep'.

16 : 10 (C) For the final phrase, while the RSV (on the basis of the LXX) has rendered 'the vintage shout is hushed', the DNV has adhered to the MT which can be easily translated 'I have hushed the shout of joy'. The subject is the Lord.

17 : 5 (B) For the MT *qāṣīr* 'harvest', read the *qal* active part. *qōṣēr* 'mower'. Cf. the AV 'harvestman' and the RSV 'reaper'.

17 : 9 (C) The DNV has rendered 'as a deserted district in the wood, or on the top of a mountain'. This translation is uncertain. The word *'āmīr* which in 17 : 6 means 'top' (of a tree), may have the more general sense in v. 9 of a high place, possibly 'mountain top'. This cannot be proved. The DSI[a] text supports the MT though the letter *w* before *'āmīr* is uncertain. The word *'āmīr* could be viewed as a further qualification of *ḥōreš* and one could translate 'high wood' or 'wood that has grown up high'. The RSV has chosen here to follow the LXX which reads 'the Amorites and the Hivites', i.e. 'the deserted places of the Hivites and the Amorites, which they deserted' (RSV). If one translates the MT as literally as possible, it is clear that the previous town dwellers are not mentioned. However, it is obvious that pre-Israelite inhabitants must be meant.

18 : 2, 7 (A) The translation of *goy qaw-qaw* (or *goy qawqaw*) is not easy. Usually a connection is made with an Arabic word for 'strength'. Thus KBL translates 'elasticity', the RSV 'mighty', the BSG 'strong', and the DNV 'imperious'.

19 : 10 (A) The DNV renders the Hebr word *šātōte(y)hā* as 'its supporting pillars'. The RSV agrees with this translation, but has given more of a paraphrase of the text, i.e. 'those who are the pillars of the land'. The form *šātōte(y)hā* is thus taken as a plur. of *šēt* 'foundation'. The indi-

cation would be that the noble or eminent persons are the foundation of the state (the LXX evidently takes the word as meaning hand-workers or weavers). Hence, over against the eminent or noble ones of v. 10a, v. 10b describes the ordinary wage earners.

23 (C) At the close of the verse, the MT reads 'and the Egyptians shall serve Assur'. This does not make sense in this context. However *ʿābad* should be interpreted in a religious sense 'to worship God', and the word *ʾet* should be viewed as the prep. 'with'. Thus the translation should be 'and the Egyptians will worship with the Assyrians' (cf. the RSV).

8 (B) The MT literally has no meaning 'and he cried a lion'. The LXX has apparently simply transliterated the Hebr *ʾaryē(h)* by ουριαν. The DNV has changed *ʾaryē(h)* into r^{e}*ʾē(h)* 'see', impv. form of *rāʾā(h)*, while the RSV has read *hārōʾe(h)* 'he who sees', or 'he who saw'. This has the support of DSI[a].

6 (C) Without changing the MT, one can translate 'with chariots, men, horses' (cf. the DNV 'with chariots, men, horsemen'). The word *pārāšīm* can mean 'horses' as well as 'horsemen'. The RSV has 'with chariots and horsemen' thereby omitting the word *ʾādām* 'man' or 'men'. The BSG has omitted the whole clause, while BH suggests that the reading should be changed to *rākab ʾărām ʿal pārāšīm* 'Aram came riding on horses'.

2 (C) The MT (cf. the DNV) reads 'the merchants of Sidon who sail the seas have enriched you' (literally 'filled you'). The RSV, however, renders 'O merchants of Sidon, your messengers passed over the sea' (cf. DSI[a]).

13 (C) The translation 'they made her a ruin' (RSV) is possible, though not altogether certain. The problem is that the verbal form is sing., whereas the verbs in the rest of the verse are plur.

11 (C) In the word *ʾorbōt*, one should evidently consider the root meaning 'to lie in ambush', or, the meaning in Arabic 'to be sly'. Thus the noun here seems to have some such meaning as 'skill' or 'tricks'.

26 : 16 (C) The RSV has 'they poured out a prayer' and the DNV 'they heaved a sigh'. While both translations are uncertain, yet in the light of the context they more or less reproduce the Hebr meaning.

26 : 18 (C) The RSV has 'and the inhabitants of the world have not fallen'. It is worth serious thought, however, that the word *nāpal* may have here the special meaning 'to be born' (cf. KBL). The translation would then be 'inhabitants of the world were not born'. Both the DNV and BSG adopt this rendering which fits in well with the opening thought of the verse.

26 : 19 (C) The MT supported by the DSI[a] ms reads at the beginning 'your dead shall live again (also) my body; they shall arise'. A slight textual change (in suff.) produces the translation 'their bodies shall rise' (RSV). The final word of the verse is the causative form of *nāpal* which could mean 'to cause to be born'. The DNV has 'the earth shall give back life to the shades', while the BSG renders 'and the earth will bring the Shades to birth'. The RSV has retained the ordinary rendering of *nāpal* 'to fall'. In this case, the object of the causative form is the dew. Thus, the RSV translates 'for thy dew is a dew of light, and on the land of the shades thou wilt let it fall'. One difficulty is that the prep. 'on' is not in the Hebr. Hence, this translation remains somewhat dubious.

27 : 8 (C) According to the MT vocalization, the first word *b*^{e}*sa'se'ā(h)* [= *bis 'ā(h) s*^{e}*'ā(h)*] means 'with measure' (RSV 'measure by measure'). This is the interpretation of the ancient versions such as Aq, Th, Tg, and the Vg. This "explanation," however, is probably too subtle to be true. KBL no longer mentions it in his dictionary, but rather explains the word as a form of the verb *s's'*, meaning to 'cry *sa-sa*', a sound that camel or donkey drivers make to hurry up their beasts, thus, 'to drive up (the animals)'. Hence, the translation can become 'by driving up' (DNV 'by driving away', and BSG 'by expulsion').

28 : 16 (C) At the close of the verse, the RSV has rendered 'he who believes will not be in haste'. The translations 'he who believes will not be agitated' and 'he who believes will not lose his head' are also quite possible (cf. Driver, JTS, 32, 1930-31, pp. 253 f.).

5 (C) The word *zārāyik* 'thy strangers', should be taken as meaning *ṣārāyik* 'thy adversaries'.

6 (B) The Hebr word *mēhem* 'out of them', has no clear meaning in this context and has been omitted by the DNV. Both the AV and RSV have rendered 'from whence come', which is a doubtful translation (cf. the LXX which, however, does not have the word 'come').

6 (C) The DNV following the MT has 'from whom the sons of Israel have deeply revolted'. The RSV renders 'from whom you have deeply revolted, O people of Israel'.

19 (C) At the beginning of the verse, the MT can be rendered 'and when it hails so that the forest comes down', or 'even if the forest should come down because of the hail'. The word *redet* is then explained as an inf. of the verb *yārad* 'to descend'. A verb *bārad* 'to hail' is elsewhere unknown in the OT, though this need not mean that it does not exist. The word *beredet* could even be derived from the verbal stem *bārad*. Nonetheless, the translation offered above remains uncertain. Some prefer to read the first word of the verse as *yārad*, perf. form of the verb meaning 'to come down', instead of the MT *bārad* 'to hail'. Thus, the RSV renders 'and the forest will utterly go down'.

2 (B) Instead of the MT 'their arm', some mss, the Tg, Pesh, and Vg read 'our arm' which fits the context better (cf. 'our arm' in both the DNV and RSV). The LXX has not only read the word 'arm' as 'seed', but it has strayed far from the Hebr elsewhere in this verse.

7 (A) In its Masoretic vocalization, the word *'er'ellām* is puzzling. It seems to be the subject of v. 7a, and, in the parallelism of the verse, it corresponds to 'messengers of peace' in 7b. Therefore, it ought to be a plur., but the MT vocalization is most obscure. Following are suggested translations:

1. 'heralds' (DNV). This rendering is influenced by the parallelism of the verse and is an old explanation.
2. 'the men of Ariel' (KBL). Thus a connection is made with Ariel, a part of Jerusalem (Is 29 : 1).

3. 'the valiant ones' (RSV). Others translate similarly by heroes or brave persons.
4. 'the heroes of "Altar-hearth" (= 'Ariel')' is the BSG rendering. This explanation combines the two previous suggestions.

33 : 8 (C) In place of the MT *ʿārîm* 'cities' (cf. the DNV and AV), it is preferable to read *ʿēdîm* 'witnesses' (RSV). It seems that the reading 'witnesses' now has the support of DSI[a].

34 : 11-12 (C) The first word of v. 12 'its nobles' is added to v. 11 by the RSV which translates 'and the plummet of chaos over its nobles'. However, retaining the traditional division here, v. 11 can be read 'he shall stretch over it the line of confusion and the plummet of chaos'. V. 12 continues 'as for his nobles, they do not proclaim the kingdom', for which the DNV has a more free rendering 'among his nobles there is not one who proclaims the kingdom'.

35 : 7 (C) The DNV attempts to follow the MT faithfully in rendering 'where jackals stay and have their lair, there will be grass with reeds and rushes'. If one omits the suff. of the word *ribṣāh* as the DSI[a] ms apparently does, a possible translation would be 'in the lair of jackals (or 'where jackals stay'), is a couch of grass with reeds and rushes' (cf. O. Eissfeldt, *Variae lectiones*, BH, 17, 1951, p. 4). The RSV translation 'the haunt of jackals shall become a swamp', is based on a conjectured reading *biṣṣā(h)* 'swamp' in place of the MT *ribṣāh* or the DSI[a] *rebeṣ*.

35 : 8 (C) The DNV has attempted to adhere to the MT by translating 'it (i.e. the way) shall be for them alone (i.e. the redeemed); neither travellers or fools shall err therein'. This rendering, then, would point to a further reason why the way is called 'a holy way', for unclean or even ordinary travellers have no access to it. This interpretation remains uncertain. The RSV has omitted from its text the words *w*^{e}*hūʾ lāmō hōlēk derek*, while the BSG has accepted a slightly altered reading *w*^{e}*hūʾ l*^{e}*ʿammō hōlēk derek*, translating 'it shall be for his people as they go along the way'.

37 : 27 (C) The DNV maintains the one main difference between this text, i.e. *š*^{e}*dēmā(h)* 'field', and the parallel passage in 2 Kings 19 : 26, i.e.

šᵉdēpā(h) 'blasted, blighted'. Here in Is the DNV translates 'a cornfield before it ripens', while the RSV (cf. also the AV) has 'blighted before it is grown', thereby making the text agree with the text of 2 Kings. The DSIᵃ ms has an interesting reading that can be translated with its immediate context 'like grass on the roofs dried up by the east wind' (cf. Eissfeldt, *op. cit.*, p. 4).

12 (C) The last word of the MT *tašlīmēnī* means 'thou dost abandon me completely' (cf. KBL). The RSV renders 'thou dost bring me to an end'. Another translation found in OTS, IX, pp. 180 f., has 'thou makest me hemmed in', i.e. thou dost surround me or besiege me. This rendering, however, is quite uncertain since it is based on a different verbal stem and assumes a form that is less usual in Hebr.

13 (C) The MT *šiwwītī* can be translated 'I make smooth, calm', or, possibly 'I try to become calm' (cf. the DNV). The DSIᵃ ms has apparently a different reading, but the text here is not clear. The RSV has 'I cry for help', which understands the verb *šiwwaʿtī* instead of the MT *šiwwītī*. The context of the verse should guide the translator here.

14 (C) Cf. the note on Jer 8 : 7 concerning *sūs ʿāgūr*.

15 (C) The form *ʾeddadde(h)* from *dādā(h)* 'to walk slowly as a mourner', should be rendered in this context 'I will walk slowly all my years'. The DSIᵃ ms appears to support the MT (cf. also the BSG 'I must go softly all my years'). The RSV has accepted a drastic textual alteration which it renders 'all my sleep has fled'.

17 (C) The MT has the form *ḥāšaqtā* 'thou hast loved', or 'thou hast bound, kept'. The form is without doubt correct. The clear meaning is that God has preserved life from the pit of destruction. Nevertheless, the RSV adopts a slightly different reading *ḥāśaktā* 'thou hast held back'. The change is unnecessary.

6 (C) The opening of the verse can be translated in two ways; either 'a voice says' (RSV), or, as the DNV renders 'listen, someone says'. The DNV clearly views the word *qōl* as an interjection 'listen'. Cf. also the beginning of 40 : 3. Following the impv. form 'call', the

Masoretes have a 3rd pers. 'and he said'. Usually this is vocalized as a 1st pers. 'and I said' (RSV). The DSI[a] ms apparently has the form of the 1st pers. Nevertheless, it is doubtful whether one should depart from the Masoretic vocalization here. The 3rd pers. can be rendered 'and someone says', or even interpreted as meaning 'someone asks the question', or 'the question is asked'. The origin of the question and the circumstances surrounding it are left undecided. Still a third textual problem in the verse is the word *ḥasdō* from *ḥesed.* It is often rendered 'beauty', but it usually means 'mercy' (AV 'goodliness'). The translation 'loving-kindness' is worthy of consideration.

40 : 7 (C) Some render 'breath of the Lord': others have 'spirit of the Lord'.

40 : 9 (C) Do Zion and Jerusalem give the good tidings or receive them? That is, are Zion and Jerusalem themselves 'the herald of good tidings' (DNV, RSV), or is someone else pictured as 'the herald of good tidings', which tidings are intended for Zion and Jerusalem (BSG 'O heralds of good news to Zion . . . to Jerusalem')? Either idea is possible in the verse.

40 : 20 (C) According to KBL, the first word in the MT *m*^{e}*sukkān* is 'unexplained'. It has been suggested that it is a type of tree or kind of wood, but this is not certain. It is likewise uncertain that it is a *pu.* part. of *sākan* meaning 'he who has benefited by' (cf. Simon, *A Theology of Salvation*, 1953, p. 246). This would give a distorted meaning. Some have considered the word *miskēn* 'poor' to be a source for the form here. The meaning of *m*^{e}*sukkān* could be, then, 'someone who has become poor'. The word *t*^{e}*rūmā(h)* 'oblation, contribution', which follows, can be connected with the verse in either one of two ways. Presuming that the translation of *m*^{e}*sukkān* is correct, one can render 'he who is too impoverished for such an oblation' (cf. the DNV), or, he can render 'he who is impoverished (chooses) for an offering' (RSV).

41 : 23 (B) Near the end of the verse, both the DNV and RSV have adopted the *Kethib* reading which has a form of the verb 'to fear'. The *Qere* has a form of the verb 'to see' (cf. the AV and LXX).

5 (B) The MT reads *w*^{e}*yābō*' 'and he shall come' (cf. the AV). Parallelism, however, calls for a synonym of the verb *rāmas* 'to tread upon'. For this reason the DNV and RSV have adopted the reading *wayyābos* 'and he trampled' (RSV 'he shall trample').

7 (C) The MT reads literally 'first to Zion, behold, behold them' (or 'these things'). The DNV has not altered the text, but for the sake of clarity it has added a few explanatory words, i.e. 'as the first (I announce) to Zion: look, there they are'. The RSV has deviated somewhat from the MT in rendering 'I first have declared it to Zion'.

4 (C) The RSV has rendered the verse according to meaning, not according to letter. It is possible, however, to translate literally the first two verbs in the verse.

6 (C) The form *'eṣṣorkā* is capable of two explanations. It can be understood as derived from *yāṣar* 'to form', i.e. 'I have formed you' (translating the impf. as a perf.). But it can also be viewed as the impf. form of *nāṣar* 'to guard, keep', i.e. 'I have kept you'. The three impf. verbs (including *'eṣṣorkā*) in the verse are all vocalized as jussives in the MT, i.e. 'I will hold you . . . and keep you . . . and I will give you'. Both the DNV and RSV have vocalized the connective 'and' in each case as a *waw consecutive*, i.e. 'and I have taken you . . .' No real difference in exegesis is involved. C. R. North, *The Suffering Servant in Deutero-Isaiah*, 1948, p. 131, says, "even if we alter the Masoretic pointing, the full effects of the initial call lie in the future. We may therefore let it stand."

10 (C) The MT has 'those who go down to the sea'. Many have suggested that the text should be changed to agree with Ps 96 : 11 and Ps 98 : 7, and thus translated 'let the sea roar'. However, the text of DSI^{a} reads the same as the MT, so one should be hesitant in making a textual change here.

20 (C) The RSV has employed the 3rd pers. throughout the verse, i.e. 'he sees', 'does not observe', 'his ears', and 'he does not hear'. Only for the last phrase does the MT employ the 3rd pers. It is doubtful whether the RSV interpretation is correct. For example, the DSI^{a}

text clearly supports the Hebr consonantal text in reading the first word as a 2nd pers. masc. sing. 'you have seen' (the LXX has the 2nd pers. plur.). The *Qere* reading indicates that the form is an inf. The reading of the verb form, however, as a 2nd pers. is definitely justified (cf. the DNV). Simon (*op. cit.*, p. 93) translates in agreement with the traditional text 'many things are to be seen, but thou observest them not; though ears are open, one does not listen'.

42 : 22 (B) In agreement with the context, read *b*^{e}*ḥōrīm* 'in holes' instead of the MT *bahūrīm* 'young men'.

43 : 14 (B) The MT reads 'I will bring down all the bars' (RSV 'break down'). The Vg follows the MT closely. On the basis of the LXX, the DNV reads *bōr*^{e}*ḥīm* 'fugitives', translating 'I will make all the Chaldeans go down to the ships as fugitives'. This interpretation, however, is dubious. The AV translation 'nobles' seems to reflect the word *b*^{e}*hūrīm*. Conjectures are many and varied, but the meaning of the verse remains obscure. Cf. Simon (*op. cit.*, pp. 248 ff.) for a brief discussion of several interpretations.

44 : 4 (C) The DNV, following the MT, has rendered 'they shall spring up in among grass' (DSI[a] and other Hebr mss have 'as among grass'). The RSV, however, on the basis of the LXX and Tg has rendered 'they shall spring up like grass amid waters'.

44 : 5 (B) The vocalization *yiqqārē'* (*niph.*) 'he will call himself', is preferable to the MT *qal* form *yiqrā'* 'he will call'.

44 : 7 (C) The literal Hebr is given in the RSV footnote. The DNV is also a possible translation of the MT 'seeing that I called the ancient people into existence, they may proclaim what is to happen in the future'. The DNV omission of *lāmō* in translation can be defended. The RSV has made a few alterations in the text, and at the close of the verse it has read *lānū* 'to us' in place of the MT *lāmō* 'to them'.

44 : 12 (C) The Hebr *maʿăṣād* means 'axe' (DNV 'the smith has an axe'). The text evidently means that he uses this tool in his work. Often, however, another form is read, i.e. *m*^{e}*ʿaṣṣēb*, *pi.* part. of *ʿāṣab* 'to fashion'

(cf. Job 10 : 8). The noun *'āṣāb* means 'idol'. Thus, the RSV has the rather attractive conjectural reading 'the ironsmith fashions it'.

14 (B) The DNV reads *kārat* 'he cuts down' in place of the MT inf. *likrot*, an irregular form containing a prep. of direction or aim. If the MT remains unaltered, it is possible to translate 'he must cut down'. The verse is admittedly difficult. Cf. the commentaries.

18 (B) KBL explains the word *ṭaḥ* as a perf. 3rd masc. sing. from *ṭāḥah* meaning 'to be smeared'. Since the verb is intransitive, the obvious thing to do is to read it here in the 3rd masc. plur. with 'their eyes' as the subject (cf. the DNV 'their eyes have been besmeared'). If the verb is retained in its sing. form, its vocalization must be understood as *ṭāḥ* from *ṭūaḥ* 'to coat, smear over'. The nouns 'their eyes' and 'their heart', then, become objects with God understood as the subject (cf. the RSV 'he has shut their eyes').

24 (C) According to the *Kethib* reading which is supported by DSI[a], the last word should really be two words meaning 'who was with me' (cf. the RSV). The *Qere* has read the two words as one, to be translated 'by myself', or 'without help', or 'completely alone' (cf. the DNV and RSV margin). This vocalization of the Masoretes can be explained if we assume the influence from the word *lᵉbaddī* 'alone', just a few words earlier in the verse.

2 (C) In place of the MT *hădūrīm* 'swellings, barricade', one should probably follow the reading of DSI[a] *hārīm* 'mountains', which is also reflected in the LXX. The suggestion in KBL that one should translate by the word 'roads' should not be accepted.

8 (B) The MT plur. form *yiprū* 'they bear fruit' makes no sense in this context. The reading of DSI[a] *yipraḥ*, impf. of *pāraḥ* 'to sprout forth' is certainly preferable. Cf. the RSV rendering 'that salvation may sprout forth'.

9 (C) According to the MT, v. 9a should be translated 'woe to him who strives with his Maker, (he is only) a sherd among potsherds of earth'. If, however, one vocalizes *ḥarśē(y)* as *ḥārāšē(y)*, i.e. with a *š* instead of

ś, the translation could become 'earthen vessel with the potter'. The rendering is uncertain.

45 : 11 (C) The MT supported by DSI[a] reads literally 'ask me about future things, command me in regard to my children, and the work of my hands'. Some have suggested that the MT form *'ōtiyyōt* 'future things' should be read as *hă'ōtī* (interrogative particle with the sign of the acc. and suff. of the 1st pers. sing.), in which case, the final letter *t* should be added to the following verbal form which becomes *tiš'ālūn*. Thus, the RSV translates 'will you question me about my children, or command me concerning the work of my hands'? However, the fact that the MT is clear as it stands and that it is supported by DSI[a], should make one hesitant in altering the text here.

48 : 1 (C) The MT reads 'from the waters of Judah'. The language is poetic or metaphorical. Some, however, by a slight textual change, read 'from the loins of Judah'. But it should be noted that nowhere else is this expression ever used to refer to the patriarch from whom the house of Judah was descended.

48 : 10 (C) Although in Hebr we might expect the prep. *kᵉ* to produce the translation 'like silver' (cf. the RSV), yet, the MT *bᵉ* 'with' is not at all impossible.

48 : 11 (C) The RSV rendering 'for how should my name be profaned' follows the LXX and L. However, since in v. 9, the 'name' has been mentioned, it is possible to translate here without addition 'how it is profaned !'.

48 : 16 (C) There is a difference of opinion on the syntactic position of the final word *wᵉrūḥō*. Some believe the translation should be 'the Lord God sent me and his spirit', i.e. not only did the Lord God send me but his Spirit sent me too. The form 'his Spirit' is then taken as a *second subject*. A second interpretation—translated the same way—could be that 'his spirit' actually is a *second object* agreeing with 'me'. But this does not make sense in this context. Still a third explanation is to translate 'the Lord God sent me with his spirit'. The sense would be that the prophet who is sent, is endowed with the Spirit

of God. Because of the various possibilities of the Hebr syntax here, the translation remains variable.

5 (C) If the word *lōʾ* is viewed as a negation and the word *ʾāsap* means 'to be gathered', the translation should be 'but Israel would not allow itself to be gathered'. If, on the other hand, *ʾāsap* means here 'to take away', the translation becomes 'but Israel shall not be taken away'. It is better, however, to adopt the *Qere* reading supported by DSI^{a}, and thus read the word *lō* 'to him', the prep. *l*^{e} with the 3rd masc. sing. suff. In this case the translation becomes 'and Israel shall be gathered to him', or 'and to gather Israel to him' (RSV 'and that Israel might be gathered to him'). Cf. North, *op. cit.*, p. 119.

7 (B) The MT *libzō(h)* may be intended to have a reflexive sense, i.e. 'to him who despises himself'. However, the DNV and RSV have read the form *libzūy* (pass. part.) *nepes* 'to one deeply despised'. The following word *m*^{e}*tāʿēb*, a *pi.* part., has sometimes been vocalized as *m*^{e}*tōʿab*, a *pu.* part., to be translated in a pass. sense.

12 (C) The MT has 'land of Sinim', which is sometimes read as *s*^{e}*wēnīm* and translated 'land of Syene' (cf. the RSV). The DNV has 'Sinites' which is evidently supported by DSI^{a}. It is possible that a region in the south is meant. Syene (Assuan) is in the south. For other interpretations, cf. KBL. It is possible that we have here "a colloquial inexactitude of terminology" (Simon, *op. cit.*, p. 253).

24 (C) The DNV has retained the MT reading in its translation 'shall the captives of a righteous man escape'. The DSI^{a} ms (cf. also the LXX) has the noun *ʿārīṣ* 'tyrant' in place of the MT *ṣaddīq* 'righteous man'. Thus, the RSV has translated 'or the captives of a tyrant be rescued'.

11 (C) The MT has 'who gird on brands', or, it can possibly be rendered 'who provide (yourselves) with brands' (DNV). On the basis somewhat of the LXX and Pesh, the RSV understands the form *m*^{e}*ʾīrē(y)*, and translates 'who set brands alight'. The change, however, is not necessary since the MT can be translated intelligibly.

51 : 2 (B) It is preferable to read the last two words with *waw consecutives* 'and I blessed him and made him many' (cf. the AV and RSV). If the vocalization of the Masoretes is followed, the obvious translation is 'I called him to bless and multiply him'.

51 : 16 (B) The MT contains the unusual expression *linṭōă'*, i.e. 'planting the heavens'. On the basis of the Pesh, the DNV and RSV have read the word *linṭōt*, i.e. 'stretching out the heavens'. The idiom 'to stretch out the heavens' is the common one (cf. Is 40 : 22).

51 : 17, 22 (B) In these two verses, the word *kōs* 'cup' or 'bowl' that follows immediately the word *qubba'at*, can hardly be translated, since the words are synonymous. Hence, the word *kōs* should be viewed as an official gloss to explain the other unfamiliar word *qubba'at*.

51 : 19 (C) With a slight change in the MT, the RSV translates the last two words 'who will comfort you'. This change has the support of DSI[a] as well as the ancient versions.

52 : 2 (C) The MT supported by the LXX has 'sit down, Jerusalem'. The RSV, BSG, and others have accepted a slight textual change that allows for the translation 'O captive Jerusalem'. This would agree with the final clause 'O captive daughter of Zion'. It is best, however, to keep to the MT.

52 : 15 (C) The Hebr verbal form *yazze(h)* has been dubiously rendered 'he shall startle' (cf. the RSV). Many suggestions on the translation of the form have been made (cf. North, *op. cit.*, p. 123). In this context, the word cannot mean 'to sprinkle'. The DNV has rendered 'to cause to jump' (i.e. 'in surprise'), an explanation based on the Arabic meaning. Vriezen (OTS, VII, pp. 203 f.) believes the form to be from *hāzzā(h)* 'to splash', which is interpreted in this context to mean 'to burst asunder'. He says, "the sense . . . might be: to cause to burst asunder, i.e. to cause to fly apart, to scatter . . . The '*Ebed* is said to make many (or large) nations retreat in great fear to all sides by his marvellous victory." This interpretation deserves consideration.

10 (C) The translation 'when he makes himself an offering for sin' (RSV) is correct. The fem. form *napšō* is taken as the subject and *tāśīm* is a 3rd pers. fem. sing. agreeing with the subject. By itself, the form *tāśīm* could be a 2nd pers. masc. sing. (cf. the AV). But, in this case, it would mean that *napšō* is the object here, which is not correct.

12 (C) Consult the commentaries for explanations of other parts of Is 53. One more example here in v. 12 will be mentioned. The RSV (cf. also the DNV) renders the first part of the verse 'therefore I will divide him a portion with the great, and he shall divide the spoil with the strong'. In this case, the two prepositions *b*^{e} and *ʾet* are both rendered 'with'. It is possible, however, that *ʾet* here is the sign of the acc. which could make the 'strong' the ones who are the spoil. The 'great' likewise, then, can be the object. Hence, it is possible to translate 'therefore I will divide him a portion of the great, and he will divide the strong as spoil'. It is clear that one's interpretation of the pericope as a whole influences the translation here.

5 (B) The words *lāhem* 'to them' and *lō* 'to him' are parallel. On the basis of DSI^a, instead of *lō*, *lāhem* should be read.

8 (C) The last two words are translated in the RSV 'you have looked on nakedness'. The translation 'nakedness' is for the Hebr *yād* 'hand' or 'side'. The DNV has 'shame'. It is probable that the word here refers to the male organ.

9 (B) In place of the MT word 'to the king', the RSV and DNV have adopted an altered vocalization, translating 'to Molech'. This change is made on the basis of the context which indicates actions and customs related to Molech worship.

3 (C) The word *ḥēpeṣ* means 'pleasure, desire, affair, business'. The translation, then, can either be 'to seek pleasure' or 'to pursue business'. The same alternatives occur in v. 13.

11 (C) The meaning of the word *ṣaḥṣāḥōt* is not certain. The root *ṣāḥah* means 'to be white, clear', and then later 'to make bright'. The RSV has 'good things' which does not say much. Both Ges-Buhl and KBL suggest 'scorched places' and refer to an Arabic word derived from

the above root meaning 'a bare plain'. The AV has 'drought' but the BSG 'rich nourishment'. Translations, thus, are quite divergent.

58 : 13 (C) See 58 : 3.

60 : 19 (C) The additional phrase 'by night' is not found in the MT but is justified in view of the DSI[a] ms and the ancient versions.

61 : 1 (C) The Hebr word *ʿānāw* (plur. *ʿănāwīm*) means someone who feels himself poor and needy before God, i.e. humble (RSV 'afflicted').

61 : 7 (C) Throughout the verse, the RSV has used the 2nd masc. plur. forms 'you' and 'your'. The MT, however, except for the phrase 'your shame', has the 3rd pers. plur. forms 'they' and 'their' throughout. In four places including the phrase 'your shame', the DSI[a] text supports the 2nd masc. plur. forms, and in the remaining two places, the 3rd pers. plur. forms. This text is probably more satisfactory, although the MT may be correct. A variation in regard to persons is a common Hebr idiom. The DNV has adhered to the traditional Hebr text.

61 : 8 (B) The MT reads 'I hate robbery with a burnt offering' (AV 'I hate robbery for burnt offering'). The word 'burnt offering' is difficult in this context. Through a slight change in vocalization that is supported by five mss and the LXX, the MT word *b*^{e}*ʿōlā(h)* 'with burnt offering' becomes *b*^{e}*ʿawlā(h)* 'with injustice'. Thus, the RSV has rendered 'robbery and wrong' and the DNV 'unjustifiable robbery'.

63 : 3 (B) According to the MT vocalization, the two imperfects in the second half of the verse should be read 'for I will tread them . . . and trample them' (AV). It is preferable, however, in keeping with the perf. verb at the beginning of the verse, to render each of the two imperfects with a *waw consecutive*, i.e. 'I trod them . . . and trampled them'. The LXX has understood this changed vocalization, and it has been followed by the DNV and the RSV.

63 : 4 (C) The MT (cf. also DSI[a]) has 'the year of my redeemed', which is generally rendered 'my year of redemption'.

: 9 (C) The *Kethib* reading has *lō'*, the negation, i.e. 'he did not afflict'. The *Qere* reading of the Masoretes has *lō* 'to him', i.e. '(there was) affliction to him' (= 'he was afflicted').

: 11 (C) In the first part of the verse, the RSV accepts the reading *'abdō* 'his servant' and translates 'he remembered the days of old, of Moses his servant'. The MT, however, has the form *'ammō* 'his people', which means that the translation should be 'he remembered the days of old, of Moses, of his people'. The next clause the RSV (cf. also the DNV and BSG) renders 'where is he who brought up out of the sea the shepherds of his flock'. This translation follows the text of DSI[a] which omits the suff., i.e. *h m ' l (h)* 'who brought up'. In this case, the *'et* which follows is clearly the sign of the acc., since otherwise, the verb form 'who brought up' would have no object. As for the MT which has the suff. at the end of the verb form 'who brought up', it should apparently be translated 'where is he who brought them up out of the sea with the shepherds of his flock' (cf. the AV). The word *'et* is thus understood to be the prep. 'with'. On the other hand, the MT could also be translated 'where is he who brought them up out of the sea, the shepherds of the flock'. This would mean that *'et* is taken as the sign of the acc., thereby making 'the shepherds of the flock' to be in apposition to the suff. 'them'. Various mss read the plur. form 'shepherds' as a sing. 'shepherd',

: 5 (C)
T, 4) The RSV (cf. also the DNV) has an interrogative sense at the end 'and shall we be saved'. This is certainly possible, though the MT has simply 'and we shall be saved'. The BSG rendering '(through our doings) we fell into guilt' is based on a drastic textual change, as is another translation 'against you we have transgressed from ancient times'. It is true that the context refers repeatedly to sin and thus, it would appear that the verb 'to be saved' seems to be out of place. If, however, we interpret the end of v. 5 interrogatively, this objection disappears.

: 7 (B)
T, 6) The MT has the form *t^emūgēnū* from *mūg* 'to shake, totter', a meaning that is difficult in this setting. On the basis of the LXX and Tg, the RSV has read a form of *māgan* 'to deliver up, over', i.e. 'and hast

delivered us into the hand of our iniquities' (RSV). The DSI[a] text is not clear at this point, though apparently it has a form of *māgad*. A few mss read a *polel* form of *mūg* to be translated 'thou hast dissolved us because of our iniquities' (cf. the AV). If the translation 'to deliver over' is accepted, another decision must be made. One must choose between 'to deliver into the hand of' (RSV), and 'to deliver over because of' (cf. the LXX which has διὰ with the acc. case).

65 : 1 (B) The MT *qōrā'* is a *pu.* perf., and is thus rendered as a pass. in the AV 'unto a nation that was not called by my name'. The context, however, makes it preferable to have an active verb here. External support for the active voice is found in the LXX and other old versions. Therefore, one should read here either the perf. form *qārā'* or the act. part. *qōrē'* (cf. the DNV and RSV). The RSV translates 'a nation that did not call on my name'.

65 : 7 (C) The RSV changes the 2nd pers. plur. forms 'your iniquities . . . your fathers' into 3rd pers. plur. forms. This is not necessary. It is better to keep to the Hebr idiom as the DNV has done.

65 : 23 (C) The word *behālā(h)* is found elsewhere in the OT meaning 'sudden terror' (cf. Lev 26 : 16). According to Ges-Buhl, it means 'sudden destruction' here in Is. The DNV has rendered it by 'early death', the RSV by 'calamity', the BSG by 'destruction', and the AV by 'trouble'. The LXX has 'curse'.

66 : 18 (C) Partly on the basis of the LXX, the RSV has translated 'for I know their works . . . and I am coming'. It seems clear that the verb 'to know' needs to be inserted at the beginning of the verse. With regard to the word 'coming', the MT has the form *bā'ā(h)*, a fem. form with neuter meaning 'it is coming' or 'it comes'. It is not said what is coming. The DNV has 'the time is coming', while the AV translates 'it shall come that I shall gather'. The text of DSI[a] has a 3rd masc. plur. form *bā'ū* which would suggest the translation 'they will come to gather all the peoples and languages.' The translation of the verse cannot be determined with any degree of certainty.

66 : 19 (C) The MT has 'Pul' but its location is unknown. Another reading is 'Put'. This district may have been the site of present-day Libya.

JEREMIAH

18 (B) In place of the MT plur. construct form *ḥōmōt* 'walls' (cf. the RSV), many mss have the sing. construct form *ḥōmat* 'wall' (DNV). Cf. the parallel reference in 15 : 20 and the notes on 51 : 58. The plur. can be understood as a plur. of massiveness.

1 (B) The first word in the Hebr 'saying' (cf. Aq and Th) appears to be the remnant of an introductory formula that read 'the word of the Lord came to me saying'. The DNV has supplied the "missing" words, though it has placed them in square brackets. On the basis of the LXX and Pesh, the RSV omits the word 'saying' and thus has no introductory formula at all.

23 (B) The prep. *min* 'from' that occurs before the word *gᵉbāʿōt* 'hills', is difficult. It is not found in the LXX and, accordingly, it has been omitted from the DNV and the RSV.

10 (B) The first word of the MT is *wāʾōmar* 'then I said'. The RSV translates it thus, thereby understanding a new sentence in the verse. It is doubtful, however, if the verse is actually a statement of Jeremiah. The context of v. 9 points to the priests, prophets, and princes as the subject of both v. 9 and v. 10. Hence, the DNV has read the first word of v. 10 as *wᵉʾāmᵉrū* 'and they said'. This change has the external witness of cod. Alex. and Aq in its favor (cf. Rudolph, *Jeremia* HAT, Erste Reihe 12, 1958, p. 30).

29 (B) The phrase *kol hāʿîr* 'the whole city' occurs twice in this verse. In place of its first occurrence, the DNV, on the basis of the LXX, has read 'all the land', which is preferable. Rather strangely, the RSV has rendered the phrase in two ways 'every city' and 'all the cities'.

7 (B) The MT *yitgōdādū* can be translated in two different ways. It can be rendered 'they gash themselves', which rendering does not fit the context here, or 'they gather themselves together in crowds' (cf. the RSV 'trooped to the houses of harlots'). On the basis of a few mss and the LXX, the DNV has accepted the reading *yitgōrārū* 'they sojourn in' (DNV 'they are at home in the brothel'). The

difference in readings is the difference between the *daleth* and the *resh.*

5 : 26 (C) The RSV renders 'they lurk like fowlers lying in wait', but this translation is not certain. Since the ancient versions do not offer a sufficient basis for the reconstruction of the text, it is advisable to keep as close to the MT as possible. The meaning of the word *šak* is not certain. Usually it is connected with the verb *šākak* meaning possibly 'to bend' in this reference. It also means 'to subside' (Gen 8 : 1). While the translation remains uncertain, one should not accept a mere conjectural reading of a commentary.

6 : 6 (B) The MT phrase *hīʾ hāʿîr hopqad* has been understood in at least three different ways:

1. The RSV has attempted to reproduce the MT by rendering 'this is the city which must be punished'. This translation understands the form *hopqad* to be derived from *pāqad* 'to visit, call to account, appoint'. Rudolph considers this a relative sentence without a relative particle, i.e. 'it has been investigated, and thereby settled'. Thus, he obtains the translation, *dies ist die Stadt von der feststeht* usw.', which, like the RSV rendering, requires no textual change (*op. cit.* p. 38).
2. Volz (*Der Prophet Jeremia*, 1928, p. 70) reads *happeqer* (with final *resh*) instead of the MT *hopqad* (with final *daleth*). This means that the verse contains the rare and almost unknown word *peqer* meaning 'licentiousness'. Köhler supports Volz and includes this word in his lexicon (KBL) citing Jer 6 : 6 as the one usage of this word in the OT. The meaning here then is 'this is the city of licentiousness'. In later Hebr, a verb *pāqar* does occur meaning 'to lead an unbridled life'.
3. A third possibility is suggested by the LXX rendering 'O lying city'. This seems to reflect a reading *haššeqer* 'falsehood'. This is the source of the DNV translation 'city of lies'.

6 : 9 (B) The parallelism of the second strophe favors an impv. form in the first strophe in place of the MT impf. 'they shall glean'. Hence, the RSV renders 'glean thoroughly' (impv. and inf. absolute). Following the LXX, the DNV reads the impv. form twice 'glean, glean'.

5 (B) Since the verse is parallel to 8 : 12, two observations should be made: first, though the vocalization is slightly different, the phrase 'they did not know how to blush' should be translated the same way in both verses; second, the expression in 6 : 15 'at the time that I punish them' (LXX 'at the time of their punishment') should be vocalized to agree with 8 : 12 'at the time of their punishment'. This allows for a more accurate rendering of the parallel texts than the RSV reflects in its translation.

8 (A) The DNV has translated this verse literally, but it does not give any real meaning. The RSV rendering 'what will happen to them', is not impossible, but it may not be correct. Some suggest the translation 'what shall I do to them', which presupposes that the verb *'āśā(h)* 'to do' has been omitted (cf. 1 Kings 11 : 25). The LXX renders the second part of this verse as 'the ones who shepherd their flocks'. It is impossible to establish with any real certainty what the text originally read.

7 (B) The word *mibṣār* is difficult. It has been vocalized *m*^{e}*baṣṣēr* 'one who searches' or 'tests' (RSV 'tester', DNV 'inspector'). Cf. the commentaries.

(B) Following the word 'places', the Hebr has the word, translated 'those who remain' which has occurred earlier in the verse. It is better to leave it out of the translation in its second occurrence as the LXX does.

(A) The DNV has 'running, they all turn away'. Since the text is obscure here, this translation attempts only to render what the probable sense is. One problem is the lack of agreement of suffixes (3rd pers. masc. sing. and 3rd pers. masc. plur.). The word *m*^{e}*ruṣā(h)* means 'walking' or 'manner of walking'. Thus literally, the clause is to be translated 'everyone turns back in his (their) walk', or 'everyone turns to his own course' (RSV). Since, however, *m*^{e}*ruṣā(h)* is derived from *rūṣ* 'to run', the BSG has rendered 'each runs his own wayward course'. Rudolph (*Jeremia*, p. 52) senses a connection between the *šāb* of v. 6 and *yāšūb* of v. 4. In v. 4 he translates by the word *fehlgehen*, and in v. 6 *jeder rennt seinen Irrweg weiter*. Thus, he has in mind a 'wrong way' here in v. 6. This thought may be borne out by v. 7 which states that the nation has disregarded God's ordinance, each one going in his own self-willed way, the wrong way before God. It would seem, then, that in translating, one needs to follow somewhat the reasoning of Rudolph.

8 : 7 (C) The translation of the word *'āgūr* is not certain. At one time it was believed that it was an adj. belonging to the *Kethib* reading of the previous noun *sūs* 'horse', thus '*flying* horse' = 'swallow'. Nowadays the two words are believed to refer to two different birds. Instead of *sūs*, the Masoretic vocalization *sīs* is accepted, meaning the 'swift', the bird which calls *si-si-si*. The following word, then, according to KBL and ZAW, 1936, pp. 288 f., must be the '*bulbul*' or '*Kurzfuss-drossel*'. On the basis of an old translation, the RSV has 'crane'. It is doubtful, however, whether the bird's name was well-known in later times. The BSG has 'swift' and 'swallow' for the two words in question.

8 : 12 (B) See 6 : 15.

8 : 13 (A) At the end of the verse, the MT reads 'and I give to them, they pass them by'. The verb *'ābar* can also mean 'to pass over something', i.e. 'and I give to them, they pass over them', but this rendering is not clear. The RSV (cf. also the DNV) has assumed a rather neutral object of the verb 'to give', i.e. 'what I gave them'. But this is not expressed in the Hebr. The verb *'ābar* is rendered 'to pass away (from)' in the RSV. Another possibility, however, is to view the form *ya'abrūm* as the object of the verb 'to give', and to regard the form at the same time as an independent relative sentence, i.e. 'those who come over them'. The sense of the text would then be that not only will there be no harvest, but also those who will execute judgment will come. Thus, one can adhere closely to the MT and translate 'I shall give them those who shall go over them' (i.e. as a judgment).

8 : 18 (B) The first word of the MT is uncertain. On the basis of a number of mss, it is generally divided into two words translated as in the RSV 'beyond healing' (cf. also the DNV).

(B) The first word of the MT *šibt^{e}kā* 'your dwelling' does not fit the
, 5) context. The LXX suggests that the consonants of the word should be divided to form two words *šūb* and *tōk*. The word *šūb* 'to repent, turn' is then taken as the final word of v. 4 (RSV, v. 5), and *tōk* 'oppression' becomes the first word of v. 6. Hence, the RSV renders 'they . . . are too weary to repent. Heaping oppression . . .' Unwillingness to repent is a well-known concept in Jer (cf. 8 : 6). While accepting the division of the MT *šibt^{e}kā* into two words, the DNV has understood the first of the two to be from *yāšab* 'to dwell', and thus it has translated the first part of v. 6 'here dwells oppression'.

5 (B) Literally, the MT reads 'I will feed them, this people' (cf. the AV).
, 14) The RSV has omitted the suff. 'them' in its translation, while the DNV following the LXX, has translated 'I will feed them', thus omitting the words 'this people'.

7 (B) Instead of the MT 'their kingdom', the DNV has followed Th and rendered 'their kings'. This is a fitting sequel to the preceding clause 'wise ones of the nations'. The RSV and AV translate 'their kingdoms' instead of the MT sing.

18 (A) The last two words read 'that they may find'. An object is apparently missing. There is no reason to emend the text, though this means that translations will inevitably vary, since one aims in translation to set forth a comprehensible sense. Thus, the RSV has rendered 'that they may feel it', while the BSG in agreement with Aq has 'that they may pay for their guilt'. Others assume that God is the object, and render 'so that they shall find me'. But in this case one would expect a verb 'to seek'. Since the text is uncertain, perhaps one can do no better than translate literally.

2 (B) The Hebr text in BH reads literally 'hear the words of this covenant and you shall tell them to the men of Judah'. If one accepts a different pointing, i.e. *dibbartem* instead of *dibbertām*, then the translation would be 'hear the words of this covenant and speak to the men of Judah'. In this latter case, these pl. verbal forms could naturally refer to the men of Judah (cf. v. 6). But to fit this text thus construed into the context

here is difficult. It is preferable to read the commands in the sing. form and refer them to Jeremiah. Thus Jeremiah is to hear the words and speak them to the men of Judah. The plur. form may have crept into the text by influence from v. 6. Also, the traditional text may be somewhat disordered (cf. the commentaries).

11 : 4 (B) The second *'ōtām* 'them' is omitted in the DNV. It can only refer to the words of the covenant mentioned at the end of v. 6. It is in place in v. 6 but not here in v. 4. In place of the second *'ōtām*, the RVS has followed the LXX translating 'all that'.

11 : 15 (A) To translate this verse literally and with meaning is well nigh impossible, Small wonder that commentators resort to various emendations! The DNV has rendered 15a 'what business has my loved one in my house? Carrying out her attempts?' This can likewise be translated 'what does it mean, that my beloved carries out her attempts in my house', or 'what right has my beloved in my house when she has done vile deeds' (RSV). These translations are all uncertain. On the basis of the LXX, one can render 'promises' or 'vows' in place of 'many things'. This means a better rendering, but it involves a textual change. In the next clause, it is practically necessary to vocalize the verb form from *'ābar* as a causative 'to make pass by' in order to obtain any sense from it. With regard to the final word, it is very doubtful whether it can be viewed as an interrogative sentence as the RVS has done. Thus, instead of 'can you then exult' (RVS), it is much better to translate 'then you will exult'. In conclusion, certainty in translation of the traditional text cannot be attained. One conclusion, however, seems to be warranted, namely, that according to this small pericope (verses 15 f.), sacrifices offer no immunity from adversity.

11 : 16 (B) The MT reads 'he (i.e. Yahweh) has set fire to it' (cf. the RSV and Rudolph, *Jeremia* p. 75). One objection to this translation is that the suff. of the prep. *'al* is fem., whereas it refers back to a masc. noun 'olive tree'. Instead of *'āle(y)hā* 'upon it', the DNV has vocalized *'ālēhū* 'its foliage' and translated 'a fire has kindled its foliage'. While this gives a satisfactory meaning, perhaps it is best to combine this

vocalization with the RSV translation and render 'he (Yahweh) has set fire to its foliage'.

: 9 (B) According to the MT, the word *'ayit* 'bird of prey' occurs twice here. It is translated once in the sing. and once in the plur. by the RSV which retains the interrogative sense of the MT. The DNV omits the word *ha'ayit* at the beginning of the verse and understands the *ha* before the second *'ayit* as the article, not the interrogative. The second word of the verse *ṣābūă'* appears to denote a multi-colored bird, *not* a 'hyena' as the LXX translates. According to v. 9a, the word does not necessarily mean 'a bird of prey' (cf. Volz, *op. cit.*, p. 144).

: 18 (B) The MT 'your head-places' has no real sense in this connection. On the basis of the LXX, read 'from your head' (cf. the DNV and p. RSV).

: 4 (B) The MT *ḥattā(h)* 'dismayed' is a *qal* perf. 3rd fem. sing. form modifying the word 'ground'. Hence, the RSV translates 'because of the ground which is dismayed'. Symm (cf. the DNV) read the form as *ḥattū*, a perf. 3rd masc. plur. form with the 'farmers' understood as the subject. In this case the translation would be 'because of the field, they (the farmers) are downcast'.

: 11 (C) The MT has the verb *'āmar* at the beginning, i.e. 'the Lord said'. The subject of the word that follows, then, is Yahweh while the two 2nd pers. masc. sing. suffixes refer to Jeremiah. The verse declares that God has been close to Jeremiah for good. The difficult form *šērītikā* (*Qere* reading) should be understood as derived from *šārā(h)* 'to set free', or 'to free'. God would even cause enemies to turn in entreaty to Jeremiah in their difficulty. In this way, the DNV has rendered 'the Lord said: if I do not free you for good ! If I do not make the enemy implore you in times of catastrophe and oppression !' On the other hand, a completely different interpretation grows out of the LXX and L translations. They have read the first word *'āmar* as *'āmēn* 'so let it be'. The word 'it', then, refers to the curse on the opponents of Jeremiah (cf. Jer 11 : 3-5 in which the last two Hebr words are to be rendered 'so be it, O Lord'). This interpretation of the verse means that Jeremiah is the subject of the verbs, and the 2nd masc. sing. suffixes refer to Yahweh. The RSV has understood the text in this way, translating 'so let it be, O Lord, if I have not entreated thee', but this rendering is uncertain. Another translation 'if I have not served thee' is based on a different reading. The RSV has translated the following clause 'if I have not pleaded with thee on behalf of the enemy'. Though this translation is not impossible from a grammatical viewpoint, yet it is unusual, since 'on behalf of' is more naturally expressed by the prep. *le* instead of the word *'et*. One conclusion is certain: a slight change in the first word of the verse (*'āmar* to *'āmēn*) produces an entirely different interpretation of the text.

16 : 7 (B) The Hebr *lāhem* 'for them' is followed by an inf. with a sing. suff. 'to comfort him' (AV 'to comfort them'). In place of *lāhem* two Hebr mss and the LXX have read *leḥem* 'bread', which reading provides a fitting parallel to the second strophe. Thus the RSV (cf. also the DNV) renders 'no one shall break bread for the mourner . . . nor shall any one give him the cup'. The same parallelism is carried over into v. 8.

17 : 1 (B) The context favors the reading 'their altars'.

17 : 2-3 (A) The text is difficult. The DNV has followed another reading in the first part of this passage, translating 'as a monument against them', and then omitting the following Hebr word 'their altars'. The RSV, however, has adhered to the MT 'while their children remember' and retained the word 'their altars'. At the beginning of v. 3, it is questionable whether one should read as Th does 'the mountains in the field' since the vocalization does not support this translation. It is also doubtful whether the RSV is right in inserting a prep. 'on', i.e. 'on the mountains in the open country', since there is none in the Hebr. Furthermore, the Hebr *bāmōte(y)kā* 'your high places' is a doubtful phrase in this context. In place of this, the DNV has rendered the words *lō' bimḥīr* 'without price' on the basis of the occurrence of this phrase in Jez. 15 : 13. This implies, then, that the negation *lō'* was originally in the text of 17 : 3 but later disappeared. Others, contrariwise, drop the negation from 15 : 13

because it is not found in 17 : 3. The RSV, however, retains the MT reading in 15 : 13 ('without price') as well as the MT omission of the negation in 17 : 3, though accepting the emended text *bimḥîr* 'as the price of' in place of the MT *bāmōte(y)kā* of 17 : 3. This produces a contrast in translation between 15 : 13 and 17 : 3. But when these texts are compared with each other, it is evident that it is better to translate them in the same way. On the whole, every translation of 17 : 2-3 remains uncertain.

: 4 (B) The MT reads 'and you shall loosen even (or 'and') by you from your heritage', which could probably mean 'through your own folly, you will loosen yourself from your heritage'. But for *ûbkā* 'and by you', it is preferable to read *yādᵉkā* 'your hand', i.e. 'you shall loosen your hand from your heritage' (RSV and DNV). For the construction of *yād* with the verb *šāmaṭ* 'to loosen', cf. Deut 15 : 3.

: 13 (B) For the consonantal text *yᵉsūray*, a substantive with suff. meaning 'my departers', the *Qere* reading of the Masoretes is *wᵉsūray*, a part. in the construct state with suff. meaning 'those who turn away from me'. The DNV has translated a form *wᵉsūrīm*, the absolute part. 'and those who turn away', while the RSV (cf. also Rudolph, *Jeremia*, p. 106) has accepted the form *wᵉsūre(y)kā* 'those who turn away from thee', thereby paralleling the preceding part. in the verse 'those who forsake thee'.

: 14 (C) This verse contains some real translation problems. The thought of snow disappearing from the rock of the field does not give any adequate sense here. Some have connected *śāday* 'field' with the Accad *šadu* 'mountain', but this is not at all certain. Ancient versions are divided in their interpretation. For this reason, it is perhaps preferable to read *śiryōn* (= Hermon, cf. Deut 3 : 9). For the greater part of the year, Mt Hermon is snow-covered. The reading *siryōn* would fit the following phrase 'snow of Lebanon'. Hence, the RSV renders 'does the snow of Lebanon leave the crags of Sirion', while the DNV has 'does the Lebanon snow ever recede from the rocks on the hill-slopes' ('mountains' or 'mountain peaks' would be even better). Both translations, however, are uncertain. In the second part of the verse, the verb *yinnātᵉšū* is puzzling. A form of *nātaš* 'to root up' does not make any sense here at all. Generally then, the form is understood as derived from *nāšat* 'to dry up'. The words *mayim zārīm* mean literally 'foreign waters'. It is doubtful whether this means here 'waters (rivers) in a foreign land', as commentaries have suggested. According to KBL, in 2 Kings 19 : 24 *mayim zārīm* means 'water to which one has no claim'. But what can be done with Jer 18 : 14? Literally, this part of the verse reads 'do the waters ever dry up, the foreign cold flowing (waters)'? The word 'foreign' might mean 'surprising, unexpected', but this does not remove the uncertainty. The word *nōzᵉlīm* in the OT has not only a participial sense, but also an independent meaning, i.e. 'streams', a synonym or parallel to *mayim* (Ex 15 : 8, Ps 78 : 44, Song 4 : 15). It is possible then, that the two preceding words *zārīm* and *qārīm* are both descriptive of *nōzᵉlīm*. The translation would then be 'do the waters dry up, the foreign cold streams'. The RSV translation 'do the mountain waters run dry, the cold flowing streams', is built on a conjectured reading *hārīm* 'mountains' in place of the MT *zārīm*. Commentaries offer still further conjectures.

18 : 15 (B) The MT reads 'but my people has forgotten me; they burn incense to false gods; they (the false gods?) have made them stumble in their ways'. Since it is unlikely that the false gods are active, it is better to change the *hiph.* impf. with suff. *wayyakšilūm* 'and they made them stumble', to the *niph.* impf. without suff. *wayyikkāšᵉlū* 'and they stumbled'. The change is supported by the LXX, Pesh, and the Vg, and has been accepted by the DNV and RSV.

18 : 17 (B) Because of the context, the verb 'to see' should be vocalized as a caus. 'I will show them' (cf. the AV, DNV, and RSV).

20 : 16 (B) Read the form *yišmaʿ* 'let him hear' in place of the MT perf. form (cf. the AV and RSV).

21 : 11 (B) The Hebr reads 'and as far as the house of the king of Judah is concerned'. Since with this verse a section begins dealing with the royal house of Judah (cf. 23 : 9 which begins a section about the prophets), it is preferable to omit the conjunction 'and' as the DNV does. The RSV has retained the conjunction 'and', i.e. 'and to the

house of the king of Judah say', but it should be pointed out that the word 'say' is not present in the Hebr.

8 (B) Because of the context here and the parallel in 16 : 15, the text should read 'where he had driven them' instead of 'where I have driven them'.

17 (B) The Hebr reads 'and everyone who walks'. On the basis of ancient versional evidence, the prep. *lᵉ* 'to' should be added, i.e. 'and to everyone who walks'. The preceding clause 'and to those who despise' favors this addition.

26 (C) The beginning of this verse is obscure. It is possible that the words *'ad mātay* 'for how long', may be an independent part of a sentence connected with the preceding verse. That is, in v. 25 the false prophets have laid claim to visions, saying 'I have dreamed'. For how long will they continue to cry out in this fashion? This interpretation means that the following part of v. 26 would have to be rendered 'is there in the heart of the prophets' = 'do the prophets intend'. This would mean, however, that the phrase 'how long' would have to be connected with v. 26 as well. To avoid using 'how long' a second time, the following clause in v. 26 could possibly be rendered 'is there something in the heart of the prophets'. However the word 'something' is not in the Hebr. The RSV has assumed that reference is made to *šeqer* 'lies', translating 'how long shall there be lies in the heart of the prophets'. At best, the translation of the verse remains uncertain. Conjectures which make a smoother translation possible obviously represent some definite interpretation.

33 (B) On the basis of the LXX and the context, a new word division should be adopted, reading *'attem hammaśśā'* 'you are the burden' (DNV and RSV), in place of the innocuous *'et mah maśśā'* 'what burden'. It is entirely possible that the punch in Jeremiah's answer preserved intact in the LXX, was deliberately toned down to what the MT has given.

39 (B) The context, backed up by several mss and the ancient versions, clearly favors the reading 'I will surely lift you up'. This means that

an *ś* should be read, i.e. *wenāśītī* 'and I will lift up', in place of the MT *š*, i.e. *wenāšītī* 'and I will forget'. Actually, in old Hebrew, there was one sign for both phonemes.

25 : 9 (B) The last two words in the MT are *ūlḥorbōt ʿōlām* 'and perpetual ruins'. This clause does not suit the context. The LXX evidently read *ūlḥerpat ʿōlām* 'and a perpetual reproach' which phrase goes well with the two preceding words 'horror' and 'hissing' (cf. the DNV and RSV). The difference in the two Hebr words is the difference between two labials, the voiceless or surd *p* and the voiced or sonant *b*.

25 : 34 (C) The last three words of the MT read 'you shall fall like a choice vessel'. The DNV has retained this text. On the basis of the LXX, the RSV understands the reading *keʾē(y)lē(y)* 'like (choice) rams' in place of the MT *kiklī* 'like a (choice) vessel'.

25 : 38 (B) For the first occurrence of the MT *ḥărōn* 'burning', it is preferable to read *ḥereb* 'sword' which has the support of about twenty mss as well as ancient versions. Two parallel references (46 : 16; 50 : 16) also lend weight to the reading 'sword'. The following word *hayyōnā(h)* in the meaning 'dove' can hardly be correct. The RSV has read 'Yahweh', i.e. 'sword of the Lord'. However, the word *yōnā(h)* can be taken as the act. part. of *yānā(h)* 'to oppress', to be understood in an adjectival sense, i.e. 'the violent sword'. In the parallel references in 46 : 16 and 50 : 16, the RSV has translated the same phrase as 'the sword of the oppressor'. But *yōnā(h)* is a fem. part. and belongs to the fem. noun *ḥereb*, thus 'the oppressing sword'.

26 : 10 (B) At the end of the verse, it is clear that one should add 'of the house' after the word 'gateway' to make the clause complete 'gateway of the house'. Various mss and ancient versions support the addition.

27 : 1 (B) Instead of the MT name 'Jehoiakim', read 'Zedekiah' in agreement with three mss, the Pesh, and the Oxford ms of the Arabic translation in the London Polyglot Bible. Considering the context in verses 3 and 12, Zedekiah is surely the correct reading in v. 1.

3 (C) The Hebr reads 'send them to the king of Edom, and to the king of Moab . . .'. The plur. suff. can only refer to the thongs and yokes that are mentioned in v. 2. Clearly, however, these are not sent to all of the kings mentioned in v. 3. The significance of the suff., then, is that it points to the true meaning or message that the thongs and yokes contain. The RSV has 'send word' with a footnote referring to the reading 'send them' found in the Hebr text.

13 (C) The RSV renders 'you have broken wooden bars, but I will make in their place bars of iron'. This means that, following the LXX, the RSV accepts a change from the MT 'you will make' to 'I will make'. This change is not really necessary. For the text can mean that though Hananiah breaks a wooden yoke in pieces, by his action he simply forges an iron yoke to take its place. Thus, it is preferable to adhere to the MT and translate 'you have broken wooden bars, but you will make in their place bars of iron'. Cf. Rudolph (*Jeremia*, p. 164) who believes a change in person is unnecessary.

1 (C) The Hebr has 'the rest of the elders'. The word translated 'the rest of' has been retained in the DNV and by Rudolph (*Jeremia*, p. 166), but omitted by the RSV on the basis of the LXX. It is not possible for us today to find out why the rest of the elders are mentioned here, but this provides no justification for changing the MT. Though the Hebr may seem to be somewhat peculiar at this point, yet it may well give the correct reading. Does *yeter* here mean 'pre-eminent'? Uncertain.

4 (B) While the RSV retains the MT vocalization 'whom I have sent into exile', yet it must be admitted that the use of the 1st pers. sing. here is somewhat strange. Thus, instead of the *hiph.* perf. 1st. pers. sing. form, the DNV has accepted the reading of a *hoph.* perf. 3rd pers. sing. and has rendered the clause 'the exiles who are carried away into exile'.

8 (C) In 27 : 9, prophets, diviners, dreamers, and soothsayers are all lumped together in a prophetic warning to steer clear of them. In the Hebr of that verse, the word is actually 'your dreams', but interpreted to mean 'your dreamers' (cf. the RSV). Likewise here in 29 : 8, it is also stated literally that the people should not listen to

'your dreams which you cause to dream'. This is correctly interpreted in the DNV to mean 'your dreamers whom you allow to dream'. Since the MT, without change, is thus capable of translation, it is not clear why the RSV has resorted to textual change to obtain the translation 'the dreams which they dream'. Neither is it clear why the same word the RSV has rendered 'your dreamers' in 27 : 9, is here in 29 : 8 translated 'dreams'.

29 : 26 (B) In place of the strange plur. *peqidīm*, one should read *pāqīd* with the old translations. Furthermore the prep. *be* 'in' should be read before the word 'house'. The RSV renders 'to have charge in the house of the Lord'.

29 : 32 (C) The Hebr can be readily translated 'and he shall not see the good'. The verb is sing., but it can be taken as a collective, and thus the translation can be 'he shall not have anyone living among this people, and they (i.e. anyone living) shall not see the good'. The text makes good sense. The RSV rendering 'to see the good' is, on the one hand, built on the LXX translation. Still, it is essentially correct and can be taken as an interpretation of the MT.

30 : 8 (B) The words 'your neck' and 'your bonds' should be read 'their neck' and 'their bonds' in agreement with the LXX and the old Latin translation. In this way a fitting connection can be made with v. 9. It is also possible that the 3rd pers. sing. suff. was the original reading, 'his neck' and 'his bonds', which would tie in with the mention of Jacob in v. 7.

30 : 23 (C) Except for one word, this verse reads exactly the same as 23 : 19. In 23 : 19 the text has the form *mitḥōlēl* 'whirling', but here in 30 : 23 the verse has *mitgōrēr*, probably a form of *gūr* 'to seize, attack', or of *gārar* 'to sweep away.' The text of 30 : 23 should then be translated 'a storm which swept everything with it'. It is definitely preferable to maintain in translation this difference between the two texts which in all other points (with the exception of a connective word 'and') are the same.

31 : 7 (B) The MT contains a prayer for deliverance 'save, O Lord thy people'.

It is clear, however, that a prayer for deliverance is hardly appropriate here in a context that is filled with gladness and joy. Hence, it is better to read with the LXX and Tg 'the Lord has saved his people' which can then be seen as the basis of the joy (cf. the DNV and RSV). Rudolph (*Jeremia*, p. 179) considers the fact that this passage is interpreted as a prayer in the traditional text *durch spätere Notzeiten veranlaszt*.

9 (C) The DNV has followed the MT and translated 'with supplication I will lead them'. The text is clear as it stands. However, on the basis of ancient versional evidence, the RSV has adopted the reading 'with consolations'.

35 (B) Following the part. *nōtēn* 'he who gives', one would expect a part. *ḥōqēq* 'he who decrees', which is actually the reading adopted by the DNV. The MT, however, has *ḥuqqōt* that can be translated '(who gives) the fixed order (of the moon and the stars)' (cf. the RSV).

11 (B) The MT reads 'and I took the deed of purchase, the sealed one, the commandment and the statutes'. This is a rather awkward construction. The DNV has added a prep. and translated 'I took the deed of purchase, the sealed one according to commandment and legal institutions'. This is essentially the rendering of the AV which places the word 'according' in italics. The sense is that Jeremiah is following closely the regulations that have to do with the purchase of property. The RSV has a different interpretation. It renders 'I took the sealed deed of purchase, containing the terms and conditions'. In this case, the Hebr *miṣwā(h)* 'commandment' would refer to the conditions agreed upon. Since, however, this use of the word *miṣwā(h)* is very unusual, it is preferable to follow the translation of the DNV.

12 (B) In place of the MT *dōdī* 'my uncle', read *ben dōdī* 'my cousin', which is the reading found in several mss and reflected in the LXX and Pesh.

43 (B) The MT *haśśāde(h)* 'the field' should be taken as a collective and translated by the plur. 'fields' (cf. the beginning of v. 44).

33 : 2 (C) The MT reads 'the Lord who made it' (cf. the DNV). It is difficult to say to what the fem. suff. 'it' refers. The LXX translators resolved the difficulty by rendering 'the Lord who made the earth', and this translation has been accepted by the RSV. Neither Rudolph nor Volz gives this as a reading, but both have proceeded to alter the text, each in his own way. Without a rather arbitrary alteration, the text is difficult to translate, which means that the sense remains obscure. The difficulty is not caused by translation: it is already present in the traditional text.

33 : 4-5 (C) Several difficulties are present here. First of all, we do not know whether the last words of v. 4 belong to what has gone before, or should be added to v. 5. Also, the RSV translation to the effect that the houses were torn down 'to make a defense against the siege mounds', is doubtful, since the MT reads only 'which were torn down for the siege walls and for the sword'.

Why should the RSV translate the prep. *'el* 'against' and immediately afterwards render the same prep. as 'before'? Where are the houses located that are mentioned in v. 4? Are they inside or outside the city walls? It is possible that buildings outside the city walls were demolished to make way for the erection of siege walls and thus, to wage war successfully (*ḥereb* = 'sword' or 'war'). In v. 5, the RSV has translated 'the Chaldeans are coming in to fight', whereas the MT should be rendered 'they are coming to fight against the Chaldeans'. The sign of the acc. is present in the Hebr text before the word 'Chaldeans'. Some mss have the prep. *'el* which also indicates a struggle against the Chaldeans. If the traditional text is translated and a fight against the Chaldeans is in view, what is it that is filled with dead bodies? Is reference made to the houses which have become ruins? Amid these various uncertainties, it is best to translate the MT as literally as possible. A really satisfactory rendering is probably not attainable.

33 : 6 (C) One can only guess at the meaning of *'ăteret*. Usually the word is taken to mean 'treasure' or 'abundance'. It might mean 'state of affairs', or it might have the meaning 'prayer', derived from the verb *'ātar* 'to pray'. In this last case, the train of thought would be 'I shall reveal (i.e. open for them) the prayer for lasting peace', meaning

'I shall give them lasting peace in answer to their prayer'. This explanation lacks proof. The RSV has 'prosperity and security' instead of 'lasting peace'.

12 (B) The DNV, supported by the LXX and Pesh, has omitted the words 'from the Lord' as being redundant. The RSV has retained them. Rudolph (*Jeremia*, p. 204) says '*Streichungen nicht ratsam*'.

14 (C) The second word in the MT is 'seven', rendered as 'six' in the RSV on the basis of the LXX. A comparison of this text with Deut 14 : 28 proves helpful. There in Deut, one finds the phrase 'at the end of three years' (RSV 'at the end of every three years'), which clearly signifies the end of a period that lasts for three years. The tithes, then, according to Deut 14 : 28, must be brought regularly in the third year and completed during that year (cf. Deut 26 : 12). Hence, the MT of Jer 34 : 14 needs no adjustment. It means 'at the end of every seven years', or 'in the seventh year of a seven-year period', or simply 'every seven years' (cf. Rudolph, *Jeremia*, p. 204).

16 (B) The MT has 'they said to Baruch' (cf. the RSV). The LXX (followed by the DNV) does not have the words 'to Baruch', thus indicating that the princes who heard Baruch read the scroll agree mutually among themselves to report the words of the scroll to the king. Then, in v. 17, they speak to Baruch.

17 (B) The final word of the MT *mippîw* 'out of his mouth' is somewhat awkward. The same word is found near the beginning of v. 18, but there it is appropriate. By a rather free translation, the RSV has taken the word in v. 17 as giving an independent interrogative sentence 'was it at his dictation'. On the basis of the LXX, the DNV has avoided the difficulty by simply omitting the word from v. 17.

12 (C) The form *laḥăliq* has been translated 'with the purpose of accepting an inheritance' (DNV), 'to take possession of' (BSG), 'to receive his portion' (RSV), and, *eine Erbteilung zu machen* (Rudolph, *Jeremia*, p. 218). Rudolph's translation is probably the best. The form is then viewed as a *hiph*. inf. of *ḥālaq* with the prep. *l*ᵉ and elided *h* (a regular

occurrence). The phrase should actually be rendered 'to make a division'. Cf. the Vg rendering *et divideret ibi possessionem*. It is probable, therefore, that Jeremiah's action here, is to be understood in the light of 32 : 6 ff.

38 : 10 (B) One ms has preserved the correct reading 'three' in place of the MT 'thirty'.

38 : 22 (B) The MT reads the verb *hoṭbᵉʿū*, a *hoph.* (pass.) form from *ṭābaʿ* 'to sink'. Thus, the RSV translates 'now that your feet are sunk in the mire'. It is possible, however, to point the form as a *hiph.* active, i.e. *hiṭbīʿū*, the whole phrase to be translated 'they made your feet sink into the mud'. This was the reading adopted by Aq, Symm, and the Vg, and, more recently by the DNV. This change has the advantage of carrying through the central theme of this dirge over the king's misery. His friends have deceived him and prevailed against him; they have (metaphorically speaking) dropped him into a miry pit and left him in the lurch.

38 : 23 (B) The MT vocalization *tiśrōp* (*qal* form) 'you shall burn', can hardly be correct in this context. The vocalization *tiśśārēp* 'it (this city) shall be burned' is obviously the correct form. It has the support of a few mss, the LXX, and Tg.

39 : 3 (B) The names should be conformed to v. 13.

39 : 9 (B) The phrase 'the rest of the people who remained' occurs twice in the Hebr, but the DNV has omitted it the second time. The RSV has translated the phrase both times, the first time by 'the rest of the people who were left', and the second time by 'the people who remained'.

40 : 5 (B) The first three words of the MT could be rendered 'and he did not yet return'. The construction is not only unusual but its meaning in this context is vague. A slight change in vocalization produces the rendering 'and when he did not yet reply', but this likewise is lacking in sense here. The RSV has 'if you remain, then return', while the DNV simply omits the words.

9 (B) The words 'by the hand of Gedaliah' in the MT can hardly be right. The LXX has 'a large cistern', which is a translation of *bōr gādōl*. This is undoubtedly the correct reading and it has been accepted by the DNV and the RSV.

1 (B) On the basis of the LXX and 43 : 2, read Azariah here instead of Jezaniah.

12 (B) The MT *wehēšīb* 'that he may make to return' does not fit the context. The prophet is attempting to resist popular pressure for a general exodus to Egypt to escape Nebuchadnezzar and a threatened exile to Babylon (cf. 43 : 3). In doing so, he emphasizes to the people the necessity of remaining in the land of Judah. Thus, instead of the MT *wehēšīb*, read *wehōšīb* 'and he will allow to dwell' (vocalization change only). The verse then becomes a promise of God with the meaning 'I will extend my mercy to you through Nebuchadnezzar so that he will let you remain right here in your own land'. Indication of this reading is given in the Vg, Aq, and the Pesh, which read, however, the first person 'I will let you remain'.

17 (B) For the first word, read *wehāyā(h)*.

9 (C) According to KBL, *meleṭ* means 'mortar', and *malbēn* 'terrace of bricks' or 'mastaba'. The RSV renders 'in the mortar in the pavement', while others have 'in the mortar under the pavement'. The translation 'under' is made on the basis of the context but it is uncertain. It is not necessary to omit *bammalbēn* as some have done.

10 (B) For the MT *weśamtī kis'ō* 'and I will place his throne', one should read with the LXX and Pesh *weśām 'et kis'ō* 'and he will place his throne'.

12(B, In place of the MT 1st pers. sing., it is obvious that the 3rd pers. sing. should be read, i.e. 'he shall kindle a fire'. The form of the 3rd pers. is in harmony with the context of v. 11 and has the support of the ancient versions. Later in the verse, the RSV renders 'he shall clean the land of Egypt as a shepherd cleans his cloak of vermin'. This means that the verb *'āṭā(h)* is taken in the sense of 'to clean from vermin', a meaning that is accepted by many (cf. von Gall, ZAW, 24, 1904, pp. 105 ff.). There also exists a verb *'āṭā(h)* 'to enwrap oneself with', but this meaning does not fit the context well here.

44 : 8 (B) The RSV follows the Hebr phrase 'that you may be cut off'. The words are found in much the same form in v. 7 and their occurrence in v. 8 is rather awkward. The DNV has omitted them from v. 8 though it is possible to render the phrase in an unnoticeable way. Rudolph (*Jeremia*, p. 240) translates *damit ihr euch den Untergang bereitet*.

44 : 9 (B) A problem exists in the *sing*. suff. of the MT reading 'his wives'. It can only refer to the preceding noun in construct state which is a *plur*., i.e. 'the kings of Judah'. Possibly the suff. could be construed to mean the wives of each successive king of the kings of Judah. The RSV has printed 'their wives' as its text but referred to the Hebr text in its footnote. Another possible solution is offered by the LXX which translates 'your princes' instead of 'his wives'. Evidently it read the form *śārē(y)kem* instead of the MT *nāša(y)w*. This change means that the LXX has, in this verse, the succession 'fathers', 'kings', and 'princes', which agrees exactly with the succession of persons noted in verses 17 and 21. For this reason, in 44 : 9 the DNV has translated 'their princes' instead of 'his wives'.

45 : 4 (B) The RSV follows the MT in retaining the last four words 'that is, the whole land'. On the basis of the LXX reading, the DNV omits these words.

46 : 9 (B) The word *tōpᵉśē(y)* in its second occurrence is unnecessary. Translate simply 'those who bend the bow'.

46 : 15 (B) The RSV has followed the LXX in rendering the opening phrase 'why has Apis fled? Why did not your bull stand'. The LXX has thus interpreted the verse as referring to the well-known Apis, the black bull-god of Memphis. It is preferable, however, to leave the MT unaltered and read with the DNV 'why has your strong one been beaten, did he not stand firm'. The 'strong one' could easily apply to Pharaoh (cf. Volz, *op. cit.*, p. 396, and Rudolph, *Jeremia*, p. 250, and

Weiser, *Der Prophet Jeremia*, 1955, p. 393, all of whom have adhered to the MT).

17 (B) The MT has the perf. *qārᵉʾū* and thus reads 'they have called there, Pharaoh, king of Egypt.' This is not a likely meaning in this context. The LXX has read the impv. form *qirʾū*, as well as the noun *šēm* 'name' in place of the MT *šām* 'there'. These vocalization changes give meaning to the verse. The translation becomes 'call the name of Pharaoh, king of Egypt'. This impv. clause is then followed by the object, the nickname by which Pharaoh is to be called.

20 (B) At the close of the verse, the MT has *bāʾ bāʾ* 'it has come, it has come'. On the basis of many mss, the LXX, and the Pesh, it is preferable to read the clause *bāʾ bāh*, the second word being the prep. *bᵉ* 'in, upon' with the 3rd fem. sing. suff. The translation then becomes 'it has come upon her' (cf. the DNV and RSV).

23 (B) The subject of the verb *yēḥāqēr* is a puzzle. Is the subject the forest, or those who cut the forest down? Following the MT 3rd masc. sing. form, the RSV has understood 'forest' as the subject and the word *kī* as concessive, translating 'though it (the forest) is impenetrable' (cf. likewise KBL, see under *ḥāqar*). The DNV, on the other hand, has adopted the reading of some *yēḥāqērū*, 3rd masc. plur. with the 'enemies' understood as the subject. It also understands the word *kī* as causative in sense, i.e. 'because they cannot be counted (searched out)'. Either meaning fits the context.

5 (B) Instead of the MT 'their valley', read with the LXX 'the Anakim' (cf. the DNV and RSV).

4 (C) The MT has 'her little ones'. On the basis of the LXX, it is better to read the word *ṣōʿărā(h)* 'as far as Zoar' (cf. the RSV). Only a slight change in the Hebr text is necessary.

5 (B) The word *ṣārē(y)* of the MT which follows the word *ḥōrōnayim*, should be omitted on the basis of the LXX and Is 15 : 5.

6 (C) The MT reads 'like Aroer in the desert', but it is a question as to

whether Aroer is meant here. The LXX has understood a reading *ʿārōd* 'wild ass', and this has been accepted by the RSV. Without change in the consonantal text, the DNV has read the form *ʿarʿār* 'a bare bush'. Cf. 17 : 6 where the word *ʿarʿār* (RSV 'shrub') is found in a similar context.

48 : 12 (B) In keeping with the context and on the basis of the external witness of the LXX and Aq, read 'his jars' instead of 'their jars'.

48 : 15 (B) The MT word *šuddad* is a *pu.* perf. with Moab as the subject, i.e. 'Moab is destroyed'. However, this makes the word *ʿālā(h)* 'he went up' difficult (cf. the additional 'out of' in the AV as an attempt to meet the difficulty). The DNV has omitted *ʿālā(h)* from its translation believing that it may have crept into the text because of the parallelism of v. 18. The RSV suggests a different solution. It has read *šōdēd*, *qal* act. part. 'the destroyer' in place of the MT *šuddad*. Thus, it translates 'the destroyer of Moab and his cities has come up', thereby making the text agree with the MT of v. 18 'the destroyer of Moab'. It should be mentioned, however, that the LXX in both verses 15 and 18 has read a pass. form.

48 : 18 (B) The MT clause 'sit down in the thirst' provides no real sense. Instead of the MT *ṣāmāʾ* 'thirst', the RSV has read *ṣāmēʾ* 'thirsty place' or 'parched ground'. On the other hand, the DNV has read *ṣēʾā(h)* 'dirt', thereby introducing a strong contrast into the text.

48 : 31 (B) The context shows that the last word should be read as an impf. 1st pers. instead of an impf. 3rd pers. This change was made in early times. The AV has retained the 3rd pers., but to do so it has had to add the words 'mine heart'.

48 : 32 (B) Read only 'Jazer' in place of 'sea of Jazer'.

48 : 34 (C) The MT begins the verse 'because of the cry of Heshbon, they utter their voice as far as Elealeh, as far as Jahaz'. The DNV has accepted this text. On the other hand, in the light of Is 15 : 4, the RSV has altered the text to secure a simpler reading, i.e. 'Heshbon and Elealeh cry out; as far as Jahaz they utter their voice'. There is

something to be said for making the text of Jer conform to Is. Nevertheless it is preferable to allow the differences between the two texts to remain.

35 (B) For the *hiph.* of the verb *ʿālā(h)* 'to go up', the DNV has read the simple *qal* form, i.e. 'he who ascends a high place'. The *hiph.* form can be retained, however, which would then refer to the offering up of sacrifice. This has the support of the context that follows which mentions incense-burning to pagan gods. Thus, the RSV renders 'him who offers sacrifice . . . and burns incense'.

39 (B) The word *hē(y)līlū* from *yālal* 'to wail' is not in the right place here. It is omitted by the LXX (cf. also the DNV). Possibly it crept into the text by influence of v. 20. The RSV rendering 'how they wail' is a free translation that attempts to fit the word into the context.

44 (C) The Hebr reads 'for I will bring upon her, upon Moab, the year of their punishment'. Though the clause might appear to be somewhat pleonastic, yet it is both understandable and translatable. The RSV, however, has read the demonstrative plur. pron. *ʾēlle(h)* 'these things', in place of the MT *ʾēle(y)hā* 'upon her'. The result is that a prep. must be added to the final phrase in order to translate 'in the year of their punishment'. Since the prep. is not in the Hebr, one should be wary of this suggested change.

45 (B) With a few mss, read *bē(y)t* 'house' instead of *bē(y)n* 'between'.

1, 3 (B) In place of the MT *malkām* 'their king', read with the old versions *Milcom*, the god worshipped by the Ammonites (cf. 1 Kings 11 : 5). When foreigners occupied the territory of Israel, it meant that there was an infringement on the position and authority of Yahweh. Thus, the name of the god Milcom here is the correct reading.

3 (B) The RSV has retained the place name 'Ai' even though no location by this name is known in Transjordan. On the other hand, the DNV has read an altered vocalization *ʿī* 'ruins', and translated 'wail, O Heshbon, for it is destroyed (in ruins)'.

49 : 4 (B, C) The MT reads literally 'why do you boast of the valleys? Your valley flows (is flooded)'. This does not give a meaning that is easily understood. Hence, it is better to follow the simpler reading of the RSV 'why do you boast of your valleys'. The following phrase 'O faithless daughter' (cf. the RSV) is found in Jer 31 : 22 where it is appropriate, but here, it is a little strange. The DNV has rendered the clause 'O presumptuous (self-assured) daughter' (cf. Rudolph, *Jeremia*, p. 264). Weiser (*op. cit.* p. 413) believes that the word 'faithless' is fitting in this context. For, in occupying Israelite territory (v. 1), the Ammonites made light of the holy right of Yahweh and brought upon themselves the apt description 'faithless daughter'.

49 : 9 (C) The RSV has taken both halves of the verse in an interrogative sense, translating 'if grape-gatherers came to you, would they not leave gleanings? If thieves came by night, would they not destroy only enough for themselves?' This is a possible translation, even though the interrogative particle is missing. The other possibility is to read the verse as a positive declaration. Thus, the DNV has 'if grape-gatherers had come to you, they would not have left any gleanings over; or thieves in the night, they would have done damage, as much as they pleased' (cf. Volz and Rudolph in their respective commentaries). In the parallel (Obad 5), the interrogative particle is present. In the light of this fact, it is preferable to retain the positive sense in Jer 49 : 9 which is well expressed in the BSG 'if grape-gatherers came to you, they would leave no gleanings behind; if robbers came by night, they would destroy to their heart's content'.

49 : 10-11 (A) The end of v. 10 and the beginning of v. 11 are very obscure. The main problem is whether the words about the orphans and widows originate from the neighbors (DNV), or from God (RSV). Rudolph (*Jeremia*, p. 266) regards v. 11 as a saying of the neighbors, but he clarifies the text by emending the phrase 'he is no more' to read 'nobody says'. Without this change, it is not easy to sense that v. 11 is a word of the neighbors.

49 : 19 (B) Read *'ărîṣēm* with the 3rd pers. masc. plur. suff. 'I will make them run away' instead of the MT 3rd pers. masc. sing. suff. This change

is quite certain in light of the LXX, the Pesh, Tg, and the *Qere* reading in 50 : 44.

21 (B) The word *qōlāh* can be omitted in translation. Cf. 50 : 46 where the word is absent from a sentence that is very similar. In 49 : 21, the RSV has attempted to read the MT 'the sound of their cry', but it is preferable to omit *qōlāh* and translate as the DNV has done 'their cry shall be heard at the Red Sea'.

23 (B) The MT *bayyām d*^{e}*ʾāgā(h)* 'in the sea there is trouble' is not certain in this context. It is better to read *kayyām dāʾăgū* which the DNV and RSV have adopted, but with this difference: the DNV reads *kayyām* with the preceding verb, thus translating 'they melt in fear like the sea'; the RSV reads *kayyām* with the following verb, translating 'they melt in fear, they are troubled like the sea'. This means a difference, too, at the close of the verse. The RSV interprets the last phrase as meaning that the sea cannot be quiet, while the DNV understands the phrase to refer to the people of Hamath and Arpad—they are not able to be quiet. It should be observed, however, that the verb *yūkāl* in the MT is sing., *not* plur.

25 (B) The DNV and RSV agree in making two slight alterations in this verse. First, the negation is omitted in order to render 'how the famous city is forsaken' (RSV). This change has the support of the Vg. Second, with the versions, the DNV and RSV omit the 1st pers. suff. on the final word. Thus, 'city of joy' is read instead of the MT 'my joyful city'. On the other hand, Weiser (*Der Prophet Jeremia*, p. 420) retains the suff., believing that the person speaking here can be viewed almost as a friend and admirer of Damascus.

2 (B) After the word 'proclaim', the Hebr reads 'set up a banner and proclaim' (cf. also the RSV). This latter clause is not in the LXX and has been omitted from the DNV. The words are comparable to what is found in 4 : 6 and Is 13 : 2.

11 (B) In place of the MT *k*^{e}*ʿeglā(h) dāšā(h)* 'as a calf treading (threshing)', read *dešeʾ* 'grass', i.e. 'as a calf at grass'. This change has the support of the LXX and the translation is found in the AV, DNV and RSV.

50 : 21 (B) The MT reads 'utterly destroy after them' which the RSV has followed. The words 'after them' have been omitted by the LXX and Pesh and also by the DNV.

50 : 29 (B) In place of *rabbīm* 'many', read *rōbīm* 'archers', which fits the context. The word *rōbīm* is derived from *rābā(h)* II. Cf. KBL under *rābā(h)* and *rab* III. Cf. also the note on Job 16 : 13.

50 : 38 (B) The MT word *ḥōreb* 'drought' fits well the following words, for, 'a drought upon her waters' (RSV) means that the waters are dried up. Yet, in the larger context, the Masoretic pointing *ḥōreb* in v. 38 is not so certain. In verses 35-37 the word *ḥereb* 'sword' appears five times in the wider sense of 'war'. It would seem, then, that *ḥereb* should be read in v. 38. The waters of v. 38 are not the Tigris and Euphrates, but the canals that are essential for irrigation. War means that these canals will be broken and neglected and thus lose their value (cf. Rudolph, *Jeremia*, p. 283). Thus, one should probably read *ḥereb* 'war' in place of the MT *ḥōreb* 'drought'.

50 : 45 (B) Read the last word as *nᵉwēhem*, cf. 49 : 20.

51 : 2 (B) Read *zōrīm* 'winnowers' not *zārīm* 'strangers' (cf. Aq, Symm, and the Vg).

51 : 3 (A) The beginning of the verse does not yield any sense. First of all, the consonants *y-d-r-k-* occur twice. The absence of vowel points in its second occurrence shows that the Masoretes felt it should be read but once. If it is read twice, the text literally can be rendered 'against him who bends, let the archer bend his bow, and against him who puts on his armor'. To make this comprehensible, the RSV, following the Masoretes, has omitted the second *y-d-r-k*, and in both occurrences of the Hebr *'el* 'unto, against', it has read the negative *'al*. Thus, it secures the rendering 'let not the archer bend his bow, and let him not stand up in his coat of mail'. But the context of the whole pericope, supported by the MT vocalization, indicates that the archers must take action against Babylon. Thus, the DNV has clearly given the text a positive rendering 'let the archer draw his bow'.

: 19 (B) On the basis of 27 mss, the Tg, and Vg, the name 'Israel' should be added (cf. the AV, DNV, and RSV). The verse, then, becomes identical with 10 : 16.

: 34 (B) Throughout the verse, translate the *Qere* readings of the Masoretes which have the 1st pers. sing. suffixes. As is done in the RSV, the last verb should be rendered 'he has rinsed me out'. The DNV has read the form as *hiddīḥānī* 'he has cast me off', a form derived from the verb *nādaḥ*.

: 39 (B) The context clearly favors the reading *yᵉʿullāpū, pu.* impf. of *ʿālap* 'to fall into a swoon', in place of the MT *yaʿălōzū* from *ʿālaz* 'to rejoice'. The ancient versions (LXX, Pesh, Tg, Vg) understood the verb *ʿālap* (cf. also the DNV and RSV). The RSV renders 'and make them drunk, till they swoon away'.

: 43 (B) The 3rd fem. *plur*. suff. in the twice-recurring *bāhēn* 'in them' is strange since it refers back to a fem. *sing*. noun 'land'. The suff. might be taken to refer to 'cities' in the land, thereby allowing the word 'land' to be omitted. The DNV and RSV have conjectured the reading *bāh* 'in it', thereby bringing the suff. into line with its antecedent 'land'.

: 49 (B) The prep. *lᵉ* 'for' should be prefixed to the words 'slain of Israel' on the analogy of 'for Babylon' in the second strophe.

: 58 (B) The MT reads 'the walls of Babylon the broad one' (cf. Weiser, *Der Prophet Jeremia*, p. 434, *die Mauer von Babel, dem weiten wird zerstört* . . .). With several mss, the LXX, and Vg, it is better to read the sing. form 'wall', and thus understand the adjective 'broad' as referring to the wall, and not to Babylon.

: 64 (B) The words 'and they shall weary themselves' should be omitted in translation as a repetition of v. 58 (cf. the DNV and RSV).

: 12 (B) Instead of the perf. *ʿāmad*, read the part. *ʿōmēd* (cf. the LXX and Vg).

: 15 (B) The DNV has rendered 'the rest of the crowd' (cf. the Tg, and AV), thus reading the word *hāmōn* which is found in the parallel reference in 2 Kings 25 : 11. The RSV has read the MT *'āmōn* translating 'the rest of the artisans', but this meaning for *'āmōn* is not absolutely certain. Rudolph reads *'āmmān* translating *Handwerker*. Cf. 39 : 9.

52 : 20 (B) The MT reads 'the twelve bronze bulls which were under'. The LXX has followed the text but then added the words 'the sea'. This is likewise the reading of the RSV. This whole clause, however, has been omitted in the DNV—and with reason. First of all, the phrase is not found in the parallel (2 Kings 25 : 16). Second, according to 2 Kings 16 : 17, king Ahaz took the brass sea from the twelve bulls and set it upon a pediment of stone. According to Mont-Gehm. (*op. cit.*, p. 461), "the brass was probably used for the tribute to Assyria" (cf. Rudolph, *Jeremia*, p. 296). The bronze bulls, therefore, had been removed some time before Jeremiah, and thus their mention here in 52 : 20 is anachronistic. It is preferable then to translate Jer 52 : 20 'as for the two pillars, the one sea, and the stands'. In keeping with 2 Kings 25 : 16, near the close of the verse read *neḥōšet* for the MT *neḥuštām*.

LAMENTATIONS

1 : 4 (C) Near the end of the verse, the MT has the form *nūgōt*, *niph.* part. fem. plur. of *yāgā(h)* 'to be sorrowful'. The ancient versions have the sense 'to take away', or 'to fall into captivity'. This means that in place of *nūgōt*, they read *nehūgōt*, *qal* pass. part. fem. plur. of *nāhag* 'to drive away'. Hence, the RSV has rendered 'her maidens have been dragged away'. Though it would be possible to understand the MT *nūgōt* as a contracted form of *nehūgōt*, yet the form *nūgōt* from *yāgā(h)* makes sense here, i.e. 'her maidens are afflicted' (cf. the DNV and H. J. Kraus, *Klagelieder*, *Biblischer Kommentar*, vol. XX, pp. 16 f.).

1 : 7 (C) The MT has a form of the word *mārūd* 'unrest, wandering', or, according to KBL 'outcast state, homelessness'. The word is then derived from a verb meaning 'to be restless'. The RSV, both here and in 3 : 19, has conjectured a noun form of *mārar* 'to be bitter'.

1 : 12 (C) The sense of the first two words *lō' 'ălē(y)kem* 'not to you' is not clear. The DNV has rendered 'does this not affect you, all you who

pass by' and the RSV similarly 'is it nothing to you, all you who pass by'. Both translations refer back to Jerusalem's sorrow and agony and interpret the verse as meaning, 'does not this distress impress you', or 'does it not mean something to you'. On the other hand, the verse may be interpreted, not in an *interrogative* sense, but with the idea of a *wish*, i.e. 'may the bitter sorrow not happen to you all of you who are passing by', or 'may it not come to you'. It is difficult to decide between the two possibilities.

13 (B) The MT reads 'from on high he sent fire into my bones and it prevailed against them'. Two slight changes give greater meaning to the verse. First, make the separation between the two phrases after the word 'fire'. Next, instead of the MT *wayyirdennā(h)* from *rādā(h)* 'to subdue', read *yōrīdennāh* from *yārad* 'to come down'. God, then, becomes the subject of the verb and the suff. refers to 'fire'. Thus the RSV renders 'from on high he sent fire; into my bones he made it descend'.

14 (A) The DNV renders 'heavy weighs the yoke of my transgressions'. The Hebr sing. verb form *niśqad*, is puzzling. An ancient explanation translates 'to be bound' (cf. the RSV 'my transgressions were bound into a yoke'), but this implies a plur. form of the verb *qāšar*. By retaining the same consonants as the Hebr text, one can read a form of the verb stem *š q d* 'to be watchful' (KBL 'keep oneself wakeful'). Thus, the BSG has 'watch has been kept over my transgressions', which means further that the BSG has read *ʿal* 'over' in place of the MT *ʿōl* 'yoke'. Another suggestion for the difficult *niśqad* is to read *hiqšā(h)* from *qāšā(h)* 'to be heavy'. This would make possible the translation 'he has made the yoke of my transgressions heavy'. Still others prefer to read *ʿālay* 'upon me' in place of *ʿōl*, as well as reading a form of *qāšā(h)* 'to be heavy'. Hence the translation 'my sins weigh heavy upon me'. The DNV retains the MT except that it reads a verb form from *qāšā(h)* in place of *niśqad*. Still another suggestion is to read *niqšā(h)* 'heavy is the yoke . . .'.

20 (C) The RSV has 'in the street the sword bereaves; in the house it is like death'. Apparently, the word 'it' refers back to the word 'sword'. A different idea is presented by the DNV 'outside the sword makes

childless, inside the pestilence'. The word *māwet* 'death' can have the sense of 'plague' or 'pestilence' (cf. Jer 15 : 2; 18 : 21). It would seem that the DNV has omitted the prep. *kᵉ* before *māwet*. The prep. is difficult here. Literally, the phrase reads 'in the house as pestilence'. Some have translated 'out of doors the sword makes childless as the pestilence (does) indoors'. This translation, however, means that the MT word order *babbayit kammāwet* has to be inverted (cf. the LXX). Others have explained the prep. *kᵉ* as the so-called '*kᵉ* of stress' (*kᵉ veritatis*), similar in sense to its meaning in Neh 7 : 2 where *kᵉʾîš ʾĕmet* means 'as faithful as a faithful man can be', or 'like a man whom one may truly call faithful'. Thus, here in Lam 1 : 20, understanding the *kᵉ* in this way, the meaning can be 'indoors pestilence (bereaves) as (pestilence can truly do)'. The translation, however, of this part of the verse, remains somewhat uncertain.

1 : 21 (C) What is meant by 'the day thou hast announced'? If it means the day of Judah's misfortune, the preceding verb should be rendered 'thou hast brought'. If, however, it means the day of judgment on the enemy, it is obvious that the verb should be translated as a future 'thou shalt bring'. The RSV follows the Pesh in translating the verb form as an impv. 'bring thou'.

2 : 11 (C) The RSV translation 'my heart is poured out in grief' is a free rendering, since the MT literally reads 'my liver is poured out to the earth'. The sentence expresses the deep anguish in the soul.

2 : 18 (C) The Hebr plur. suff. in the phrase 'their heart cries aloud', can be explained by viewing the people collectively. The following phrase, 'the wall of the daughter of Zion', is strange. As it stands, one can propose that in this way the all-inclusive nature of the complaint is shown, i.e. all whom the wall of Zion surrounds.

3 : 22 (C) At the close of the first clause, the MT reads 'we are not worn out,' or 'we have not perished'. The meaning would be that we are not worn out because the Lord loves us and remains faithful. Thus the DNV has 'it is because of the steadfast love of the Lord that we have not perished' (cf. also the AV). The RSV, however, has here followed the Pesh and Tg, and translated 'the steadfast love of the Lord never

ceases'. This means that in place of the MT *tāmnū*, the RSV has read *tammū*, its subject becoming *ḥasdē(y) yahweh*.

56 (C) The MT has a form of the word *rᵉwāḥā(h)* 'respite, relief', followed by a form of the noun *šawʿā(h)* 'call for help', the translation of the whole clause being 'do not close your ear to my call for help, that I may find relief'. The RSV has left one of the two words untranslated. The translation is somewhat uncertain.

6 (C) The RSV has rendered 'no hand being laid on it', but it rightly indicates in a footnote that the Hebr is uncertain. The problem is the verb form *ḥālū* which apparently comes from *ḥūl*. Ges-Buhl still give *ḥūl* as a separate stem meaning 'to smite', but KBL does not. Is the meaning of the whole expression here 'they did not turn helpful towards it'? The verb *ḥūl* regularly means 'to turn, turn to, whirl' (cf. KBL). Kraus (*op. cit.*, p. 67) believes that the verb here means 'to tremble' (cf. Ps 55 : 5, etc.). The translation would thus be 'hands were not trembling in it'. That is, so sudden is the judgment that the inhabitants have no time even to tremble. Another possible stem for *ḥālū* may be *ḥālā(h)* 'to be weak, ill', i.e. 'her hands were not weak'. The thought would be that Sodom felt smug and self-sufficient when sudden judgment struck the town. The translation remains uncertain.

7 (C) The exact meaning of the last word *gizrā(h)* is not known. It is clearly to be linked to the verb *gāzar* 'to cut'. Thus, some have suggested that the noun here means the 'form' or the 'cut' of their body; others have proposed 'the structure of the veins'; still others have thought of tattooing. Since there is this uncertainty, it is best to select a "neutral" translation. The RSV has 'form', i.e. 'the beauty of their form', and the DNV has 'appearance'. Some such meaning seems to be intended but a more precise indication of the place where the beauty resides does not seem possible.

17 (C) The RSV renders 'in our watching'. The Hebr word apparently means an observation post.

EZEKIEL

1 : 10 (C) The words 'in front' and 'at the back' have been added in the RSV. Commentaries are not in agreement here. Cooke (*The Book of Ezekiel*, ICC, 1937, p. 14) proposes the rendering 'the face of a man and the face of a lion were on the right of the four of them, and the face of an ox and the face of an eagle were on the left of the four of them', thus making v. 10b parallel to v. 10a (cf. also Fohrer, *Ezechiel*, HAT, 12, 1955, p. 11). Zimmerli (*Ezechiel*, BK, Lief. I, p. 1) translates literally as does the DNV which renders 'as for the likeness of their faces, each had the face of a man and the face of a lion on the right side; and the four had the face of an ox on the left side; and the four had the face of an eagle'.

1 : 11 (B) The DNV has omitted the first word believing that it has no place here, and that its omission makes for a smoother reading. Both the LXX and L omitted it in their translations. The RSV 'such were their faces' (cf. also the AV) is a free translation attempting to make it a summary of the description contained in v. 10.

1 : 14 (B) For the final word *bāzāq*, one should undoubtedly read *bārāq* 'lightning' (cf. the final word of v. 13). The Vg and Tg understood *bārāq*.

1 : 15 (C) The RSV renders 'one for each of the four of them', while the DNV has 'in front of all four'. Both translations are uncertain since the MT reads literally 'in agreement with their four faces'. The final word of the Hebr, *pānā(y)w* is often left untranslated. Accordingly, one should translate 'I saw a wheel upon the earth beside the living creatures, the four of them'. Cf. also the commentaries, among others, Cooke (*op. cit.*, p. 16), Fohrer (*op. cit.*, p. 11), and Zimmerli (*op. cit.*, p. 6).

1 : 18 (C) The RSV rendering 'and they had spokes' is very dubious. The MT reads literally 'and their rims—they had height and they had fear (= inspired fear)'. Since this does not give an adequate sense, a different text has been sought. The LXX apparently read a verbal form of *rā'ā(h)* 'to see' in place of the noun *yir'ā(h)* 'fear'. Thus,

Cooke renders 'and they had felloes, and I looked at them, and behold, their felloes were full of eyes'. One should probably assume that the word *gōbah* 'height' is present in the text by reason of dittography. The translation, therefore, remains very uncertain.

6 (B) For the MT *'im lō'* 'if not', it has been suggested that one should accept the reading of the versions, which omits the negative. Probably no textual change is needed. Cooke (*op. cit.*, pp. 39-40) holds to the translation 'verily had I sent thee'. He explains that *'im lō'* has here lost its literal meaning and is used emphatically; "the clause which follows must be taken as a virtual hypothesis, 'had I sent thee . . .' " Cf. also the RSV 'surely, if I sent you to such' (DNV—'if I send you'). In any case, no negation should be translated.

12 (B) The DNV has followed the MT 'blessed be the glory of the Lord' (cf. also the LXX), but it has placed the phrase between dashes. The RSV, however, has read a well-known conjecture *b*ᵉ*rūm* 'as it arose', for the MT *bārūk* 'blessed (be)'. The RSV translates 'and as the glory of the Lord arose'.

15 (C) The *Kethib* reading or consonantal text has the form *wa'ăšer*, and the clause containing it should be rendered 'I came to the exiles of Tel Abib, who lived by the river Chebar, and where they lived, there I stayed'. The *Qere* reading, however, has the form *wā'ēšēb*, i.e. 'and I lived where they lived; and I stayed (lived) there'. The *Kethib* reading is preferable.

4 (C) The Hebr has the verb form *śamtā* and the prepositional form *'ālā(y)w* and is to be translated 'and you shall lay the punishment . . . upon it'. The RSV has understood the forms *śamtī* and *'āle(y)kā* and hence translates 'and I will lay the punishment . . . upon you'. This change gives a much better sense. On the basis of v. 6, one can omit the form *'ālā(y)w* from translation in v. 4, and simply render the form *w*ᵉ*nāśā'tā* 'and you shall carry the injustice (or punishment) of the house of Israel' (instead of *śamtā*, cf. Zimmerli, *op. cit.* p. 95 f.).

7 (C, B) The MT reads at the close of the verse 'and have not acted according to the ordinances of the nations', i.e., not even according to the

ordinances on the standards of the nations, let alone the ordinances of God. Numerous mss do not have the negation, and thus the RSV omits it, translating 'but have acted according to the ordinances of the nations'. Hence, the text would mean that the ones who are addressed have not acted according to God's commandments, but have gone in the way of the nations (cf. 11 : 12). It is not easy to explain, however, why a negation, if not original, was later introduced into the text. It is simpler to believe that the negation is original and that it was omitted from various mss in order to soften the severity of this statement. Near the beginning of the verse, the word *hămonkem* is apparently an inf. construct form with suff. from an unknown verb *hāman*. It has been thought to be a denominative of *hāmōn* 'noisy crowd' which would allow for the RSV translation 'because you are more turbulent'. The reading *hamrōtkem* 'your rebelliousness' is generally accepted (cf. the DNV 'because you are more rebellious than'). Cf. Cooke, *op. cit.*, p. 66.

5 : 15 (B) The first word *w^{e}hāy^{e}tā(h)*, 3rd pers. sing. fem. 'and she shall be', should be pointed *w^{e}hāyītā*, 2nd pers. masc. sing. 'and you shall be'. The 2nd pers. is favored by the ancient versions.

6 : 6 (B) In place of the MT *w^{e}ye'š^{e}mū* 'and they shall be guilty', one should read with Symm, the Pesh, and Tg, the form *w^{e}yēšammū* 'and they shall be ruined' (cf. the DNV and RSV).

6 : 9 (B) The context shows that the *niph.* form *nišbartī* 'I have been broken' cannot be right. Various old versions including the Tg show that the form should be active, i.e. *šābartī* 'I have broken' (cf. the DNV and RSV).

7 : 7 (C) The meaning of the word *ṣ^{e}pīrā(h)* is unknown (cf. also v. 10). In Is 28 : 5 it means 'diadem', but this meaning does not fit here. In later Hebr, the word means 'plaited edge', or 'basket work'. Here, the word may be interpreted as 'doom', or 'the time of judgment', but this meaning is not at all certain. Ancient versions apparently could only guess at the meaning. The translation 'sunset', 'end' is suggested in VT, IV, 1954, p. 278. It is preferable to translate 'doom' as several have done. Some threatening sense seems to be present in the word.

0 (C) The DNV translation 'rod' follows the MT *maṭṭe(h)*. In v. 11 'rod of wickedness' is sufficiently clear and may help to explain v. 10. If this reading of v. 10 is correct, one can consider also the word *ṣᵉpīrā(h)* of 7 : 7 as an object otherwise unknown. Thus, the word *maṭṭe(h)* 'rod' can be retained in v. 10 without replacing it by *muṭṭe(h)* 'injustice' as the RSV does. It is best to translate v. 10 as literally as possible.

3 (C) At the close of the verse, the MT has 'and everyone, in his iniquity his life, they will not hold their own'. The meaning is vague. The Vg, which gives otherwise an understandable translation, has *et vir in iniquitate viae suae non confortabitur*. Thus, it disregards the suff. of the word *ʿāwōn* 'iniquity'. The sense may be that their 'life' consists of crime and hence the translation 'and none whose life is nothing but iniquity will hold his own'. The ancient versions offer no help. If one adheres to the MT, he can only produce an uncertain translation. In place of the final word, a reflexive verbal form *yitḥazzāqū*, some have suggested the causal form of the same verb as the true reading, i.e. *yaḥăzīq*. It is then possible to consider the word 'life' as the object of this verb and render as the RSV does 'and because of his iniquity, none can maintain his life'. This certainly provides an excellent sense, but it labors under the disadvantage of an unusual Hebr word order.

0 (B) Since the sing. verbal form with suff. *śāmāhū* 'he placed (used) it', does not fit the context, it is preferable with the old versions to read a plur. form *śāmūhū* 'they used it' (cf. the DNV and RSV). A plur. form agrees with the plur. verb 'they made' which is found later in the verse. In reading 'their beautiful ornament', the RSV has followed the Pesh and Symm which understand the suff. as plur., referring to the people. The MT sing. suff., however, can be retained and the translation read 'the decorative magnificence of it'. The 'it' would refer to the silver and gold mentioned in v. 19. The sing. suff. in the word *bō* connected with the verb *ʿaśa(h)* in 7 : 20, favors this view.

2, 23 The MT word *ṣāpūn* means 'hidden', thus 'the precious' or 'the valuable'. The RSV has rendered 'precious place' although the word 'place' is not found in the Hebr. At the beginning of v. 23, the MT has the clause 'make a chain'. The meaning is not clear. The RSV has read the word *battōq*, translating 'make a desolation' viewing these words as a continuation of v. 22. The translation is not certain.

8 : 2 (B) The MT has the word *'ēš*, i.e. ('appearance of) fire' (DNV). The RSV following the LXX has accepted the reading *'îš*, translating ('appearance of) a man'. Chap. 1 : 26 has been used as an argument for the LXX translation, but the immediate context in 8 : 2 seems to favor the MT.

9 : 7 (B) The RSV has followed the MT closely, translating ' "Go forth." So they went forth, and smote in the city'. However, since it is somewhat unusual to translate two perf. forms after an impv. in such a way, it is preferable to take all the verb forms as imperatives. Thus, the DNV renders 'go away, go away and smite down in the city'. The Pesh fully, and the LXX partially, support this translation. Some have chosen to omit the second verb and translate 'go forth and smite in the city'.

10 : 17 (B) The form *'ōtām* 'them', the sign of the acc. with the 3rd masc. plur. suff., should be pointed *'ittām* 'with them', the prep. *'et* with the 3rd masc. plur. suff. The LXX supports this change which is accepted by the DNV and RSV.

11 : 3 (C) Two different lines of interpretation are possible in this verse. The DNV and RSV translations explain the text as meaning that the people who give wicked counsel feel themselves safe. No one needs to be concerned about the possibility of the city's destruction so that houses will need to be built. That time is not near. The other possible sense is to take the text as an interrogative sentence (cf. the RSV footnote). The idea, then, is that those who remain in Jerusalem after the first deportation of 597 B.C., reject the prophetic warning of impending judgment. They feel that they are so safe that they can unmolested proceed to build their houses. Cf. the commentaries, especially Cooke (*op. cit.*, p. 122), Fohrer (*op. cit.*, p. 60), Zimmerli (*op. cit.*, pp. 243 f.).

11 : 19 Cf. Ezek 17 : 7.

21 (C) At the beginning of the verse, the RSV reads *'ēlle(h)* 'as for those', in place of the MT *'el lēb* 'to the heart'. The translation is uncertain, and at the same time, the change does not introduce any new element into the text.

3 (C) The last part of the Hebr text can be translated and understood in three different ways due to three possible usages of the particle *kī*. First, the translation can be 'perhaps they will understand (see) that they are a rebellious house'. Here the word *kī* is rendered 'that' and thereby introduces an objective sentence. Second, the text can be translated 'perhaps they will repent (see) because they are a rebellious house'. In this case, the particle *kī* is causal and indicates the need there is of repentance. The sense is, that such repentance may occur, but it is not at all certain that it will. Still a third possibility is 'perhaps they will understand although they are a rebellious house'. In the word 'although', the concessive force of *kī* appears. Framed in this way, the sentence points out clearly the possibility of repentance. Thus, the translation of this part of the text is controlled by the particular usage of *kī* that a translator is attracted to in this context. A definite choice must be made.

5 (B) The MT 'bring outside through it' (*hiph.* causative verb), should be changed to the simple *qal* form 'go out through it'. The old versions support this change (cf. also the DNV and RSV). The RSV (but not the DNV) has accepted a similar alteration in v. 7.

10 (A) The Hebr reads only 'the prince, this oracle in Jerusalem, and the whole house of Israel who are in their midst'. The RSV and DNV translations agree here in rendering 'this oracle concerns the prince in Jerusalem and all the house of Israel who are in it' (RSV). This translation is about the best that can be made though it involves considerable guess-work. By virtue of the ancient versions and 12 : 12, the word 'prince' should be retained as these translations suggest. Cf. Cooke, (*op. cit.*, pp. 131, 134), Zimmerli (*op. cit.* pp. 255, 265 f.).

12 (B) The MT reads 'they dig through the wall in order to bring out through it'. The sense is that people other than the prince shall dig

the hole. On the other hand, the RSV has translated 'he shall dig through the wall and go out'. This involves two changes. It has, in the first place, read the verb as a sing. with 'the prince' taken as the subject. And, second, instead of the MT causative inf. form 'to bring forth', it has read a simple impf. sing. form 'and he shall go forth'. It is possible, however, to retain the MT as it is.

13 : 2 (C) The MT reads 'prophesy against the prophets of Israel who are prophesying'. The plur. part. form in the text may well indicate the industrious nature of these foolish prophets—they are always prophesying something. However, the RSV and others have followed the suggestion of the LXX to the effect that the impv. form should be read in place of the part. Hence, the RSV has rendered 'prophesy against the prophets of Israel, prophesy'. One objection to this rendering is its repetition of the impv. form 'prophesy'.

13 : 11 (C) It is possible that the word *w^{e}ʾattēnā(h)*, fem. plur. pron., 'and you', should be taken with the following word. The translation would then be 'and you, great hailstones, will fall'. The RSV has omitted the pronoun. Other translations, including the LXX, have understood the vocalization *w^{e}ʾett^{e}nā(h)*, impf. 1st pers. sing. of the verb *nātan* 'to give'. The translation would then be 'a deluge of rain I will bring'. This rendering is improbable since, in this context, 'hailstones' and 'gale' are subjects. It is more likely, then, that 'rain' is also a subject, not an object.

13 : 18 (B) The word *yāday* is to be understood as a dual form like *yādayim*. This latter form is found in a few Hebr mss and the Tg.

13 : 20 (C, B) Since the word *n^{e}pāšōt* 'souls' is the true plur. of *nepeš*, the DNV has omitted the words *ʾet n^{e}pāšīm* at the close of the verse. Probably the text has been damaged. Some have proposed here the conjecture *ʾōtām ḥopšīm* (cf. the RSV 'go free like birds'). This conjecture is based on Deut 15 : 12, 18 and Jer 34 : 9, where one finds the phrase *šillaḥ ḥopšī* 'to let go free'. Even if one omits the words in question, however, the translation 'to set free' is implied in the text.

The MT clause 'with which you hunt the souls like birds' occurs not only at the close, but earlier in the verse as well. Since the idea of freedom like that of the birds seems to be present, it is possible to translate the final clause 'I will let go free the souls that you hunt like birds'.

4 (B) Near the close of the verse, the consonantal text reads *bāh* 'by it' whereas the Masoretes (*Qere* reading) have understood *bā'* 'coming' (cf. the DNV and AV 'that cometh'). On the basis of the Tg and the occurrence of the identical phrase at the end of v. 7, the RSV and others have adopted the reading *bī* 'by myself'. Thus, the RSV has the translation in both v. 4 and v. 7 'I the Lord will answer him myself' (cf. Cooke, *op. cit.*, p. 151 and Zimmerli, *op. cit.* p. 301).

4 (A) The difficult form *lᵉmišʿī* is usually translated 'in order to clean', or 'to your cleansing' (cf. the Tg). Both Aq and Th have 'for salvation', while the Vg renders *in salutem*. It is grammatically possible that the form is to be taken from a verb 'to behold', thus here 'for my beholding'. The context, of course, points to the cleansing of the child. One must exercise care in translating a word that is unknown elsewhere, so as not to give it too precise a meaning (cf. Cooke, *op. cit.*, pp. 162 f., Zimmerli, *op. cit.* p. 334).

7 (A) At the beginning of the verse, the MT reads 'a great multitude (myriad) I made you as'. This does not give any meaning. The DNV has rendered 'I made you grow up as' and other translations have followed the idea of 'growing up'. An attractive suggestion is to read the first word of v. 7 either as in impv. of a perf. with a *waw consecutive*, and then relate the text directly to the end of v. 6. Thus, the RSV arrives at the translation 'live and grow up like a plant of the field'. But, in this case, one has to omit the verb form *nᵉtattīk*. It may be possible, however, to translate 'live, grow up, I shall make you as a plant in the field'. The superlative expression in the following clause 'an ornament of ornaments' has been rendered in the DNV 'to full beauty', meaning 'to mature beauty'. The RSV, on the other hand, has 'at full maidenhood', a translation that is based on a slight textual change (cf. Cooke, *op. cit.*, pp. 163, 166, Zimmerli, *op. cit.* p. 355).

16 (A) Near the end of the verse, the DNV has translated 'never has anything of this sort happened before', while the RSV renders 'the

like has never been'. Though these translations contain some guesswork, they are probably the best that can be offered. Cf. the Vg which expressed the phrase plainly *sicut non est factum neque futurum est.*

16 : 19 (C) At the close of the verse, the RSV renders 'you set before them for a pleasing odor, says the Lord God'. Thus, the word *wayyehī* has been left untranslated. This word probably means 'and this is indeed how it happened', thereby strengthening the preceding description. This is a possible rendering of *wayyehī* but not entirely certain. It is not advisable to view these final words of the verse as an introduction to v. 20, but rather they should be taken as the conclusion to v. 19. It should be noticed that with the exception of v. 19, verses 15-20 all begin with verb forms in the 2nd pers. fem. sing. (verses 16, 17, 18, 20, all begin with exactly the same verb).

16 : 57 (C) The MT has the words *k^{e}mō ʿēt* 'like the time', or 'like at the time'. It is difficult to make sense out of this clause. If it is correct, it would mean probably that the reproach which comes upon Jerusalem is compared to that which came upon Aram and the neighboring countries. Historically, 'the time of the reproach of the daughters of Aram' is not at all clear. Textually, the verse states clearly how the neighboring pagan states delight in Jerusalem's downfall. Thus, instead of the obscure *k^{e}mō ʿēt*, it is preferable to read *kāmōhā ʾatt^{e}* 'now you have become like her'. With respect to the phrase 'reproach of the daughters of Aram', one should note that numerous mss read 'Edom'. It is a fact that the names 'Aram' and 'Edom' are sometimes confused in the OT (cf. 2 Sam 8 : 13 and 1 Chron 18 : 12). This phrase itself means either the reproach which the daughters of Aram themselves experience, or, the reproach which the daughters of Aram heap upon Jerusalem. This second meaning is certainly preferable in this context (cf. RSV 'an object of reproach for ...').

17 : 5 (A) One can do nothing with the two consonants *q ḥ* at the beginning of v. 5b. Probably at an early date the text was unreadable. Apparently the MT has simply preserved a part of a word that was originally longer. In translation, one can either omit the two consonants, or, as a substitute for them, use a verb such as 'to place'.

: 7, 8 (B) On the basis of the ancient versions and the sense of the verse itself, one should read *'aḥēr* 'another' (cf. the AV, RSV, etc.) instead of the MT *'eḥād* 'one'. The same change should be made in 19 : 5, and possibly in 11 : 19 where the RSV text has 'one heart' but its margin 'a new heart' (literally 'another heart'). Cf. Cooke, *op. cit.*, p. 128. In v. 8, in place of the MT *hī' šᵉtūlā(h)* 'it was planted', the RSV has read *hū' šᵉtālāh* 'he transplanted it'. The reason for the change is insufficient. Actually, the heart of the matter is the translation of the prep. *min* at the end of v. 7. If the prep. is the '*min* of separation' meaning 'from', then the RSV rendering may be correct. But *min* often expresses comparison. In this sense, the translation in verses 7-8 is both clear and meaningful, i.e. 'and shot forth its branches towards him, that he might water it more than the bed where it was planted. It was planted in good soil by abundant waters'. It is also possible that the prep. *min* here is 'the *min* of negation' which would mean that the translation could be 'that *he* might water it, and *not the bed* where it was planted'. It is apparent, then, that in interpreting the word *min* in this context, there is no necessity for textual change nor for translating the verb *šātal* in two different ways (i.e. 'plant' and 'transplant') as the RSV does. (cf. Zimmerli *op. cit.* p. 372, 381).

: 17 (B) The sign of the acc. with suff., *'ōtō*, should be vocalized as *'ittō*, prep. with suff., i.e. 'with him'. The translation, then, is 'to deal with him' in *bonam partem*, i.e. 'to help'. The same change should be understood in several places in Ezek (cf. 10 : 17; 38 : 9) which Cooke calls "a real variation in popular speech" (*op. cit.*, pp. 35 f.).

: 21 (C) In place of the MT word 'fugitive', numerous mss read the form *mibḥārā(y)w* 'his choice ones' (RSV 'the pick').

: 9 (C) The noun *'ĕmet* can be rendered adverbially 'truly'. Thus, one can translate 'has kept my ordinances truly'. The LXX suggests a metathesis in the text since it reads *'ōtām* '(to do) them' instead of *'ĕmet* (cf. the RSV). This would mean that the suff. 'them' refers back to the antecedent 'ordinances'. Apparently v. 19 supports this change though the MT makes sense as it stands.

: 5 (B) Cf. 17 : 7.

19 : 7 (C) The MT reads 'and he knew his widows'. If one insists on retaining the MT here at all costs, then the word *yāda'* must be taken in a sexual sense. This is possible. But, in place of the Hebr word *'alm^enōtā(y)w* 'his widows', a strange clause in this context, Th and the Tg suggest the reading *'arm^enōtā(y)w* 'his strongholds' (cf. the RSV). Furthermore, since it is uncertain as to whether the word *yāda'* means here 'to destroy', it is difficult to fit it into the context. Hence, some have suggested in its place the reading *yidda'* from *dā'ā(h)* 'to desire' (RSV 'he ravaged'), or *yārōă'* from *rā'a'* 'to break'. Cf. Cooke, *op. cit.* p. 211, Zimmerli, *op. cit.*, p. 418f.

19 : 8 (C) The MT reads 'then the nations set against him from the provinces on every side'. In place of the MT *m^edīnōt*, the RSV has accepted the conjectured reading *m^eṣūdōt* 'snares', and thus renders 'then the nations set against him snares on every side'. The change is not necessary.

19 : 10 (B) The MT *b^edām^ekā* has been rendered literally by the AV 'in thy blood', but such a meaning in this context is impossible. The LXX has translated 'like a pomegranate flower', and similarly, the Tg has given a non-literal rendering. More recent translations vary widely. The *Africaans Bibel* has 'in your time of rest', thus understanding a form from *dŏmī* 'stillness, rest'. The BS renders *comme toi* which means it has understood a form from *dāmā(h)* 'to be like'. The *Zürcher Bibel*, BSG, and RSV, have conjectured the word *b^ekerem* 'in a vineyard', which, though it gives sense, is a translation that is both flat and obvious. The DNV has proposed the word *d^emī* 'half' which, in Is 38 : 10, indicates the noontide or prime of life. Thus, it renders 'in your bloom', i.e. in the prime of your life. This translation, however, is only a guess. Cf. Zimmerli, *op. cit.* p. 419.

20 : 37 (B) The DNV and AV follow the MT in reading 'I will bring you into the bond of the covenant'. The RSV has chosen to follow the LXX which omits the word 'covenant', translating 'I will let you go in by number'. But, in view of the fact that the other ancient versions (Aq Th, Pesh, Vg, Tg) have retained the word 'covenant', it is preferable to retain the MT at this point. Cf. Zimmerli *op . cit.* p. 437.

20 : 38 (B) The verb 'enter', although sing., should be translated as a plur.

No textual change is involved. A sing. form is used in Hebr because the persons are viewed as individuals.

10 (A) In these two verses the MT reads literally 'the staff of my son scorns
T, 15) all wood', and 'staff that scorns'. The sense escapes us entirely.
13 One commentator believes that the text is not only void of meaning
T, 18) but beyond hope of correction! The word 'staff' might be rendered 'sceptre' or 'rod', and 'wood' brings to mind images or idols. The 'son' is unknown. The plain fact is that there are too many questions without answers. The DNV has chosen to translate the text literally, and to place this section in v. 10 between dashes, thus indicating that the connection of this clause with the rest of the verse is obscure. The RSV has vocalized the consonants *m'st* as 2nd pers. masc. sing. perf. forms in both verses, i.e. 'you have despised', thereby understanding 'my son' as a vocative. This raises the difficulty, however,, in that the verb *mā'as* is construed with a double acc. It means also that the translation 'rod' must be adopted. The BSG regards 'rod of my son' as a vocative, and relates it to what precedes in the verse. Its translation in brackets has 'or shall we make mirth, O rod of my son, despising every tree'. In conclusion, one must admit that every translation is doubtful and every textual emendation somewhat arbitrary. Cf. Zimmerli, *op. cit.* p. 470.

22 (C) The MT reads 'into his right hand comes the lot for Jerusalem,
T, 27) to set battering rams, to open the mouth with slaughter'. The RSV omits the words 'to set battering rams' and replaces the MT *reṣaḥ* 'slaughter' with *ṣeraḥ* 'cry'. While it is undoubtedly a war-cry that is uttered, yet that cry means destruction and murder, Thus, the MT *reṣaḥ* is undoubtedly the correct text. From the phonetic standpoint, the two Hebr words could easily be confused.

24 (B) The RSV has rendered 'you shall be taken in them', i.e. in your
T, 29) sins and transgressions. This follows the LXX. Other translations, also on the basis of the LXX, read differently. The *Zürcher Bibel* has, *um ihretwillen*, and Bertholet (*Hesekiel*, HAT 1936, p. 76) gives the translation *für sie*. Nevertheless, it is preferable to follow the MT which reads 'with the hand', i.e. by force. This is done by the BSG and the DNV as well as by Cooke (*op. cit.*, p. 234).

21 : 27 (C) (MT, 32) The MT has 'even this shall not be' (or 'was not'). The meaning is apparently that it will not always remain a heap of ruins (cf. the context). But a question surrounds the Hebr here, since the masc. vb. *hāyā(h)* following the fem. demonstrative pron. is suspicious. Some adopt the translation of cod. Vat. of the LXX which has 'woe be to her! Such a one she shall be until . . .' but this represents a considerable divergence from the MT. Others adopt the emendation *'ōt* 'sign' or 'trace' instead of the MT *zō't* 'this'. Hence, the RSV renders 'there shall not be even a trace of it'. Fohrer, however, points out that this suggestion violates the context. For, since it has been emphatically stated that a heap of ruins shall remain, it can then hardly be immediately added that no trace shall remain (*op. cit.*, p. 125). Thus, if one feels it necessary to deviate from the MT, the text of cod. Vat. is to be preferred.

21 : 28 (C) (MT, 33) The form *hākīl* could be a *hiph.* inf. of *kūl* 'to contain', but this gives no adequate sense to the passage. It could also be, however, a shortened form of the *hiph.* inf. of the verb *'ākal* 'to eat, devour'. If, then, too much importance is not attached to the caus. form of the inf., the translation, accordingly, could be 'polished to devour'. Other translations, based on textual changes, are 'to destruction' and 'to glitter' (RSV).

22 : 4 (C) The MT reads 'and you have come to your years', which the DNV explains as meaning 'you have reached the limit of your years'. The change of the MT *'ad* 'until' into *'ēt* 'time' is supported by two mss as well as the ancient versions. This allows for the translation 'the appointed time of your years has come'.

22 : 16 (B) The first word of the MT is a *niph.* form of *ḥālal*, *not* of *nāḥal* as the LXX and AV indicate. The MT form is a 2nd pers. fem. 'you shall be profaned', i.e. Jerusalem (cf. V. 1-16). The RSV has followed the first pers. form of the LXX and translated. 'I shall be profaned', i.e. God. As Cooke points out (*op. cit.*, p. 242), this would mean that "it will be Israel's fault if Jahveh is dishonoured for casting out his people: the heathen will say that he was unable to protect His own."

22 : 24 (B) The RSV (cf. the AV) follows the MT and translates 'a land that is

not cleansed'. The DNV has accepted the LXX translation 'a land that is not moistened' which fits the parallelism of the verse better.

25 (B) Both the DNV and RSV follow the LXX in reading 'her princes' (*n^{e}śīʾe(y)hā*) in place of the MT *n^{e}bīʾe(y)hā* ('her prophets'). The change is favored by the context which indicates that the prophets are first mentioned in v. 28.

21 B) Read 'the Egyptians' in place of the MT 'out of Egypt'. Near the close of the verse, in place of the Hebr word *l^{e}maʿan* 'for the sake of', some suggest that the reading should be *l^{e}maʿēk*, *pi.* inf. of *māʿak* 'to press' (cf. the RSV). Cooke even believes that the MT is the result of an "attempt to modify objectionable words" (*op. cit.*, p. 252). But, it is noteworthy that in 23 : 3, the word *māʿak* in a similar context is present and allowed to stand. Hence, taken as a whole, the chapter is extremely realistic, thus making a theory of modification in this verse questionable.

: 23 (C) The MT has the word *q^{e}rūʾīm* 'those who are called', which the DNV has rendered as 'important people'. This is an uncertain translation. Usually the word *q^{e}rōbīm* 'warriors' is read, which is the word used in 23 : 5 (MT) and v. 12. The word *q^{e}rāb* means 'battle'.

: 24 (B) The Hebr word *hōṣen* is unknown. From the context, one can surmise some such meaning as 'multitude'. This opinion is accepted by the DNV which has 'with many (carts)'. The ancient versions do not help us much, though, on the basis of the LXX, the RSV renders 'from the north'.

: 34 (C) The MT has 'to gnaw its sherds'. The RSV has followed the suggestion of the Pesh and rendered very freely 'and pluck out your hair'. On the basis of the Tg, one can produce the translation 'to finish the dregs thereof', or 'to consume to the dregs'. Cf. Cooke (*op. cit.*, pp. 255, 262) who cites various other conjectures.

: 42 (C) The *Kethib* reads the act. part. *sōb^{e}ʾīm* 'drunkards', or, possibly the pass. part. *sūbāʾīm* (= *s^{e}būʾīm*) meaning 'drenched with wine', both forms derived from *sābāʾ* 'to drink' (cf. Cooke, *op. cit.*, p. 263). The

Qere reading has *sābā'īm* which is perhaps intended to denote the name of a tribe (cf. Cooke, *ibid.*). The text is rather obscure, but, for this reason, it is best to adhere as closely as possible to the traditional form and translate 'drunkards'.

23 : 43 (C) The MT is hardly translatable. Cooke (*ibid.*) gives a summary of the treatment of this verse by the various ancient versions. The RSV is based on the LXX. Does the MT perhaps mean 'I said about her, who had grown old (literally 'withered', cf. Josh 9 : 4) through adultery: do they practice harlotry with her'?

23 : 44 (C) The text reads 'they went in to Oholah and to Oholibah, women of lewdness'. Since the plur. form *'iššōt* is most unusual, the text is somewhat doubtful. One suggestion is to change the form into a sing. *'ēšet*. Another idea that forms the basis of the RSV rendering, is to read a verbal form *la'ăśōt* 'to commit'.

24 : 5 (B) The MT has *hā'ăṣāmīm* 'the bones'. On the basis of the immediate context and v. 10, one should probably read *hā'ēṣīm* 'the logs', thus translating 'burn the logs under it'. Except for this change, the DNV keeps to the MT in this verse whereas the RSV accepts some further alterations.

24 : 10 (B) An altered reading *wehārēq hammārāq* 'empty out the broth' (RSV) is often accepted in place of the MT *weharqaḥ hammerqāḥā(h)* 'and mix the spices' (AV 'spice it well'). The noun *merqāḥā(h)* means 'ointment-pot', but it is possible that we are here to recognize another form of the noun, i.e. *merqāḥ* 'scented herbs'. The form of the verb *rāqaḥ* found here, could mean 'to mix herbs', so the text could mean approximately 'add herbs to'. This is an attempt to translate the MT so that it is understandable.

24 : 12 (C) The initial words 'she has made the troubles tired' are puzzling. The word *hel'āt* is apparently a *hiph.* perf. 3rd pers. fem. sing. from the verb *lā'ā(h)*. This means that the subject is the pot that is described in this passage. Thus, the sense evidently is that all was in vain. Whatever was tried, the layer of rust remained. However, the text is usually altered to read *ḥinnām nil'ētī* 'in vain I have wearied myself' (RSV).

: 17 (C) At the close of both of these verses, the MT supported by the LXX
: 22 reads 'and do not eat the bread of men'. Cooke (*op. cit.*, pp. 270 f.) interprets the expression as meaning 'bread of the people' or 'ordinary bread'. The DNV explains the clause as meaning 'bread that the people bring'. It is entirely possible that there is an allusion in this speech to some particular custom of mourning. Friends or relatives may have customarily brought bread to the mourners. In the light of these things, then, there is no need to change the text as the RSV has done in reading *'ōnīm*, i.e. 'bread of mourners' (Hos. 9 : 4).

: 5 (B) The insertion '(cities of) the Ammonites' is an attempt to clarify the text. The LXX has the word 'city' in the sing. form.

: 8 (C) The MT has 'Moab and Seir'. 'Seir' does not suit this context which concerns an 'oracle against Moab' (verses 8-11). The 'oracle against Seir' is next in order (verses 12-14). Still, the question arises as to whether for this reason it should be omitted from 25 : 8. After all, a translation must be based on the text that has been handed down to the church. A translation intended for religious and church use is quite different from a commentary aimed at theologians. Perhaps 'and Seir' could be placed between brackets or dashes.

: 9 (C) Translations tend to omit the phrase *mē'ārā(y)w* 'from its cities' (cf. the RSV). Fohrer (*op. cit.*, p. 145) omits the word but translates *dass sie keine Städte mehr haben ohne Ausnahme* (literally, *von seinem Ende an*). The DNV reflects the MT as it is, and then following the word 'cities' translates as Fohrer does, i.e. 'so that there are no cities any more, with no single exception'. In this translation, then, there is no mention of the 'frontier' (cf. the RSV) in a literal sense. Of the form *miqqāṣēhū*, Cooke says, "the last word may be given the meaning 'in its whole extent', a condensed expression for 'from one end to the other', from south to north" (*op. cit.*, p. 283).

: 10 (C) The phrase 'that the sons of Ammon may be remembered no more' seems out of place in this section. It ought to be found in the dirge against the Ammonites in 25 : 1-7. Here, in verses 8-11, one senses that the nation that nobody should remember should be Moab. The RSV has attempted to resolve the question by simply omitting the phrase 'sons of Ammon'. It is questionable, however, whether such a correction should be introduced in translation, even if one believes the correction to be established.

26 : 17 (C) The DNV has followed the MT closely. It must be admitted that the word *nōšebet* has been understood differently in ancient translations. If the word is kept, the sentence can be translated 'how you have vanished, O inhabited one, from the seas' ('from the seas' thus related to the verb *'ābad*). Hence, it would mean that Tyre was populous because its seatrade flourished. On the other hand, instead of the MT *nōšebet*, *niph.* part. of *yāšab* 'to dwell', some read the form *nišbatt^e*, *niph.* perf. 2nd fem. sing. of the verb *šābat* 'to cease'. In this case, though, one should omit the word *'ābadt^e* at the beginning. Then the translation becomes 'how you have vanished from the seas'.

26 : 20 (B) The DNV has 'and does not rise again in the land of the living' and the RSV 'or have a place in the land of the living'. These translations represent a change in the text on the basis of the LXX. The MT reads literally 'and I shall give an ornament in the land of the living'. It is possible, however, that the negative phrase that precedes continues its influence into this final phrase. This would allow for the translation 'so that you will not be inhabited, and I will not make (you) an ornament in the land of the living'. This translation is far from certain, though the influence of the preceding negation is quite clear.

27 : 6 (B) The MT has the puzzling phrase 'daughter of Ashurim'. The solution is that the two Hebr words should be read together as one, as the Tg did, i.e. *bit'aššurīm* which refers to some kind of cone-bearing or evergreen tree. KBL identifies the *t^e'aššur* as the 'cypress', the RSV as 'pine', and the DNV as 'fir-wood'.

27 : 8 (C) The MT reads 'your skilled men, O Tyre'. In objecting to this reading, Cooke says, "the senators of Tyre could hardly be sailors in the ship which represents Tyre! The context speaks of a crew furnished by subject towns" (*op. cit.*, p. 299). Thus, in place of *ṣōr* 'Tyre', Cooke and others conjecture the reading *ṣemer* (RSV 'skilled men of Zemer'), presumably situated north of Tripoli in Syria. The uncer-

tainty of the conjecture, however, presents a good reason for retaining the MT reading. Moreover, the suff. 'your' in 'your skilled men, O Tyre', can hardly be explained as a textual corruption.

15 (C) The LXX reading 'Rhodes' (cf. the RSV) in place of the MT 'Dedan' fits well into the geography of the passage, since Dedan occurs in v. 20 in its usual place among the districts in Arabia. However, it is a question whether the LXX is correct. Cooke (*op. cit.*, p. 301) believes it is unlikely that ivory and ebony would be imported to Tyre by way of Rhodes. He thus prefers to keep the MT.

16 (C) Instead of the MT 'Aram', many mss as well as Aq and the Pesh read 'Edom' (cf. 16 : 57).

17 (C) If the text has been handed down correctly, the word *minnīt* apparently designates a place in the Ammonite territory, famous for its wheat. The next word *pannag* is unknown. It would seem to designate a kind of food, perhaps a cake or pastry. Some prefer to read *paggag* and thus translate 'early figs'. Instead of 'wheat from Minnith', some render 'wheat and olives', while others suggest 'wheat and spices'.

19 (C) The MT phrase *w*^{e}*dān w*^{e}*yāwān* is an enigma. The RSV translates 'wine' thus understanding the word *yayin*. Cf. the commentaries.

23 (C) Since 'the traders of Sheba' are mentioned in v. 22, some (cf. the RSV) omit them from v. 23. But, if v. 23 indicates locations in southern Arabia, 'the traders of Sheba' should be kept in the text, if necessary, by placing the clause between dashes. Cooke (*op. cit.*, p. 305) believes that the names in v. 23 are locations in Mesopotamia, but Fohrer (*op. cit.*, p. 157) emphatically affirms that they are in South Arabia.

24 (C) The RSV translation 'bound with cords and made secure' (cf. also Cooke, *op. cit.*, p. 306), apparently refers to the packing for shipping of the previously mentioned choice materials. The translation could also be 'in plaited and twisted ropes' (DNV 'in plaited cableropes'). In this case, the text cites another article of merchandise. The final word of the verse in the MT 'in your market place' should

be retained. The change suggested in the RSV 'in these they traded with you', adds nothing to the verse in view of its beginning.

27 : 25 (C) The MT can be rendered 'ships from Tarshish conveyed your merchandise'. This means that the sense of 'caravans' should be attached to the word *šārōt* which is derived from *šūr* 'to journey' or 'to descend'. The translation is thus somewhat free, but it is possible. In the RSV rendering, 'traveled for you with your merchandise', a prep. *bᵉ* must be added before the word *maʿărābēk*. Cf. the commentaries.

27 : 32 (B) In place of the MT 'like silence', read 'destroyed' along with the Pesh and Tg (cf. the AV, RSV, and DNV).

27 : 34 (B) The first word *ʿēt* 'time' in the MT, should be read *ʿattā(h)* 'now'.

28 : 12 (B) The MT has 'you are the sealer of the model', which must mean something like 'you show complete proportion' (cf. Cooke, *op. cit.*, p. 315). Instead of *ḥōtēm* 'sealer', the RSV (cf. also the ancient versions) has read *ḥōtam*, translating 'you were the signet of perfection'. The DNV rendering 'thou art perfect of figure' is somewhat free, but it does express the meaning well.

28 : 13 (C) The translation 'your engravings' for the word *nᵉqābe(y)kā* is not certain. The word may mean 'perforated ornaments' suitable to be hung or fastened on a garment. The stem *n q b* means 'to bore through' (cf. G. R. Driver, JTS, 1944, pp. 13 f., and W. F. Albright, BASOR, 1948, 110, p. 13, ann. 39).

28 : 14, 16 (C) The MT literally reads 'you, a cherub, anointed, guarding, and I placed you'. In place of the word 'anointed', the translation 'extensive' could be used (cf. the Vg *extentus*). In this case, one appeals to Aram where a verb *mᵉšaḥ* means 'to measure'. Somewhat freely, the DNV has rendered 'you were a guardian cherub, with widespread wings; I had given you a place'. The 'prince of Tyre' is thus compared to a cherub (cf. also Fohrer, *op. cit.*, p. 164). If this explanation is accepted, v. 16 can read unaltered 'and I drove you out, O guardian cherub'. If, however, in v. 14 one prefers to read the first word as the prep.

’et ‘with’ instead of the MT pron. *’att*^{e} ‘you’, thus making the cherub a companion or guardian of the prince of Tyre, then he must deviate from the MT in v. 16 and vocalize *w*^{e}*’ibbadkā*, i.e. ‘and the guardian cherub drove you out’ (RSV), instead of the MT *wā’abbedkā* ‘and I drove you out (O guardian cherub)’. The connection between verses 14 and 16 is important. Whether one chooses to follow the MT where the prince of Tyre and cherub are identified as one, or to follow a reading in which they are distinguished as two distinct personages, it is necessary to see that verses 14 and 16 are in agreement.

7 (B) The MT has ‘you made to stand’, a verbal form from the root consonants *‘ m d*. The Pesh read these consonants in a different order, i.e. *m ‘ d*, a root meaning ‘to shake’. The MT, then, is probably an error of metathesis for the more original reading of the Pesh. Both the DNV and RSV have accepted the Pesh reading ‘made . . . to shake’.

9 (B) The MT reads the 3rd pers. ‘because he has said’ which may be by influence of v. 3 where the 3rd pers. is found in the same phrase. In v. 9, however, the context calls for the 2nd pers. ‘because you have said’. The ancient versions also favor the 2nd pers.

5 (C) Instead of *kūb*, an unknown word, the name *lūb* ‘Libya’ is usually read.

9 (B) The MT reading *baṣṣīm* ‘in ships’ is accepted by the DNV and AV which translate ‘(messengers) in ships’. Similarly, Cooke (*op. cit.*, p. 332) believes that the word ‘ships’ fits the context. On the basis of the LXX, however, the RSV translates ‘swift (messengers)’, thereby reflecting the reading *’āṣīm* ‘hastening’ from *’ūṣ*.

16 (C) The Hebr reads ‘and Nof (= Memphis) enemies by day’. The translation ‘enemies’ can just as easily be ‘distresses’. It is indeed possible that the MT represents the true text and that something very significant is added to what has already been stated concerning the town Memphis. Hence, the translation ‘and Memphis—enemies by day’! Translations and commentaries, however, have generally accepted the conjectured reading *w*^{e}*nipr*^{e}*ṣū ḥōmōte(y)hā* ‘and its walls

broken down', thus referring back to the description of No (= Thebes).

30 : 18 (B) The MT reads *ḥāśak* (with the letter *sin*) 'it holds back', i.e. its light. Without consonantal change, one can read *ḥāšak* (with the letter *šin*) 'it becomes dark' (cf. the AV and RSV).

31 : 3 (B) The MT reads 'behold Assyria was a cedar in Lebanon'. The DNV has translated in this way and set forth its Scriptural heading for 31 : 1-18 as 'Assyria, a warning and example for Egypt'. The question arises, however, as to whether we ought to think of Assyria here at all. Instead of the MT *'aššūr 'erez ball*ᵉ*bānōn* 'the Assyrian (was) a cedar in Lebanon', the RSV has accepted a suggestion found in the critical notes of BH to read *'ašw*ᵉ*kā l*ᵉ*'erez ball*ᵉ*bānōn* 'I will liken you to a cedar in Lebanon'. This conjecture has apparently some support from the context since it gives an answer to the question that immediately precedes 'whom are you like in your greatness'. If this conjecture were adopted, it would mean that this entire section to the end of the chapter is concerned not with Assyria's greatness and fall, but with Pharaoh's fate and the fate of his people. The text has had still another explanation. Some have felt that in place of *'aššūr*, the text should read *t*ᵉ*'aššūr* 'a pine tree'. In this case, 'cedar in Lebanon' would be an explanatory note on this rare word, i.e. 'behold a pine tree, a cedar in Lebanon'. Cf. 27 : 6. Near the close of the verse, with the LXX read *'ābōt* 'clouds' in place of the MT *'ăbōtīm* 'boughs'. The same change should be made in v. 10 and v. 14.

31 : 10 (B) Instead of the MT 'because you . . .', in view of the context, one should read 'because it . . .' Cf. also the note on 31 : 3.

31 : 14 (B) See 31 : 3.

31 : 15 (C) The RSV has omitted the word *kissētī* 'I covered'. Literally, the MT reads 'I will cause to mourn, I covered upon it, the deep' ('the deep' is the rendering of *t*ᵉ*hōm* 'the deep primeval waters'). Admittedly, the word *kissētī*, added without connection to the previous verb, is difficult to reproduce. It would appear that someone who is going to mourn covers himself with a garment of mourning. Perhaps the

reference is to God who is going to cover the 'deep' with such a garment and thus cause it to lament. The DNV has attempted to give the sense in this way, translating 'for his sake (*'ālā(y)w*) I covered the flood in mourning'. With respect to meaning, this translation is clearly correct.

17 (C) At the close, the MT reads 'and his arm, they lived in his shadow among the peoples'. The words 'and his arm' may be in apposition to 'they'. That is, 'his arm', or 'his strength' could mean metaphorically 'his helpers'. What follows would then be a relative sentence without a relative pronoun. This is possible. The translation, then, can be 'his helpers who had lived in his shadow, in the midst of the peoples'. This rendering is supported by Ezek 30 : 8 and 32 : 21. The word 'helper' can also be read if the consonants of *zᵉrōăʿ* are interchanged to *ʿōzēr*. The RSV, however, follows the LXX in this verse reading a verbal form '(they) shall perish' in place of the Hebr word 'and his arm'. This involves a textual change.

3 (C) The MT 'they will haul you up in my net' pictures the various peoples as an instrument in the hand of God. There is not much point then to a change to the 1st pers. 'I will haul you up in my net' as the RSV suggests on the basis of the LXX and Vg.

5 (C) The MT *rāmūt* is puzzling. Can it mean 'high heaps of bodies', or, is it derived from *rāmā(h)* 'to throw', thus meaning 'that which is thrown away', or 'refuse', or 'carcass'? One cannot be certain.

9 (C) The Hebr reads 'when I bring your destruction among the nations'. The meaning is apparently that God will effect the break-up of the Egyptian empire among the nations who will witness the event (cf. Cooke, *op. cit.*, p. 348). However, in place of the MT *šibrᵉkā* 'your destruction', the LXX has read *šibyᵉkā* 'your captivity'. Hence, the RSV has 'when I carry you captive among the nations'.

20 (B) The DNV has left the text unaltered and attempted to reproduce its meaning with the rendering 'a sword is given, drag (Egypt) away, with all its multitudes'. The RSV, however, has harmonized its text somewhat with v. 25, which, among other things, means that it has

dropped the second occurrence of *ḥereb* 'sword' in v. 20. The RSV renders 'and with her shall lie all her multitudes'.

32 : 25 (B) The MT has a sing. verb 'he is placed', whereas the context requires a translation in the plur. Among other witnesses, the LXX and Tg have a plur.

32 : 27 (C) The MT has 'with the fallen mighty men of the uncircumcised'. The text is translatable, and the DNV has chosen to adhere to it. Among the old versions, however, the LXX (cf. also now the RSV) has read *mē'ōlām* 'of old' in place of the MT *mē'ărēlīm* 'of the uncircumcised'. Cf. Cooke (*op. cit.*, pp. 353 f.), and Fohrer (*op. cit.*, p. 179) who regards 'of the uncircumcised' as a dogmatic gloss. Instead of '*ăwōnōt*, iniquities, the RSV has read *ṣinnōt*, shields'.

32 : 32 (C) The vocalization indicates the translation 'I spread my terror in the land of the living' while the *Kethib* reading has 'I spread his terror'. The Tg, however, indicates the reading 'he spread his terror'.

34 : 12 (C) One possible translation of the Hebr is 'as a shepherd seeks out his flock in the day when he is in the midst of his sheep which are dispersed'. A second translation is also correct, i.e. 'as a shepherd seeks out his flock in the day when among his sheep some are dispersed'. The first word *baqqārā(h)* can be described as an Aram inf. This indicates that one can expect other linguistic peculiarities here. Hence, it is not certain if the suff. attached to the inf. *hĕyōt* refers to the noun *rō'e(h)* 'shepherd' (cf. the first translation given above), or, to the word *ṣō'n* 'flock' (cf. the second translation above). This second possible rendering is somewhat unusual but it is entirely possible. Thus, the RSV rendering on the whole reproduces this sense, which does not at all mean that a textual change is necessary.

34 : 16 (B) The DNV follows the MT which reads 'and the fat and the strong I will destroy' (cf. also Cooke, *op. cit.*, p. 376 who retains the MT). On the other hand, the RSV adopts the suggestion of the LXX and translates 'and the fat and the strong I will watch over'. This represents a doubtful reading and means quite a different exegesis of the verse.

: 29 (C) The MT *maṭṭāʿ lᵉšēm* apparently means ‘plantation for renown’, or a plantation “which shall be so productive as to be famous” (Cooke, *op. cit.*, p. 379). The RSV rendering ‘prosperous plantations’ requires the reading *šālōm* or *šālēm*, but this change is not needed.

: 31 (C) The MT has ‘the sheep of my pasture; you are men and I am your God’. Often the word *ʾādām* ‘men’ has been omitted on the grounds that it is possibly a later explanatory addition. The question must be faced, however, as to whether a ‘translation’ which is intended not for scientific use, but for the church and the cause of religion, should omit *ʾādām* even though it were shown to be “explanatory.”

: 6 (C) This is part of the section 35 : 5-9 that contains a prophecy against Edom. Here in v. 6, the text reads literally ‘if you have not hated blood’. Since the words ‘as I live’ come at the beginning, the clause in question must signify ‘you have surely hated blood’. The MT can only make sense in this context if it means that Edom hated his blood relationship with Israel, and by action, disowned it and disdained it (v. 5). It is a remarkable statement. Considering Ezek 22 : 4 and other references, however, many believe that the LXX suggestion is best, i.e. that the text should read here *bᵉdām ʾāšamtā* ‘because you are guilty of blood’. This change provides an acceptable meaning.

: 11 (B) On the basis of the LXX and the context, read *bᵉkā* ‘among you’ in place of the second occurrence of *bām* ‘among them’.

5 (C) At the end of the verse, the word *migraš* could be taken as an inf. formed as an Aram inf. from *gāraš* ‘to drive out’. The translation would then be ‘in order to drive it (i.e. the land) out for a spoil’. But, the object ‘land’ does not suit the verb very well. Some have suggested that *migrāš* is a noun here meaning ‘meadow-land’. The translation, in this case, would be ‘in order that the meadow-land of it (i.e. of the land) become a spoil’. But this is also strange. Thus, in agreement with one ms, the form *mōrāšā(h)* should probably be read. This makes possible the RSV translation ‘that they might possess it and plunder it’. The DNV, however, has not accepted this change but rendered the clause freely ‘to plunder it thoroughly’.

36 : 20 (B) The first word is a sing. verbal form. According to the context, it should be translated with a plur. form.

37 : 19 (B) The MT reads literally 'and I will join them to it, the stick of Judah'. With a slight textual change, translate 'I will join with it the stick of Judah'.

37 : 23 (B) The MT 'I will save them out of their dwelling places' does not make sense in this context. Symm suggests that a very slight change in the text should be made to read 'I will save them out of their backslidings'. This gives an excellent meaning (cf. the DNV and RSV).

37 : 25 (B) The RSV follows the MT in reading 'your fathers'. The DNV, like the LXX, has 'their fathers'.

37 : 26 (B, C) The Hebr reads 'and I will give them'. Does this mean 'I will give them a place' (cf. the AV)? One can translate as the Tg does 'I shall bless them', but this does not mean that this reading ever existed in the Hebr text. In place of the first occurrence of *'ōtām*, one should understand the pointing *'ittām* 'with them'. Cf. 17 : 17.

38 : 9 (B) Read the final word as *'ittāk* 'with you'.

38 : 21 (A) The text reads literally 'I will summon against him to (or, in respect to) all my mountains, a sword' (cf. Cooke, *op. cit.*, p. 415). Ancient versions had their difficulties in this verse. For example, the cod. Vat. mentions neither 'mountains' nor 'sword'. This text has become the basis of the RSV rendering 'I will summon every kind of terror'. But, it should give pause for thought that both cod. Alex. and the Scheide papyrus mention a 'sword'. This fact would indicate that *ḥereb* is original in this text. The DNV has the translation 'on all my mountains'. Though not strictly literal, this is a possible rendering.

39 : 11 (A) The Hebr text 'place, there, grave' is rendered by the RSV 'a place for burial'. The Hebr construction is not a common one. It is necessary to combine the last two words 'there a grave' and allow these words to depend on 'place'. In Hebr, this dependence is ex-

pressed by the construct relationship. Thus, the DNV has translated 'a place where a grave will be'. This is grammatically possible and, in essence, agrees with the RSV. In place of the MT *šām* 'there', various ancient versions have understood the vocalization *šēm* 'name', i.e. 'a place of a name, a grave'. The meaning is that Gog will have a place in Israel which will be called after him, but that place will be his grave. This would introduce a kind of irony into the text. Cooke believes that this alteration "does not suit the context so well" (*op. cit.*, p. 419).

: 14 (C) The Hebr reads 'to bury the travelers, those left behind'. This could mean 'to bury those of the travelers who are left behind'. The LXX omitted the word 'travelers' and its example is often followed.

ap. -48 Many difficulties face the translator in reproducing these chapters accurately. Among the details of the temple construction, a great number of architectural terms are used, some of which are not clear. The list of problem passages that follow indicates those places where the DNV deviates more or less from the MT. It will be obvious that other translations in many places express various other opinions.

: 15 (B) The MT reads twice 'at the front'. Read 'from the front' and 'up to the front'.

: 16 (B) Translate the next to the last word *ʾayil* as a plur. 'jambs'.

: 44 (B) On the basis of the LXX, the RSV has adopted a more detailed text at the beginning of the verse. Moreover, for the MT 'rooms for singers'(?), the RSV with the support of the LXX has rendered 'two chambers'. Again, instead of the MT 'that at the side' and 'east gate', the RSV has rendered respectively 'one at the side of the north gate' and 'south gate'. The LXX also has 'south gate' which does fit better into the text as a whole. The RSV more or less agrees with the DNV.

: 7 (B) For the MT *w*^{e}*kēn* 'and so', the DNV following the LXX has read *ūmin* 'and from'. The RSV has evidently understood *w*^{e}*kēn* (*min*) since it translates 'and thus one went up from'.

41 : 9 (B) Instead of *bē(y)t* 'house', read *bē(y)n* 'between' (cf. the LXX).

41 : 11 (B) Although the MT has a sing. form 'and the entrance' since the separate entrances are in view, one should translate it by a plur. form. The RSV and AV render 'and the doors'.

41 : 16 (C) Cf. also 40 : 16. Probably *ḥallōnīm 'ăṭumōt* are 'windows framed with stone' (cf. Fohrer, *op. cit.*, p. 226, who renders *Rahmenfenster*). The translation is very uncertain. The stem *'āṭam* means 'to stop, close'. We apparently have here an architectonic technical term, the exact meaning of which eludes our grasp.

41 : 20 (B) In place of the MT *wᵉqīr* 'and a wall', read *laqqīr* 'on the wall' (cf. the AV and RSV). This change is verified by a comparison of v. 25. The final word of the verse, 'the temple', has been retained by the DNV but omitted by the RSV. The Masoretes have given the word a special punctuation possibly indicating thereby that they believed it to be out of place. Also, since v. 21 begins with the same word 'temple', it can easily be omitted from the close of v. 20.

41 : 22 (B) In place of the MT 'its length', read with the LXX 'its base' since the length has already been mentioned.

42 : 3 (C) According to Fohrer (*op. cit.*, p. 236), the word *'attīqīm* means *Absätze im felsigen Gelände . . . die sich aus dem Höhenunterschied zwischen dem oberen und dem unteren Vorhof ergaben.*

42 : 4 (B) The MT 'road of one cubit' does not make sense. The DNV (cf. the RSV) has followed the LXX and translated 'and a hundred cubits long'.

42 : 8 (B) For the MT *wᵉhinnē(h)* 'and behold', the DNV (cf. also the RSV) has read *wᵉhēnnā(h)* 'and those'. The change has the support of the LXX.

43 : 3 (B) Two textual changes should be made in this verse. First, instead of the MT 'like the vision of the vision which I saw', one should translate 'the vision which I saw', And second, for the MT 'when I came', read 'when he came', i.e. Yahweh. It is evident that Ezekiel

himself took no part in the destruction—that was the work of God (cf. Cooke, *op. cit.*, p. 463). A few Hebr mss and Th are external witnesses for this change.

6 (B) Instead of the MT *middabbēr* 'after speaking', it is obvious that one should read *mᵉdabbēr* 'one speaking'. Cf. also the next to the last word in 2 : 2 where a similar change should probably be made (cf. the LXX). The DNV is undoubtedly correct in interpreting the speaker as Yahweh (cf. Cooke, *op. cit.*, p. 463). It should be mentioned that the form *middabbēr*, if retained, could be taken as a *hithp.* part.

7 (B) Near the end of the verse, as an alternative translation for the MT *peger* 'carcass', the RSV margin has 'monuments' (cf. the JBL, 1948, pp. 55 ff.). Cf. also v. 9. In Lev 26 : 30, the RSV does not give the alternative translation. The last word of the MT *bāmōtām* 'in their high places' is omitted by the RSV (Cooke, *op. cit.*, p. 464, calls the word 'an explanatory gloss'). Many Hebr mss read *bᵉmōtām* 'in their death', i.e. 'after their death', which is the reading the DNV follows.

13 (B) Read *ḥē(y)qō(h) 'ammā(h)* (cf. the RSV).

14 (B) In place of the last two words, read either *raḥbō 'ammā(h)* or *rōḥab 'ammā(h)* 'a breadth of one cubit'.

17 (B) The MT has *pᵉnōt*, an inf. One can read the part. *pōnōt*. In either case the translation should be 'face east'.

5 (B) For the word *'ōtāk*, see the note on 17 : 17. In the latter part of the verse, the DNV has followed the MT and translated 'mark the entering in of the house through all the entrances of the sanctuary'. On the other hand, the RSV has followed a conjecture mentioned in the critical notes of BH, translating 'mark well those who may be admitted to the temple and all those who are to be excluded from the sanctuary'.

7 C) Literally, the MT reads 'to profane it, my house', for which the DNV has 'to profane my house', thereby omitting the suff. The RSV has omitted the words 'my house' and, accordingly, related the suff. of the word *lᵉḥallᵉlō* to the word 'sanctuary' that comes immediately

before. Later in the verse, the Hebr reads 'they have broken my covenant', which, in this context, must refer to foreigners. The question then arises as to how foreigners can break the covenant between Israel and God. If one follows the MT, the final words of the verse should be rendered 'above all your abominations', *not* 'with all your abominations'. On the basis of some ancient versions, the RSV has translated 'you have broken my covenant with all your abominations'.

44 : 19 (B) The words 'into the outer court' are found twice in the Hebr text. Translate them only once.

44 : 26 (C) The Hebr has 'and after he is cleansed (i.e. after establishing his purity), they will count off seven days for him'. Num 19 : 11 indicates that a person who touches a dead body will be unclean for seven days. It would seem, then, that the seven days mentioned here in Ezek 44 : 26 come after the defilement. Thus, the RSV has accepted the translation of the Pesh and rendered 'after he is defiled, he shall count for himself seven days, and then he shall be clean'. This translation suggests that the order of events here is as follows; defilement, a period of seven days, a state of purification, and the bringing of a sacrifice (Ezek 44 : 27). However, in the Hebr of v. 26, even if the Pesh translation 'after his defilement' should be accepted, there is no mention of being clean. The Pesh supplies this at the end of the verse and thereby gives the RSV reason for adding the words 'and then he shall be clean'. But, should one follow the Pesh at this point? The LXX clearly supports the MT in reading 'after his cleansing they will count off seven days for him'. In connection with the requirement of Num 19 : 11, Ezek 44 : 26 apparently means that "in the case of priests, on account of the holiness of their calling, an additional period of seven days is required" (Cooke, *op. cit.*, p. 487) before they may once more fulfil their cultic duties. Hence, the first two words of Ezek 44 : 26 'after he is cleansed', affirm that the requirement of Num 19 : 11 has been met, while the rest of Ezek 44 : 26 sets forth the "extra" requirement for the priest.

44 : 28 (C) The MT reads 'and it shall be to them for an inheritance: I am their inheritance'. It is generally agreed that at some time the negation

dropped out of the text. For this reason and with the support of the Vg, the translation should be 'they shall have no inheritance', thereby putting the text in agreement with Deut 18 : 2, 5.

: 1 (B) Following the word *rōḥab*, the MT has 'ten thousand'. On the basis of the LXX and the clear meaning of the context in verses 3 and 5, one should read 'twenty thousand'.

: 5 (B) At the close of the verse, the Hebr reads 'twenty rooms' which cannot possibly be correct. Following the LXX, read *ʿārīm lāšābet* 'cities to live in'.

: 12 (A) The DNV gives a literal translation of the Hebr text, and thus, translates that which is given in a footnote in the RSV. The RSV text follows the LXX. Later commentaries believe the LXX is correct since the text aims to say that the mina is 50 shekels, and not 60, as the MT apparently gives it in its very strange form. Cf. Cooke, *op. cit.*, pp. 498 f., and K. Galling, BRL, cols. 186 f.

: 15 (C) If the text is correct, the word *mašqe(h)* means here 'the well-watered land', a sense that it likewise has in Gen 13 : 10. The MT as it stands can be translated, and thus the DNV has adhered to it. The LXX has not rendered the text literally, and thus many have followed its example and translated 'families'. Others have understood the word *miqne(h)* 'cattle' in place of the MT *mašqe(h)*.

: 21 (B) The MT reads at the close of the verse 'feast of weeks, days, unleavened bread shall be eaten'. Since the passage has to do with the Passover ritual, the feast of weeks can hardly be referred to. Thus, instead of 'weeks', one should read the numeral 'seven' as the LXX has done. It is possible to combine the word 'feast' with the preceding word and translate as the RSV has done 'you shall celebrate the feast of the passover'. But since it is not usual to find the word 'feast' combined with 'Passover', it is better to follow the DNV and understand the word 'feast' to go with the following phrase 'during the feast of seven days, unleavened bread will be eaten'. Note that in v. 23, the seven days of the feast are likewise mentioned.

46 : 6 (B) The plur. form *t^{e}mīmim* 'complete, without blemish', in its first occurrence, should be taken as a sing.

46 : 10 (B) The last word should be read as a 3rd pers. sing. verb 'he shall go out' instead of the 3rd pers. plur. of the MT. Cf. the end of v. 9 where the same verb occurs, and in which the Masoretes have clearly indicated their preference for the sing. form. A great number of mss have also written the sing. form *yēṣē'* in both references.

46 : 14 (C) The MT reads at the close 'as a cereal offering to the Lord, perpetual ordinances continually'. Apparently, the plur. noun 'ordinances' refers to the various regulations that are mentioned in the preceding verses—these hold good for all time. The DNV has adhered to the MT even though it is quite usunual. Some mss, however, support the sing. noun *ḥuqqat* 'ordinance'. This evidently means that in early times a simpler text was proposed. A further textual change from the MT *'ōlām* 'for ever' to the form *'ōlat* 'burnt offering' (RSV) has very slim support.

46 : 16 (C) The MT can be translated 'if the prince makes a gift to any of his sons—it is his inheritance; it shall belong to his sons'. This is a clear sentence as it stands. But, since v. 17 states that the prince gives one of his servants 'a present out of his inheritance', many believe that this indicates how v. 16 should be read. For example, the RSV suggests for v. 16 the rendering 'if the prince makes a gift to any of his sons out of his inheritance', i.e. out of the inheritance of the prince. This makes verses 16 and 17 parallel to each other. But it means a change in text and in punctuation, i.e. *minnaḥălātō* must be read instead of the MT *naḥălātō*, and the changed form must be connected with what precedes it. At the close of the verse, the RSV translates 'it is their property by inheritance', the word 'by' standing for the prep. *b^e*. A better translation is 'it is their property as inheritance', which interprets the prep. as the "*b^e* essential" (cf. Cooke, op. cit., p. 515).

46 : 19 (B) The MT reads literally 'unto the chambers, the sanctuary, unto the priests' which the RSV has interpreted as meaning 'to the north row of the holy chambers for the priests'. This change places the text here in substantial agreement with 42 : 13 where we find mention

of the holy chamber where the priests eat. Thus, in 46 : 19 it would appear that we should omit the article and read *b*^{e}*liškōt haqqōdeš* 'in the chambers of the sanctuary', and then read further *'ăšer lakkōhănîm* 'which are to the priests'.

: 22 (C) The meaning of *q*^{e}*ṭurōt*, apparently a pass. part., is not established. The verb *qāṭar* can mean 'to bind', or, possibly 'to close'. This suggests for *q*^{e}*ṭurōt* the meaning 'enclosed space' or 'forecourts'. According to the Mishna, tract. Middot II 5, "inclosed" (*q*^{e}*ṭurōt*) indicates "only that they (i.e. the courts) were not roofed" (cf. *The Mishnah*, translated by H. Danby, p. 592). On the basis of the LXX, the RSV has rendered 'small courts'. But this means an emendation of the text from *q*^{e}*ṭurōt* to *q*^{e}*ṭannōt*. The tradition of the Mishna does not support this conjecture.

: 2 (C) The RSV has 'to the outer gate that faces towards the east'. This translation is obtained by interchanging the words *derek* and *happōne(h)*. The DNV has retained the MT word order, but for the sake of clarity it has added a word. It renders 'to the outer gate, to (the gate) which faced to the east'. Both translations give the same meaning.

: 8 (A) Very early, considerable uncertainty surrounded the latter part of this verse. The text is obscure and the proposed solutions are many (cf. Cooke, *op. cit.*, pp. 520, 523). It is clear that the MT punctuation has a caesura after the word *'ărābā(h)* 'plain'. Accordingly, the RSV has allowed the first part of its translation to pause with 'plain', i.e. 'and goes down into the Arabah;'. The DNV, on the other hand, includes the two words following 'plain' in the sentence before making a pause. It renders 'flows down to the Arabah, and comes into the sea'. What follows in the Hebr is quite incomprehensible 'to the sea (the water) which is made to go out'. Again, on the basis of the ancient versions, emendations have been offered. For example, the reading that is supposed to lie behind the Pesh, is also the starting point for the RSV, i.e. 'the stagnant waters'. Cooke (*op. cit.*, p. 520) states several reasons why he believes the Pesh is wrong. At the same time, one should not consider the RSV translation impossible. It senses a difference between the waters at the beginning of v. 8 that are in full movement (the part. definitely indicates this), and the waters at the end of the verse that may be described as 'stagnant waters' because flow has ceased. The DNV has not chosen any of the proposed textual changes, but has tried to reproduce the meaning of the text as it is by translating 'it is poured out into the sea, so that its waters become healthy'.

47 : 9 (B) Instead of the MT dual form 'two rivers', read the sing. 'the river' (cf. the RSV).

47 : 10 (B) The Hebr has 'a place to spread out nets they will be'. The plur. 'they' is vague. It is better to follow the ancient versions and read a sing. here, i.e. 'it will be a place'.

47 : 17, 18, 19 (B) Three times the form *w^{e}ʾēt* occurs in the MT in connection with three different directions, north, east, and south. Since the fourth direction is found in v. 20, and since the Hebr form there is clearly *zōʾt*, the demonstrative pronoun ('this is the west side'), it is obvious that *zōʾt* should be read for *w^{e}ʾēt* in each of the three previous statements of direction. The difference between *w^{e}ʾēt* and *zōʾt* as far as the Hebr consonants is concerned, is hardly noticeable.

48 : 22 (C) The text states that the 'prince' also receives a strip of landed property, parallel to the territories of the tribes. In the middle of the 'prince's' property, however, are the sections which belong to the Levites and the priests, and that which is regarded as a possession of the holy city. Thus, v. 22 can be translated 'except for the property of the Levites and except for the property of the city, which lie between that of the prince (literally 'in the middle of what belongs to the prince'), that which lies between the territories of Judah and Benjamin will be for the prince'. It is not necessary, then, to follow the RSV in omitting the prep. *min* at the beginning of the verse, nor to make v. 22 a continuation of v. 21. It is better actually to make v. 22 begin a new sentence. Moreover, it is unnecessary with the RSV to omit the words 'property of the Levites'. The following diagram makes clear the probable situation in verses 21 - 22.

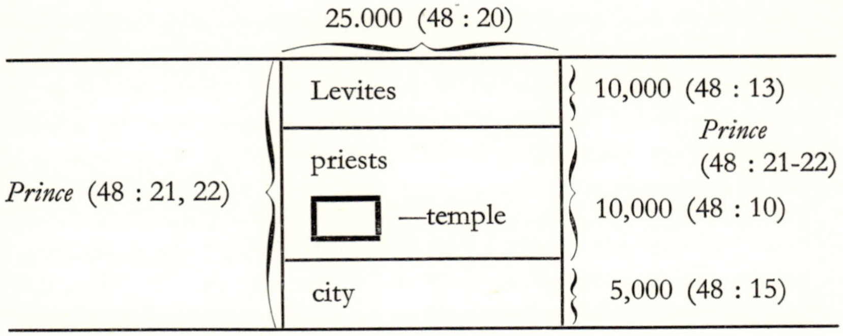

29 (B) The Hebr has ‘from an inheritance’. For the construction of this noun with the verb *nāpal*, cf. 45 : 1 and 47 : 22 and their translations. Thus, 48 : 29 should undoubtedly read ‘which you shall allot as an inheritance’. The DNV agrees with this substantially, though its wording differs slightly. It seems clear, then, that in place of the prep. *min* we should read b^{e}, just as b^{e} is used in 45 : 1 and 47 : 22.

34 (B) For the Hebr ‘their gates three’, translate ‘three gates’, or ‘likewise three gates’.

DANIEL

17 (C) The initial words *hēn ʾītay* have often been rendered ‘behold’ or ‘see’ (cf. the Vg *ecce enim*). But it is doubtful whether the Aram *hēn* can be translated as ‘see’. Montgomery (*The Book of Daniel*, ICC, 1927, pp. 206, 209) does not consider this translation possible (cf. also KBL). The word *hēn*, then, should be rendered ‘if’. The sense of what follows could be ‘if our God whom we worship is able to deliver us’(cf. the RSV margin). This would seem to imply that there is some doubt as to God’s power to save which is probably the reason why some translations have adopted the rendering ‘behold’ or ‘see’ for *hēn*. However, in the light of v. 18, the sense would be that God might leave the three youths to their fate, not because of His inability to effect a deliverance, but because of other reasons that would keep Him from interfering. A different interpretation is found in the RSV text which renders ‘if it be so, our God whom we serve is able to deliver us’. In this case, the clause ‘if it be so’ means ‘if the king’s command simply has to be obeyed’.

3 : 21 (C) According to the RSV note, the translation 'mantle' and 'tunic' is uncertain. KBL renders *sarbāl* as 'trousers or cloak', or 'the long oriental overalls'. For the word *paṭṭiš* (?), KBL suggests 'coat' or 'trousers', and for *karb*^{e}*lā*(*h*) 'a high pointed cap'. Clearly, articles of clothing are intended. The DNV has 'mantles', 'trousers', and 'caps'. Cf. Montgomery (*op. cit.* pp. 211 ff.).

4 : 8 (C)
(MT, 4 : 5) The RSV translates 'spirit of the holy gods'. The Aram has the plur. form for the noun 'god' as well as for the adj. 'holy'. One could defend the translation by the plur. since it is the pagan king Nebuchadnezzar who is speaking. Similarly, the heathen Pharaoh says of Joseph that a 'spirit of the gods' is in him (Gen 41 : 38). It is interesting to note that in the Gen reference, the RSV renders 'Spirit of God'. Here in Dan 4 : 8 it is possible, then, to render 'spirit of the holy God'. The plur. form of the noun does not oppose this, while the plur. form of the adj. can be explained as an assimilation to agree with the nominal form. Cf. Josh 24 : 19 where the plur. noun and plur. adj. should be translated in the sing., i.e. 'a holy God'. Montgomery (*op. cit.*, p. 225) not only prefers a translation in the sing. here in Daniel, but emphatically denies that there is any 'polytheistic expression' found here. The same expression is found in 4 : 6, 15 (RSV, 4 : 9, 18), and in 5 : 11, 14. Naturally, the writer of the book has interpreted such an apparent, polytheistic expression in a monotheistic way.

4 : 9 (C)
(MT, 4 : 6) According to the traditional text, the king asks Daniel to tell not only the explanation, but also the 'visions'. The Aram reads 'the visions of the dream which I saw and its interpretation tell me'. However, according to what follows, the king himself tells Daniel the 'visions'. Hence, usually the word *ḥezwē*(*y*) is changed to *ḥăzī*, and the translation becomes 'here is the dream . . . interpret it' (cf. Montgomery, *op. cit.*, p. 226, and the RSV).

5 : 3 (C) On the basis of 5 : 2 and the ancient versions, the RSV adds 'and silver' after the word 'gold'.

6 : 6 (C)
(MT, 6 : 7) For the stem *r*^{e}*gaš* KBL has 'enter thronging'. Hence, the DNV (cf. the RSV margin) has 'to urge impetuously', which would express the violent emotion and indignation found among the satraps and

those with them who were intent on seeing Daniel's influence ended. Cf. also 6 : 12, 16 (RSV, verses 11, 15). In 6 : 12, one can render 'to rush in' or 'to rush to'. On the other hand, Montgomery (*op. cit.*, pp. 272 f.) supports the translation 'to come by agreement' (cf. the RSV text), in the belief that the joint action or plot of the opposition against Daniel is in view.

18 (C) The RSV has 'no diversions were brought to him' while the DNV
T, renders 'he let nothing be brought to divert him'. The translation of
19) the Aram word *daḥăwān* is not certain. The word has been thought to indicate concubines as well as various kinds of food and music. Since the king spends the night fasting, apparently in strict seclusion, it is best to translate the word *daḥăwān* by 'diversion', a fairly general word. The form of the diversion is not known. Montgomery (*op. cit.*, p. 276) accepts this rendering as a "non-committal translation of an obscure word."

1 (C) The words *rēʾš millīn* can mean 'beginning of the matter' (cf. Montgomery, *op. cit.*, pp. 283 f., and KBL). The translation, accordingly, would be 'then he wrote down the dream. Beginning of the account'. The word *ʾămar* remains untranslated. What points to this as the true sense is the phrase in 7 : 28 *sōpāʾ dī millᵉtā* 'the end of the matter'. The RSV, however, offers a different translation for *rēʾš millīn*, i.e. 'the sum of the matter'. But it is questionable whether *rēʾš* here means 'sum' or 'main point'.

15 (C) The RSV has 'my spirit within me' (cf. also the DNV). This translation is not certain, since the word *nidne(h)* poses a problem. Some suggest that the word comes from *nᵉdan* 'sheath', but in this case the vocalization should be *nidnā(h)*, not *nidne(h)*. A slight change in this word and the preceding word produces the reading *bᵉgīn dᵉnā(h)*. which allows for the translation 'on account of it'. Both the LXX and Vg seem to point to this as the correct reading and translation.

12 (C) Translation difficulties face one here. The RSV has 'and the host was given over to it (i.e. 'the horn') together with the continual burnt-offering through transgression'. On the other hand, it is possible that the word *ṣābāʾ* 'host' here means 'worship'. Also, instead of translating the verb 'was given over', it is possible to render 'was

established'. The words 'to it' (RSV) are not actually in the Hebr text. Moreover, the prep. *'al* rendered 'together with' in the RSV, can also mean 'against' or 'opposite'. Finally, it is possible to render 'in transgression' instead of 'through transgression'. Hence, the DNV has arrived at a translation considerably different from the RSV. The DNV renders 'a form of worship was established in transgression against the continual burnt-offering'. This would mean that the text speaks of sinful, heathen worship, by which the sanctuary was desecrated. In the next part of the verse, the RSV has rendered 'and truth was cast down to the ground'. This means that in place of the pointing of an active verb form in the MT *tašlēk*, the RSV has adopted a pass. form *tušlak*. The DNV, however, has adhered to the MT vocalization *tašlēk*, and apparently taken 'the horn' as the subject. Its translation has 'it cast down the truth to the ground' (cf. Montgomery, *op. cit.*, pp. 336 f). By 'truth' is here meant 'the true religion' or the religion that remains faithful to the law.

8 : 13 (C) The second half of the verse is difficult. The Hebr reads literally 'how long the vision, the continual burnt-offering and the desolating transgression, the giving of both the sanctuary and of the host, the trampling'. It is clear that the words need to be fit together to make a comprehensible and meaningful sentence. Montgomery translates 'for how long is the vision: the Constant, and the desolating Iniquity, the giving of both sanctuary and host to trampling' (*op. cit.*, p. 341). This translation follows the MT closely and can readily be used as a starting-point in the translation of the verse. By 'the Constant' is meant the continual burnt-offering or daily sacrifice. According to Montgomery, the 'vision' refers to all that follows. The contents of the vision are the abolishment of the continual burnt-offering, the desolating Iniquity that replaced it, and the trampling of both sanctuary and host. The 'iniquity' or 'transgression' may indicate the foreign form of worship that was established. On the meaning of 'host', cf. Montgomery (*ibid*).

8 : 27 (C) The RSV translates the first three words 'and I Daniel was overcome'. The Hebr verb form here is a *niph.* of *hāyā(h)* 'to be'. Cf. Dan 2 : 1 where a *niph.* of this verb also occurs and where the translation should be 'it was all over with his sleep' (RSV 'his sleep left him').

In this light, it is better to translate 8 : 27 'it was all over with me', or 'I was worn out' (cf. the DNV). Montgomery, however, believes that 8 : 27 cannot be explained on the basis of 2 : 1, and that the verb form of 8 : 27 comes *not* from *hāyā(h)* 'to be', but from *hāwā(h)* 'to fall'. Hence, his translation reads 'I was befallen', i.e. 'I was stricken' (*op. cit.*, pp. 355 f.).

17 (C) Usually, translations follow the lead of Th and render 'for thy own sake, O Lord'. The change involved in the MT is slight, while it brings the text into agreement with 9 : 19.

22 (C) The first word of the MT *wayyāben* means 'and he made to understand'. The LXX, followed by the RSV, has apparently understood the word *wayyābō'* 'and he came'. This reading would seem to have the support of the context of v. 21 where the approach of Gabriel is noted. Th, however, (followed by the DNV) translates 'and he made me understand', although in reality, the word 'me' is not present in the Hebr.

24 (C) The RSV renders the last two words 'to anoint a most holy place', though its footnote indicates correctly that the MT is indefinite as to whether it is a place, a thing, or a person. In Hebrew usage, however, as Montgomery points out, "the term is used always of sacrosanct things or places: of the tent of meeting, the temple, its *debīr* or *adyton*, of the territory belonging to the temple, the altars, holy vessels, incense, sacrificial flesh, etc." (*op. cit.*, p. 375). The idea is wide-spread among both Jews and Christians that the Messiah is actually indicated in the clause (Montgomery, *op. cit.*. p. 376). The DNV has not chosen this Messianic interpretation, but has left the matter open as far as possible by rendering 'something most holy'.

26 (C) The RSV has 'and after the sixty-two weeks, an anointed one shall be cut off, and shall have nothing'. The translation 'and shall have nothing' is not certain since the MT has simply *wᵉ'ē(y)n lō* 'and not to be to him'. This can mean 'he shall not have', or 'there is not to him', i.e. 'he has not'. But what is the object? Th has supplied an object, i.e. *krima* 'guilt' which does not necessarily mean that Th reads a different text. His rendering is the basis of the DNV translation

which has 'while there was nothing against him', i.e. judicially. Others have taken the text to mean that the anointed one shall be cut off, not for himself, but in the place of, and for the benefit of others. Thus, the clause has been explained as a prophecy of the substitutionary death of Jesus Christ. Today, however, many agree that the destruction of 'an anointed one' refers to the martyred high priest Onias III (cf. 2 Maccabees 4 : 23-34). Another problem, later in the verse, is latent in the clause 'its end shall come with a flood'. The suff. may refer to 'the prince to come' whom one should probably identify with Antiochus Epiphanes, the foreign oppressor. Thus, the translation may be 'his end'. The RSV has rendered the suff. as neuter 'its end', but, does this mean the end of the city or the sanctuary, or both? Or, does it mean the end of the people? The answer is not clear.

9 : 27 (C) The MT reads 'and he shall make strong the covenant for many'. This allows for two different explanations. First, the RSV has 'and he shall make a strong covenant with many'. The sense would be that the prince or ruler shall make a strong alliance with the disloyal Jews who choose his side. The covenant, then, is between the foreign prince or oppressor and the faithless Jews of his time. But a second explanation is suggested by the DNV translation to the effect that the ruler will make the covenant hard, strong, or heavy, for the many. This idea means that the covenant is God's covenant with his people, and this prince will make it difficult for many faithful Jews to continue to maintain the covenant with Yahweh, their true religion (cf. Montgomery, *op. cit.*, p. 385). Cf. the commentaries for the remainder of the verse, especially Montgomery, *op. cit.*, pp. 386 ff. As for translation, it is best to render the text literally even though the meaning thereby may not be clear. In this passage both the DNV and RSV have kept as close as possible to the traditional text.

10 : 13 (C) The MT has 'I was left there'. Attempt has been made by various explanations to keep this text, interpreting it as meaning 'I kept the upper hand', i.e. because Michael came to his rescue. This is, however, a dubious rendering of the *niph.* form of the Hebr verb *yātar*. It is better here to follow the LXX and Th in translating 'I left him there', the 'him' referring to Michael (cf. Montgomery, *op. cit.*, p. 412).

: 6 (C) The MT has 'he that begat her'. However, the context does not seem to refer to 'her' father. Hence, without change in the consonantal text, one can read the form *yaldāh* 'her child', which is the RSV rendering (cf. Montgomery, *op. cit.*, p. 430).

: 7 (C) The MT has *minnēṣer* 'from a branch', though in conjunction with the following word, one should translate 'one of the branches of her roots', or 'a branch from her roots'. No textual change is needed. A similar construction is present in the translation of v. 5 'one of his princes'.

: 17 (C) The MT 'and upright ones' can hardly be correct here. Probably, one should read *mē(y)šārīm*, the same word as in 11 : 6, and thus translate 'and he shall bring terms of peace and perform them' (RSV), or, more literally 'and an agreement with him he shall make' (cf. Montgomery, *op. cit.*, p. 441). It is possible that the individual intended is the one who shall come with the power of his whole kingdom. Somewhat less probable is the DNV explanation 'he shall try to secure power over the whole kingdom of the other, and he will come to terms with him (i.e. the other)'.

: 18 (C) The RSV renders 'but a commander shall put an end to his insolence; indeed he shall turn his insolence back upon him'. This is an example of tautology that Montgomery accepts (*op. cit.*, p. 443). The difficulty lies in the MT word *biltī* which is translated 'indeed' in the RSV. This is a negation 'not' but an unusual occurrence of it, since *biltī* is generally found with an inf. Thus, numerous emendations have been proposed, an example of which is the LXX 'with an oath'. All such suggestions imply that the word *qāṣīn* 'commander' is the subject of *yāšīb*, thus making a tautology unavoidable. The DNV, however, has taken *biltī* as a negation and accepted a different subject for *yāšīb*. The sense would thus be that the commander ends the arrogance of the insolent one without the insolent one being able to pay the commander back with arrogance. Or, as the DNV has rendered 'but a commander shall make him stop his insolence without his being able to revenge his insolence'. The translation remains uncertain since the interpretation of the text is made difficult by the puzzling word *biltī* (cf. Montgomery, *op. cit.*, pp. 443 f.).

HOSEA

The Hebr text of Hosea is difficult and in many places changes have been adopted. Since it is impossible in a book of this kind to deal fully with all of the problems, only a few examples are given.

4 : 4 (B) The Hebr apparently reads 'and your people as those who quarrel with the priests' (?). The DNV and RSV suggest the vocalization *'imm^ekā* 'with you', in place of the MT *'amm^ekā* 'your people', and the reading *rībī hakkōhēn* instead of the MT *kimrībē(y) kōhēn*. Thus, the RSV translates 'for with you is my contention, O priest'. Various commentaries have other suggested conjectures.

4 : 18 (C) The beginning of the verse is difficult. The MT *sār* can be a perf. of the verb *sūr* 'to give way, turn aside'. The difficulty is that the word *sob'ām* is probably the subject, meaning 'their drinking', or 'their drink', or even 'their intoxication' (as a result of much drinking). The translation, then, could possibly be 'when their intoxication is ended (they practise fornication)', or 'when they have stopped drinking (they practise fornication)'. The prophet is apparently expressing how the people go from bad to worse, i.e. when they have had enough to drink, they turn to dissipation and immorality. The RSV has accepted an altered reading, i.e. *sōd sōb'īm* 'a band of drunkards'. With a slight change in text the latter part of the verse can be rendered, 'her shields have fallen in love with shame'. The word 'shields' should be understood in a figurative sense, i.e. 'rulers'. The DNV renders 'their shields love shame', which means that *hēbū* is changed into an inf. abs. from the verb *'āhab*. On the other hand, the AV has translated 'her rulers with shame do love, Give ye'. This indicates that the AV has interpreted *hēbū* as an impv. of the verb *yāhab* 'to give', a sense that is very doubtful in this context. Furthermore, the prep. 'with' is not present in the Hebr. The RSV renders 'they love shame more than their glory'. This has partial support from the LXX which rendered the final word of the Hebr as though it were 'pride' or 'insolence'. Accordingly, KBL suggests that in this case *māgēn* means 'insolent' (cf. Driver, JTS, 34, pp. 383 f.). If this suggestion is correct, then the translation can be 'they love the shame of the insolent ones', or 'their insolent ones love

shame'. Cf. H. W. Wolff in *Dodekapropheton* (Bibl. Komm. XIV), 1957, pp. 89 f.

2 (C) The beginning of the verse presents some real problems. A slight change in text allows for the translation 'they have made deep the pit of Shittim' (cf. the RSV and the commentaries). This conjecture, however, is not based on the ancient versions, which, in turn, offer no help in unraveling the puzzling MT. Two other translations are 'the unfaithful have made a deep pit' and 'they have made the pit of unfaithfulness deep', but both are uncertain.

: 11 (C) The final word of the MT is *ṣāw* 'commandment', which does not make sense in this context. Probably the reading *šāw'* 'vanity' (= idolatry) should be adopted (cf. the LXX and RSV). While this interpretation is the best, it is uncertain.

: 7 (C) The MT has *kᵉʾādām* 'like Adam' (cf. the account in Gen), though the question remains as to the meaning of the breaking of the covenant by Adam. The Vg has *sicut Adam* which rendering follows the MT. The MT may mean 'like men, humanly'. On the other hand, since the adverb *šām* 'there' occurs in the next clause, perhaps one should adopt a slight change in text to produce the reading *bᵉʾādām* 'in Adam' or 'at Adam' which may designate a place of this name near the Jordan river where, at some time, a covenant was broken. The meaning is not clear. It is conceivable that the MT as it is might mean 'like the people of Adam'.

: 9 (C) The first word *ḥakkē(y)* is generally thought to stand for *ḥakkōt*, inf. of the stem *ḥākā(h)* 'to wait for, spy upon, lie in wait'. Instead of the noun *ḥeber* 'company', the RSV following the example of the versions (cf. the Pesh) has read a verbal form 'are banded together'. It is possible, however, to retain the noun form and translate 'like a gang of robbers, the company of priests lies in wait'.

: 12 (C) The RSV renders 'I will chastise them for their wicked deeds'. This translation has thus interpreted the verbal form *'aysirēm* as derived from *y s r* 'to chastise'. This is possible. Others believe the stem to be *' s r* 'to bind, shut up'. Since the verse depicts God as trapping Ephraim like birds are trapped, *ʾ s r* might have the meaning here 'to catch'. The final word is rendered 'for their wicked deeds' in the RSV which results from the reading *rāʿātām*, whereas the Hebr text has *ʿădātām* 'their congregation'. Thus, a literal translation for the last part of the verse would be 'in agreement with the preaching to their congregation'. This rendering is very unlikely. Generally, the word *ʿēdā(h)* means 'congregation', but in Judg 14 : 8, one finds *ʿēdā(h)* meaning 'a swarm (of bees)'. Here in Hos 7 : 12 it could mean 'swarm', that is swarm or flock of birds. The word *šēmaʿ* from *šāmaʿ* 'to hear', possibly means here 'noise' or 'tumult'. These considerations point to the rendering 'I shall bind (catch) them as soon as there is noise in their crowd', i.e. as soon as I notice that there is a large swarm of birds, I shall catch them. The MT can thus be retained. Cf. the DNV translation 'as soon as their swarm becomes noisy, I will take them captive'.

7 : 16 (C) The first part of this verse is most difficult. Every attempt at translating the MT produces an uncertain result. Literally, the text has 'they turn back, not, height' (?). Thus, some translations have 'they turn, but not upwards', i.e. their conversion is not genuine. But this is uncertain. Another suggestion is to emend the text to read 'to Baal', but this means omitting the negative *lōʾ*, whereas the ancient versions retain the negative in their respective translations. Still another possibility is to lengthen out the word *ʿāl* so that it becomes a verbal form *yōʿil*, thus allowing for the translation 'they turn to that which has no use' (i.e. idols); or some read *ʾēlay* '(but not) to me'.

8 : 10 (C) The second part of the verse is puzzling. The consonants *w y ḥ l w* can be read as follows:

wayyāḥēllū (MT)	'and they shall begin'
weyēḥēlū	'and they shall suffer'
weyōḥīlū	'and they shall expect'

Translated literally, the rest of the verse has 'a little from the utterance of the king of princes' (probably the king of Assyria). But what does this mean? One translation has 'they shall begin to decline because of the burden of the king of princes', but the translation 'decline' for *ʿmeʿāṭ* 'little', is very doubtful just as the translation 'begin' for the verb is uncertain. The AV renders 'and they shall sorrow a little for the burden of the king of princes'. But actually, they would have to suffer greatly! The DNV has 'they have little to hope for from the utterance of the king of princes'. Another possibility is 'they have little to expect from the burden of the king of princes', i.e. one should not think too lightly about it. All of these suggested translations are built upon the MT. If one adopts the LXX as his basic text, then the result is similar to the RSV translation 'and they shall cease for a little while from anointing kings and princes'. This means that the main verb is taken as *ḥādal* not *ḥālal*, and that an inf. of *māšaḥ* is read instead of *maśśā'*, and that the connective *wᵉ* 'and' is to be inserted after the word *melek* 'king'. However, even if these changes should be accepted, nothing is really known about an anointing of *śārîm* 'princes'.

13 (C) The remarkable *habhābay* has had detailed discussion in commentaries. It might denote some kind of animal, but probably those who connect the word with the verb *'āhab* 'to love' are correct. It is possible, then, to agree with the RSV rendering 'they love sacrifice'. But it is also possible to vary this translation somewhat, i.e. 'they like to bring sacrifice, meat, and they eat of it'. Every translation has the cloud of uncertainty about it.

6 (C) The verse begins with a perf. which is followed by several imperfects. It is possible, however, to understand the perf. as part of a conditional sentence, i.e. 'if they have escaped (literally 'gone away') from destruction, Egypt will assemble them'. The readings *yēlᵉkū 'aššūr* 'they will go to Assyria', or *hōlᵉkîm 'aššūr* 'they are going to Assyria' are not only conjectural, but they introduce into the text a deportation to Assyria which is probably out of the question. On the other hand, a literal translation has to face the question as to the meaning of 'destruction' in this context. The AV has 'they are gone because of destruction', a translation that is grammatically not impossible.

10 (C) Literally the Hebr reads 'they have consecrated themselves to shame'. The word 'shame' (*bōšet*) most probably is a synonym for Baal-Peor that has just been mentioned. The question arises as to

whether the translation here should be 'shame' (= disgrace). If Hosea refers to Baal as the god who was a 'disgrace' to Israel, the word 'disgrace' can remain in the translation here (cf. Saul's son and successor who had both the name *Ish-baal* and *Ishbosheth*). On the other hand, if one believes that the name of Baal in Hos 9 : 10 was later replaced by the despicable *bōšet*, then the word Baal should probably be restored in translation. But this is not altogether necessary.

9 : 13 (A) This verse is puzzling. The ancient versions do not shed much light upon it. The DNV has attempted to reproduce the text literally in rendering 'Ephraim as I had seen it was a Tyrus planted in a field; but now Ephraim must hand over his sons to the murderer'. In the first part of the verse it is uncertain whether 'God' is the subject of the verb 'to see', and if the Hebr word *ṣōr* means Tyre. Furthermore, it is not certain that the reading *šᵉtūlā(h)* is actually correct, nor is it clear to what it refers. The one positive contribution of the versions is their lack of mention of Tyre. The LXX takes 13a as more or less a parallel of 13b. Thus, to parallel the second part in which Ephraim delivers his sons to the slaughter, the LXX in the first part makes Ephraim's sons become the spoil of the chase. This means that the text has to be changed drastically. The RSV has not held back from doing this in translating 'Ephraim's sons, as I have seen, are destined for a prey'. There is another possible solution to the problem here. Since, in v. 13b, an inf. follows the prep. *lᵉ*, this may be the case in 13a. That is, one can vocalize *lᵉṣōr* as *lᵉṣūr* 'to gather, bind'. Also, because v. 13b has the word 'people' (literally 'his sons') as the object of the inf. *lᵉhōṣī'* 'to bring forth', so the suggested vocalization *lᵉṣūr* may have a similar object in the word *šᵉtūlā(h) bᵉnāwe(h)* 'planted in a field'. Since *šᵉtūlā(h)* is a fem. pass. part., it can mean 'that which is planted in a field', and even 'those who are planted in a field'. It does not seem impossible that here, couched in poetical terms, the writer may be indicating the people who lived in the country, i.e. the population. Thus while retaining the Hebr consonantal text as it stands, it is possible to translate as follows 'Ephraim, as I see it (or 'have seen'), shall bind together those planted in a field (i.e. his own people), yea, Ephraim shall hand over his sons to the murderer'. The meaning of the whole verse would be that Ephraim works out his own destruction. It is clear that this translation cannot be proved

beyond doubt to be correct, but it seems to be worth considering and perhaps it will open up new and fruitful discussion on this most difficult text.

3 (B) Generally the difficult word *qāḥām* is considered to be a verbal form with suff. from *lāqaḥ* 'to take' (with the loss of the unaccented initial consonant *l*ᵉ). However, this means a form of the 3rd pers. whereas the context calls for a form of the 1st pers. It is perhaps better to follow the LXX and Tg and read 'I took them up in my arms' (LXX = 'him' instead of 'them'). This means two textual changes should be made. First, for *qāḥām* one should read *'eqqāḥēm*, 1st pers. sing. impf. with the 3rd masc. plur. suff. And second, the word 'his arms' should be changed slightly to read 'my arms'.

7 (C) Like many passages in Hosea, this verse, especially its beginning, has challenged the ingenuity of many commentators. Most of the "solutions" involve textual changes which are not always clear nor always based on versional evidence. The word *tᵉlū'īm* can be taken as a plur. pass. part. meaning 'hung up, suspended'. The noun *mᵉšūbā(h)* can mean 'faithlessness' or 'apostasy' (cf. 14 : 4). Thus, with the 1st pers. sing. suff. the meaning could be 'the turning away from me'. Hence, the translation of the first part of the verse can be 'my people is hung up on the turning away from me', i.e. my people persists in its apostasy from me' (RSV = 'my people are bent on turning away from me'). The remainder of the verse has been rendered 'and even if they call to Him (i.e. God) on high, He shall not lift them up', or 'even if they call to Him on high, they shall not lift themselves up together' (cf. the *'al* here with 7 : 16). A different vocalization of *'al* yields the translation 'yoke'. Thus the RSV has 'so they are appointed to the yoke (literally 'they call it, i.e. the people, to the yoke') and none shall remove it'.

: 8 (C) The MT, literally translated, has 'Ephraim said, verily I am rich,
T, 9) I have made myself a fortune. All my possessions—they do not find in me an injustice which is sin'. Apparently Ephraim concludes from his great material prosperity that he is rightly related to God and that his wealth surely means that God is pleased with him. Moreover, if he were unjust or disobedient to God's law, punishment would be

inevitable and his social position less prosperous. This is a possible explanation of the verse. But even if this interpretation should be correct, the above translation meets with some objections. The translation 'an injustice which is sin' definitely cannot mean that there is an injustice which is not sin. Rather the text means 'an injustice which is surely sin'. With the aid of the LXX, the RSV arrives at a different translation for this latter part of the verse, rendering 'but all his riches can never offset the guilt he has incurred'. This means that 'his riches' is read instead of the MT 'my riches', that *ḥāṭā'* 'he has incurred' is read instead of *ḥēṭ'* 'sin' of the Hebr, and that *māṣā'* is understood to mean 'to be sufficient for' or 'to offset' (cf. Lev 12 : 8). Thus the RSV takes this part of the verse to be the observation of the prophet on Ephraim's boast of his self-sufficiency. Cf. the commentaries.

JOEL

1 : 4 (C) Either the verse describes four different kinds of locusts or it indicates the four stages in the development of the locust. According to KBL *gāzām* is a 'caterpillar', while the RSV renders it 'the cutting locust' (others 'the shearer'). The word *'arbe(h)* is 'the fully developed locust with wings' (KBL), translated 'the swarming locust' in the RSV. The third word *yeleq* according to KBL is 'the creeping, unwinged phase of locust', rendered 'hopping locust' in the RSV and by others 'the hopper'. The fourth word *ḥāsīl* is given as 'cockroach' in KBL but as 'destroying locust' in the RSV, and by others, 'the stripper'. The verb *ḥāsal* clearly means 'to eat everything bare'. Thus, it is difficult to translate precisely the creatures with their several characteristics.

1 : 10 (C) The RSV renders 'the wine fails'. If the form *hōbīš* is viewed as derived from *yābēš*, the translation can be 'the wine is dried up' (cf. the AV and BSG)).

1 : 17 (C) The RSV rendering 'the seed shrivels under the clods' is uncertain. However, the Hebr verb *'ābaš* is explained as a cognate of the verb *'abasa* in Arabic meaning 'to dry up, shrivel'. Another suggested but rather improbable translation here is 'to rot'. Instead of the

rendering 'clods', some have suggested that *megrāpā(h)* here means 'spade' or 'rake' (KBL).

2 (C) The MT followed by the DNV has *kᵉšaḥar* 'like dawn'. The RSV without change in consonants has adopted a different vocalization, i.e. *kišḥōr* 'like blackness'.

6 (C) The DNV renders 'all faces became pale with fear' while the RSV has 'all faces grow pale'. According to KBL, the word *pā'rūr* means 'glow', i.e. all faces gather glow, or glow with excitement. But another explanation is that the faces gather the 'blushing' or hold back the 'blushing' and thus become pale. Hence, the DNV and RSV translations are just as probable as the explanation offered in KBL.

7 (C) The RSV translates 'they do not swerve from their paths'. In a note, the RSV mentions that it is following the LXX since the Hebr should really be translated 'take a pledge'. It is true that *'ābaṭ* means 'to take a pledge' in the simple *qal* form, but here the form is the *pi.* intensive. KBL here not only cites another meaning for *'ābaṭ*, i.e. 'to tear, rend in pieces', but also refers to a note by G. R. Driver who compares the Arabic *'abaṭa*. The Arabic verb means 'spoiling or disturbing what is sound or intact'. Thus, without a change in the text, Joel 2 : 7 can be rendered 'they shall not break line'. The DNV has translated rather freely 'they do not walk among each other'.

23 (C) The RSV translates 'for he has given the early rain for your vindication', while the AV has 'for he hath given you the former rain moderately'. In both cases, the word *mōre(h)* is rendered 'early rain' which is possible. But *mōre(h)* can also mean 'teacher'. Similarly, the word *liṣdāqā(h)* can mean 'as it ought to be' or 'moderately', but also 'according to righteousness'. Thus, the phrase *mōre(h) liṣdāqā(h)* can be translated 'a teacher of righteousness' as the DNV does in its rendering 'he gives you the teacher of righteousness'. In the OT, the sending of rain in its season is often made dependent on listening to the law and obedience to the commandments of God (Lev 26 : 3, 4; Deut 11 : 13, 14; 1 Kings 8 : 35, 36). Hence, the possibility of an alternative rendering here should be acknowledged. The feeling of

the translator on the sense of the passage will, of course, be one determining factor in his translation.

3 : 11 (B) (MT, 4:11) The first word *ʿûšû* is rather strange for it is apparently the impv. form of the verb *ʿûš* 'to help' cf. KBL. But how does this meaning fit the verse? For this reason, many read either *ḥûšû* from *ḥûš* 'to hasten', or *ʿûrû* from *ʿûr* 'to awake'.

AMOS

2 : 13 (C) The DNV renders 'I will cause it to creak under you as a cart creaks which is filled to overflowing with sheaves'. The metaphor of the creaking cart serves to emphasize the moaning and groaning of the people in their terror and distress. Another translation is 'I will make it totter beneath you as a cart tottereth that is full of sheaves' (cf. Harper, *Amos and Hosea*, ICC, 1936, p. 61). KBL likewise offers the translation of the verb 'to totter' in this context. The RSV has 'I will press you down in your place, as a cart full of sheaves presses down'. A certain amount of uncertainty is present in the translation of the verse.

2 : 15 (B) The form *yᵉmallēṭ*, *pi.* impf. occurs twice in this verse (once in the preceding verse). In its first occurrence here the translation of the whole clause should apparently be 'he who is swift of foot shall not save'. Are we to understand that there is an unexpressed object of the verb, i.e. 'he shall not save his life'? Note that the object *napšô* is expressed with the verb in its second occurrence. It is possible that in its first occurrence, on the basis of the LXX, the *pi.* form *yᵉmallēṭ* should be pointed as a *niph.*, i.e. *yimmālēṭ*, to be translated with the negative as 'he shall not escape' (DNV) or 'shall not save himself' (RSV).

3 : 3 (C) The RSV has rendered the clause well 'unless they have made an appointment'. Another possibility is 'unless they have come to an agreement' or 'unless they have got together'.

3 : 9 (B) The MT has 'Ashdod' which the DNV has retained. The RSV, however, following the LXX, has translated 'Assyria' which has the

advantage of the context where another great power 'Egypt' is mentioned.

11 (C) The word *ṣar* can mean 'distress', but more probably here it means 'enemy'. Hence, the RSV has 'an adversary shall surround the land', which though not altogether literal, is possible. On the other hand, it is possible to follow the MT closely and translate 'the enemy!' And all around the land!' The expressions would thus be taken as the excited cries of the prophet.

12 (C) A question surrounds the last two words of the MT *dᵉmešeq ʿāreś*. KBL suggests that the meaning is the inlaid ivory couches of Damascus, thus a 'Damascus-bed'. Others propose 'the silk damask'. Harper (*op. cit.*, p. 82) says, "we have a picture of Samaria's nobles lying free from care on soft couches". The DNV has 'the soft garment'. The RSV has rendered 'part of a bed' but it is not clear what the basis of this translation is. Some have conjectured the word *rōʾš*.

3 (B) The MT has a *hiph.* (active) form 'you shall cast'. This does not suit the context and so, retaining the same consonants, it is better to point them as a *hoph.* (passive) form 'you shall be cast forth' (RSV) or 'you shall be dragged away' (DNV). This change to the passive form has the support of the LXX. Aq, however, interprets the verb as active.

5 (C) The RSV translates 'offer a sacrifice of thanksgiving of that which is leavened' which reflects a possible sense of the prep. *min*. Since, however, Lev 7 : 12 specifies that in the sacrifice of thanksgiving *unleavened* cakes must be used, the reference here in Amos appears contradictory. This could be explained by understanding that the instruction of Lev 7 : 12 is of a later date, or by understanding that in northern Israel there was prevalent a custom different from that in Judah. On the other hand, it is possible to interpret the prep. as the *min* of privation which allows for the translation 'offer a sacrifice of thanksgiving without that which is leavened'. This translation is grammatically possible and puts the verse in agreement with Lev 7 : 12.

9 (A) Various translations reflect the difficulty in translating the word

harbōt. Some have the rendering of the construct *harbōt* with the following word as 'many of your gardens', others 'the multiplying of your gardens', still others 'much mildew', and finally some have taken *harbōt* alone as an adverb meaning 'most' or 'often'. Perhaps all of this is one reason why some have proposed the conjectured reading *heḥĕrabtī* 'I laid waste' (cf. the DNV and RSV). Cf. Harper (*op. cit.*, pp. 99 f.).

4 : 10 (C) The DNV (cf. also the BSG) has rendered 'I have killed your young men with the sword when capturing your horses'. Thus, the prep. *ʿim* is taken to mean 'at the same time as'. Harper (*op. cit.* p. 101) believes *ʿim* here has the meaning 'besides'. The RSV is rather free in its rendering 'I carried away your horses.

5 : 11 (B) The sing. form *maśʾat* should be read as a plur. *maśʾōt* (cf. the LXX, the AV 'burdens', DNV 'presents', and RSV 'exactions').

5 : 26 (B, C) The Hebr order 'your images, your star-god' is usually inverted in translations. It is probably impossible to end satisfactorily the discussion on whether one should translate 'but you have carried around' or 'you shall take up'. Cf. the RSV and the commentaries, for example Harper (*op. cit.*, pp. 137 f.).

6 : 12 (A) In the second half of the verse, both the DNV and the RSV insert the word 'sea'. In the Hebr text the word *yām* 'sea' is obtained by taking the plur. ending of *bᵉqārīm* as an independent word, and thus reading *babbāqār yām* 'with oxen the sea'. Many accept this change although the ancient versions do not support it.

8 : 3 (C) The RSV has 'they shall be cast out in silence' but this translation is uncertain. It is possible to render with the DNV 'in every place he casts (them) out! Be silent!' In keeping with this idea, Harper says, 'so deep is the despair, and so great the danger, that silence is enjoined by those who are removing their dead" (*op. cit.*, p. 182). Thus, keeping to the MT, the word *hās* can be explained either as an adverb (RSV) or as an impv. (DNV).

8 : 8 (B) Instead of *kāʾōr* 'like the light', one should read *kayᵉʾōr* 'like the

Nile'. This secures a close connection with the end of the verse as well as with 9 : 5. Furthermore, many Hebr mss as well as the LXX and Tg support this reading.

OBADIAH

B) The Hebr *laḥmᵉkā* 'your bread' does not give any sense here. The LXX omitted it. It is possible that in translation a word such as *'ōkᵉlē (y)* should be supplied, and thus the translation could be 'they who ate your bread' (cf. the AV). Still another possibility is to vocalize the word as a plur. part. with suff., i.e. *lōḥăme(y)kā* 'they who eat your bread' or 'they who eat bread with you' (cf. the DNV), but the RSV has 'your trusted friends'. The thought apparently in the RSV is that whoever dines with another person is supposedly his friend.

(B) With a bit of good will, the MT can be translated 'the exiles of this army of the Israelites'. The phrase 'this army' is puzzling here and it has been supposed that the word *haḥēl* indicates the name of some place or district. According to 2 Kings 17 : 6, the king of Assyria exiled Jews of the northern kingdom, Israel, to a place called *ḥalaḥ* 'Halah' in Assyria. Perhaps then, *haḥēl* should be read *ḥàlaḥ* denoting this Assyrian town. An additional factor supporting this argument is the clause that comes later in the verse 'the exiles of Jerusalem'. Accordingly, the RSV renders 'the exiles in Halah who are of the people of Israel'. A further difficulty in the verse is the relative pron. *'ăšer*. The RSV and others have read the form *yirᵉšū* 'shall possess' (both *'ăšer* and *yirᵉšū* are found in the next part of the verse). The DNV, on the other hand, has read *'ereṣ* 'land' instead of *'ăšer* in the first part of this verse.

MICAH

5 (B) The MT reads literally 'what (are) the high places of Judah'. The DNV has added between brackets 'the sin of', i.e. 'what is the sin of the high places of Judah'. This is a clarifying addition because of the parallel phrase in the first part of the verse 'transgression of Jacob'. The RSV has followed the LXX reading 'what is the sin of the house of Judah'. This provides no translation for *bāmōt* 'high places'. It may be that in place of *bāmōt*, the LXX reads *ḥaṭṭaṭ (bē(y)t*.

1 : 11 (A) The last phrase of the verse reads literally 'takes away from you his (or, its) standing place'. This is rendered literally in the RSV but it does not make a great deal of sense. Points of contact with the context escape us and thus any construction or reconstruction of the text becomes very subjective. The DNV has attempted to clarify the text by translating 'prevent you staying there', but this is uncertain.

2 : 4 (C) The RSV translates 'he changes the portion of my people'. Since the verb *mūr* means 'to exchange', the sense of the sentence is that 'the inheritance of my people' is transferred to other hands (cf. the DNV). In the following clause, the verb *mūš* in the *hiph.* form means 'to remove (something)' or 'to make (something) give way'. Whereas the Hebr has *lī* 'for me', the meaning probably is that the inheritance is removed so that it is actually withheld 'from me'. Hence, the RSV is perhaps essentially correct in translating 'how he removes it from me'. The last three words of the verse are difficult. The DNV renders the MT 'he divides our fields to the rebellious'. Instead of the form *šōbēb*, the RSV suggests that the word *šōbē(y)nū* 'those who take us captive' should be read. Thus the RSV renders 'among our captors he divides our fields'. But textual change is not necessary in view of the adequate translation the DNV has given for the MT. Another possibility, however, is that *šōbēb* can be an inf. of *šūb* 'to bring back'. The object of the inf. would then be 'our fields' while the verb *yeḥallēq* 'he shall make the division' or 'he shall divide it in parts', can become an independent sentence. Furthermore, the word *'ē(y)k* 'how' that occurs shortly before, can also be connected with *yeḥallēq*. The translation would then be 'how shall he divide the parts, to restore our fields (to us)'. Cf. Eerdmans, *Essays in Masoretic Psalms*, OTS, I, pp. 185 f.

2 : 8 (A) The text reads 'and yesterday my people takes action as an enemy'. The DNV has translated the Hebr word *'etmūl* 'yesterday' as 'for a long time'. A change in text in which the verb is read as a 2nd pers. masc. sing. instead of the 3rd pers. masc. sing. results in the translation 'but you rise against my people as an enemy' (RSV). This means also that the word *'etmūl* is divided into two words *'attem* 'you ' and *le* here meaning 'against'. In the following clause, the word *'eder*

'splendor, magnificence' is used here in the sense of 'robe of state' or 'mantle' which is actually the meaning of *'adderet*. It may be that the original text here had *'adderet* and the final consonant *t* dropped out by haplography. Moreover, in place of the word *śalmā(h)* 'garment', it is perhaps preferable to read *šālēm*, the consonant *h* then to be taken as the article before the following word. In this way the RSV arrives at the translation 'you strip the robe from the peaceful'.

3 (B) The Hebr has literally 'and lays them apart as in a pot and as meat in a kettle'. The DNV renders 'and lays them apart as meat in a pot or in a kettle'. The LXX has rendered the word 'meat' twice though with two different words. This means that it read *kiš'ēr* instead of the MT *ka'ăšer*. The RSV follows the LXX 'and chop them up like meat in a kettle, like flesh in a caldron'.

6 (A) In the vocalized text the second phrase of the verse has apparently a verbal form 'and it shall become dark'. By a slight change in vocalization only, the verbal form can be made a substantive meaning 'darkness'. Most translations follow this change in vocalization which expresses the meaning well.

10 (B) The sing. part. 'who builds' should be understood as a plur. (cf. the LXX and Tg) since in the whole context the subject is in the plur. number. The AV, DNV, and RSV, have all translated the part. in the plur.

10 (A) The Hebr word *gōḥī*, impv. of a verb meaning 'to break out' or 'to break loose', is not clear in its meaning in this context. Usually, one chooses another verb with the meaning 'to groan, cry out, moan' that fits the context better.

13 (B) The RSV footnote indicates that in the MT the verb 'to devote' is in the form of the 1st pers. sing. The 1st pers. clearly does not fit the context. However, no change in pointing is necessary since one can view the form as being the archaic 2nd pers. fem. sing.

1 (C) The MT reads 'now, make incisions, daughter of the band'. The
T, Hebr words *bat gᵉdūd* can designate the members of the band or part-

4 : 14) ners in the band. The sentence could also be rendered 'gather together ye partners in the band'. However, if in place of *bat gedūd* one reads *hitgōdēd*, the inf. belonging to the preceding verbal form, the translation becomes like the BSG rendering 'now you will cut yourselves deeply'. The RSV on the basis of the LXX understands the forms to be from the stem *gādar* and renders 'now you are walled about with a wall'. This rendering fits the context but it requires a textual change.

5 : 5 (B) (MT, 4) Instead of the word *be'armenōtē(y)nū* 'in our palaces', the LXX read *be'admātēnu* 'upon our soil'. This secures the parallelism 'land . . . soil' which is perhaps preferable to the Hebr (cf. the RSV). The DNV has kept to the MT.

5 : 6 (B) (MT, 5) Should the text be rendered 'he shall deliver', i.e. God, or 'they shall deliver'? Perhaps it is better to adopt a plur. pers. here which could then be taken to refer back to 'the shepherds and princes' mentioned in the previous verse. The statement would then be understood as a reckless claim of the people.

6 : 10 (A) The beginning of the verse is not clear. The translation 'another man' is not certain nor does it make sense. The DNV has taken the clause 'treasures of wickedness' as subject. Moreover, it has read some form similar to *hayēš* since its translation reads 'are there not yet'. In addition, for the sake of clarity, it has inserted the prep. 'in'. The RSV translation 'can I forget' is based on a change in text that has often been adopted.

6 : 16 (B) The MT reads literally 'he shall guard himself the decrees of Omri'. This contains no satisfactory sense in this context. The DNV has attempted to solve the problem by rendering the sentence in the pass., i.e. 'for the statutes of Omri are maintained'. On the basis of the ancient versions, it is possible to read the first word of the MT as a 2nd pers. form, i.e. 'for you have kept' (RSV). This has the further support of the context since later in the verse, a verbal form in the 2nd pers. is used. Later in the verse, the RSV renders 'your inhabitants' instead of 'its inhabitants' and 'the scorn of the peoples' instead of 'the scorn of my people' (cf. the LXX). The DNV here keeps to the MT, which has an intelligible meaning.

(C) The Hebr literally has 'on the evil (their) hands to do good' which the DNV has translated as 'the hands are good to do evil'. Whether this is a correct translation or not, the Hebr apparently means that they are out to do evil though they appear to want to do good. The RSV renders 'their hands are upon what is evil, to do it diligently'. Later in the verse, the RSV translates literally 'and the great man utters the evil desire of his soul'. The DNV has a free translation here 'the great man speaks at his own pleasure'. Possibly the verb *dābar* here means 'to follow' (cf. KBL, *dābar* I) like the Arabic word *dabara*. The translation would then be 'the great man follows the desire of his soul', i.e. he does what he wishes to do.

2 (B) The Hebr reads 'from Assyria and the cities of Egypt'. It is quite clear that instead of *ʿārē(y)* one should read *ʿădē(y)* (*resh* for *daleth*), i.e. 'from Assyria to Egypt'. Likewise at the end of the verse, on the basis of the LXX, one should read 'from sea to sea and from mountain to mountain' in place of the MT 'and sea from sea and mountain to mountain'.

4 (B) The sing. form *šōkᵉnī* should probably be read as a plur. *šōkᵉnē(y)* 'inhabitants of' or 'who dwell' (cf. the LXX). This would accord with the plur. form *yirʿū* later in the verse. Cf. v. 15 where the RSV translates the Hebr sing. 'him' by 'them'.

9 (B) The Hebr has 'their sins' but the parallelism of the verse calls for the reading 'our sins' which the LXX has.

NAHUM

3 (B) The DNV has followed the MT in reading *mᵉqōmāh* 'her place', the suff. referring to 'earth' or 'world'. The RSV, however, has read the form as *qāmā(y)w* 'his adversaries', translating 'he will make a full end of his adversaries'. The change has the support of the LXX though with this qualification: the LXX reads the form with the latter part of the verse which the RSV does not.

9 (B) The Hebr apparently reads 'Yahweh will utterly destroy; then oppression will not raise its head again'. BH suggests the reading 'his opponents do not rise up a second time'. This change, which is void of versional support, was apparently introduced by an inter-

pretation of v. 8 where 'opponents' are mentioned. Partly on the basis of the LXX and partly by conjecture, the RSV changed the text to read 'he will not take vengeance twice on his foes'. This is not an established translation, and thus it is better to adhere to the MT.

1 : 10 (C) The verse is difficult. The words 'and like their drunkard drunken' are puzzling, though perhaps they mean 'drunken to their drunkard's nature'. The words have been omitted by some as a dittography of the preceding words (cf. the RSV). The word *'ukk^{e}lū* undoubtedly connects with what follows, i.e. 'they are consumed like dry stubble'. The last word of v. 10, *mālē'*, is rendered as 'completely' in the DNV. However, the RSV has read the word as *hălō'* and made it the first word of v. 11. V. 11, then, becomes interrogative in sense 'did one not come out from you'. The DNV retains *mālē'* in v. 10 and understands v. 11 as a positive sentence 'from you came forth someone'.

1 : 11 (C) See 1 : 10.

1 : 12 (B, C) The RSV notes that the first part of the verse is uncertain. The textual difficulty lies in the word *w^{e}kēn*. Literally, the passage reads 'if in full strength (or 'strong') and likewise numerous, and likewise shall they be cut off'. Since *w^{e}kēn* occurs twice, it is possible that it could be omitted in its first occurrence. It is also possible to translate 'although they are in full strength and likewise numerous, thus they shall be cut off'. The thought evidently is that not only are they strong in their vast numbers, but also in the total dedication of strength and power of each one—quantitatively and qualitatively. The RSV has a free rendering 'though they be strong and many' while the BSG through a drastic emendation of the text, has arrived at the translation 'when many days are fulfilled'. It is not advisable to follow a conjecture of this kind. A translation problem is also present in the word *w^e'ābār*. The form is sing. and its subject is not clear from the context. Since the Tg (cf. also the RSV) reads the verb in the plur., it is advisable to do this in translation. The RSV renders 'they will be cut off and pass away'.

2 : 3 (B, C) (MT, 4) The translation 'steel' has been proposed for the word *p^{e}lādōt*. Hence, the DNV has 'in the fiery light of the steel stand the chariots'.

Others think a metathesis has occurred, i.e. *p*^{e}*lādōt* appeared in the text later by an interchange of the consonants of the original *lappīd* 'torch'. This explanation would mean that the translation should be 'like the fiery light of torches, the chariots'. The RSV has 'the chariots flash like flame' which rendering implies a slight change in text including the reading *lappīd*. In the final clause, for the MT *b*^{e}*rōšīm* 'cypresses', the DNV has 'lances', the idea being that the lances are made of cypress wood. KBL no longer mentions this possibility in his lexicon. The LXX has read *pārāšīm* 'horses' which has been accepted by the RSV (= 'chargers'). The final word of the verse *hor'ālū* comes from *rā'al* which, according to Ges-Buhl, means here in its *hoph.* form 'to be shaken' or 'to be waved'. A different view is that the verb should be connected with *r*^{e}*'ālā(h)* 'a veil', thus associated with the dressing or adorning of horses with plumes. The RSV translates the last two words as 'the chargers prance'.

7 (C) The first word of the MT *w*^{e}*huṣṣab* has been taken by some as a
T, 8) verbal form to be translated 'and it is decided' or 'it is established'. Others have viewed the word as a woman's name (cf. the AV), but this idea lacks support. The RSV has accepted the reading *huṣ*^{e}*'ā(h)* 'she is carried away' in place of the MT *w*^{e}*huṣṣab*. Furthermore, the RSV rendering 'its mistress' reflects a reading *ba'ălātāh* instead of the MT *hō'ălātā(h)* 'she is carried (up)'. And finally, the RSV has apparently inverted the order of the first and second words, translating 'its mistress is stripped, she is carried off'.

8 (A) The MT words *mīmē(y) hī'* 'since the days of her (she)' consist of
T, 9) the strange combination of a construct noun followed by a pers. pron. The ancient versions provide no help. If one retains the reading *mīmē(y)*, it is, of course, to be traced to the noun *yāmīm* 'days' (cf. the AV 'of old' and the DNV 'as long as it exists'). Ordinarily, however, one would not expect a construction of this kind with the separated pers. pron. The common idiom is the noun with the suff. Some believe *mīmē(y)* is a case of dittography and thus omit it from translation. The pers. pron. in this case, underscores the subject Nineveh, and a literal translation would be 'and Nineveh, she is like a whirlpool, while they take to flight'. Another possible solution is

to accept an emendation of the text here as the RSV does in translating 'Nineveh is like a pool whose waters run away'.

2 : 11 (C) (MT, 12) The MT word *mirʿe(h)* 'pasture' does not suit the context since it comes from the stem *rāʿā(h)* 'to graze'. By an interchange of consonants one should read here *m^{e}ʿārā(h)* 'cave' which does fit well into the context.

2 : 13 (B) (MT, 14) In place of the 3rd fem. sing. suff. in the MT word *rikbāh* 'her chariots', the LXX has the suff. of the 2nd pers. sing. fem. This suits the context much better. Thus the translation should be 'your chariots' (cf. the DNV and RSV).

3 : 7 (C) On the basis of the LXX, the RSV reads the last word as 'for her' instead of the MT 'for you'. It is doubtful, however, whether this change is necessary. The MT is not hard to translate and its sense is clear (cf. v. 7 as a whole). A similar situation exists in v. 9 where the MT has a 2nd pers. 'your', but translated 'her' in the RSV. Here a more plausible case might be made for the change. The use of the 2nd pers. in v. 8 may have influenced the transmission of the text of v. 9. It is perhaps better to translate 'her' in v. 9, but to retain the 'you' in v. 7.

3 : 9 (C) See v. 7.

3 : 17 (C) For the word *ṭaps^{e}rayik* KBL refers to the Accad *ṭupšarru* 'tablet-writer'. His translation is 'official for recruiting', thus having a military function in view. In the translation 'writer', this military accent is probably not adequately expressed. The DNV has 'officials' and the RSV 'scribes' with a marginal reading 'marshalls'. It is preferable to use some word from the official language of the state.

HABAKKUK

1 : 9 (C) The word *m^{e}gammat*, construct form of *m^{e}gammā(h)*, is not known. One should probably translate the word as a noun. There is a stem *gmm* which apparently means 'to have in abundance' or 'to collect', but this meaning does not help much here. Humbert (*Problèmes du*

livre d'Habacuc, 1944, p. 37) proposes a derivation from *g-m-m* which makes it possible to translate *mᵉgammā(h)* as 'totality'. Thus he suggests the translation 'the totality of their countenances', but this suggestion is only a guess. According to tradition, the noun should have the meaning 'aspiration', i.e. 'the aspiration of their faces'. As for the word translated 'their countenances', Humbert suggests 'their glance'. This is possible since the full expression used elsewhere *nātan pānīm ʾel* means 'to cast one's eye upon'. The following word of 1 : 9 *qādīmā(h)* means 'toward the east'. Thus the translation of the three words in question can be 'the aspiration of their countenance is to the east'. This seems unlikely, however, since in the context the reference is to the Chaldeans who come *from* the east. Thus the DNV has explained *qādīm* as 'east wind'. This is quite possible, since, at the beginning of the verse, it is said that the Chaldeans come to commit violence. As a parallel thought then, the text may be saying that the aspiration of their countenance (perhaps 'advance guard'?) is like an east wind or the Sirocco that Palestine fears. All that this discussion attempts to do is to translate an obscure text. In departing from the MT some prefer to read *mᵉgurat* 'horror' instead of *mᵉgammat*, and *qēdmā(h)* in place of *qādīmā(h)*. Hence, the translation 'horror of them (literally 'the horror of their countenances') goes before them' (cf. also the RSV). The translation is based on an emended text, but it does give a plausible meaning.

4 (C) The MT has the fem. form *ʿuppᵉlā(h)* 'swollen' or 'puffed up', and a literal translation would be 'behold, puffed up, not right is his soul in him'. Some suggest that in the place of *ʿuppᵉlā(h)* a masc. sing. part. of the same stem should be read which would allow for the translation 'behold the puffed up one, whose soul is not right in him'; others suggest a noun form 'behold, the wicked'. To a great extent the translation depends on the relationship between v. 4a and 4b. It is clear that v. 4b speaks of 'the righteous'. If a contrast exists between 4a and 4b, the question arises as to whether 'the wicked' is present in 4a. It is possible that the phrase 'not is his soul right in him' describes the wicked. Since in 4b the righteous 'live', one would expect that 4a should describe how the wicked die or pine away. Accordingly, it has been suggested that in place of *ʿuppᵉlā(h)*, one should read *ʿullap zū* which makes possible the translation 'he whose

soul is not right shall give way' (cf. Humbert, *op. cit.*, pp. 44 f.). the RSV has 'behold, he whose soul is not upright in him shall fail'.

2 : 5 (C) The traditional text is difficult to fit together. The sentence at the beginning reads literally 'how much more, the wine, acting disloyally, man, reckless, and he shall not have rest'. The RSV attempts to render the MT without change 'moreover, wine is treacherous; the arrogant man shall not abide'. The Habakkuk scroll from *Qumran* may shed some light here. In this place it has the word *hōn* 'wealth' instead of *hayyayin* 'the wine', and the imperf. form *yibgōd* instead of the part. *bōgēd* from the same stem. On the basis of this text, the translation of Hab 2 : 5 can be 'how much more, wealth deceives the reckless man; he shall know no rest'. Though this translation is uncertain, yet it does give a plausible meaning and deserves consideration (cf. Millar Burrows, *op. cit.*, plate LVIII, Habakkuk-Scroll, Col. VIII, l. 3).

2 : 15 (C) The MT reads 'woe to him who makes his neighbor drink, mixes your wrath (with it); yea, also makes drunk'. For this sentence the RSV has rendered 'woe to him who makes his neighbors drink of the cup of his wrath, and makes them drunk'. This means that in place of *meₛappēăḥ*, the RSV reads *missap* 'of the cup'. Humbert (*op. cit.*, p. 55) prefers to read a noun form *mispaḥ* to which he assigns the meaning 'glass of wine'. This reading, however, is uncertain since the noun is not known elsewhere. The Habakkuk text of *Qumran* (*op. cit.*, plate LX, Col. xi, lines 2-3) backs up the consonantal text of the MT except that it has 'his wrath' in place of 'your wrath'. This change in suff. can be accepted and hence, the translation can be 'woe to him who gives his neighbor drink, mixes his wrath with it, yea, also makes drunk'.

2 : 16 (C) The MT form *hē'ārēl* means 'be uncircumcised' or 'show your uncircumcision', i.e. 'uncover yourself'. A rearrangement of the consonants of the word yields the reading *hērā'ēl* 'stagger' (RSV) which reading is now supported by the *Qumran* scroll. This does not mean, however, that the reading of the MT is incorrect. It is always much more likely that a difficult reading gave way to an easier one, than vice versa. At any rate, the MT can be translated.

7 (B) The form *yeḥītan* from *ḥātat* (?) 'to terrify' should be read as *yeḥittekā* 'will terrify you'. The LXX supports this change, and internally, the context requires a 2nd pers. sing. suff.

(A) The MT contains a most difficult clause *šebuʿōt maṭṭōt ʾōmer*. A witness to the inherent difficulties is the AV that has resorted to various insertions in order to produce some intelligible sense. It renders '(according to) the oaths of the tribes, (even thy) word', but even with these insertions the sentence has little meaning. The DNV interpretation of the verse is based on the fact that the first phrase mentions a bow. It was reasoned, therefore, that probably the following clause makes mention of some kind of weapon. Hence, it was believed that *maṭṭōt* should be rendered 'arrows' instead of 'tribes' (this agrees also with v. 14). Then the word *šebuʿōt* 'sevens' was viewed as an indication of a great quantity—an abundance of arrows would then be a 'word' or a 'proverb' (*ʾōmer*). One could then render 'sevens of arrows tell a tale' or 'an abundance of arrows tell a tale'. This translation, however, was not accepted, and thus the DNV finally rendered 'you have provided yourself with an abundance of arrows'. In this case, the starting point was the supposition that the first consonant of *šebuʿōt* should be read as an *ś* in order to make the word *śābaʿtā*, a verbal form from *śābaʿ* 'to satisfy oneself' or 'to provide oneself with an abundance'. The resulting translation, of course, is uncertain. If the verb *śābaʿ* is accepted as present here in some form, one can just as well conjecture an intensive form with a transitive meaning, i.e. 'you have satisfied your arrows'. It is difficult to interpret the word *ʾōmer* which the DNV has simply omitted. Some believe the word 'quiver' should be inserted, and that the translation should be 'you have satisfied your quiver with arrows', i.e. completely filled your quiver (cf. the LXX). The RSV has adopted yet another reading, rendering 'and put the arrows to the string'. For details on this text, cf. Humbert (*op. cit.*, pp. 61-63) who translates *tu rassasies sa corde . . . de traits.*

11 (C) The RSV renders the word *zebulā(h)* in their 'habitation'. The vocalization of the MT indicates the translation 'to the dwelling' (direction), or 'in the dwelling' (locative). The word *zebul* can mean 'dwelling' or 'residence' or something like this. Although

some uncertainty is present (does the word *šemeš* actually belong to the preceding verse?), still a fairly accurate translation is possible.

3 : 13 (C) The MT reads 'thou didst crush the head from the house of the wicked'. In omitting the phrase 'from the house', the RSV reflects a particular exegesis of the verse. The complete sentence may contain a metaphor, i.e. the destruction of the enemy is like the destruction of a house—a complete demolition from the roof to the foundation that is laid bare fully. It is possible to understand the inf. absolute 'the uncovering' as meaning 'thou hast uncovered'. Moreover, Hebr usage allows for the translation of the perfects in the verse as presents. And, finally, one can vocalize the MT *ṣawwā'r* 'neck' as *ṣūr* 'rock'. Thus, this final part of the verse can be translated 'thou hast uncovered the foundations unto the rock'. On the other hand, the RSV believes the verse depicts the complete extermination of the people, and thus its translation has 'laying him bare from thigh to neck.' While this translation retains the MT reading *ṣawwā'r* 'neck', yet it offers a debatable translation for the MT *yᵉsōd* 'foundation' or 'pedestal'.

3 : 14 (C) The suff. 'his' in the MT clause 'thou didst pierce with his arrows' is somewhat difficult. The suff. can only mean 'his own arrows' but it can hardly refer to the arrows of the wicked. It is better, then, to accept a change in suff., i.e. from the 3rd pers. to the 2nd pers. masc. sing. 'with thy arrows'. The word *perez* is also difficult. It probably means 'warriors' (RSV), but it is also possible that it implies 'leaders' or 'commanders' as the ancient versions indicate.

3 : 16 (C) The translations 'under me I trembled (as regards) my steps', i.e. 'my steps trembled under me' (cf. the RSV) and 'I walked with trembling steps' are both uncertain. The word 'steps' implies a reading *'ăšūray* instead of the MT *'ăšer* which here can have no meaning either as a conjunction or as a relative particle. Even the LXX indicated the reading 'steps'. The change of the verbal form from the 1st pers. 'I trembled' to a 3rd pers. in which the 'steps' become the subject, is not necessary, for the word 'steps' can be an acc. of relation. Some have rendered 'on my place I tremble' which indicates that *taḥat* is a noun meaning 'place' instead of a prep. meaning 'under'. This does not seem to be likely.

ZEPHANIAH

: 3 (C) The MT has 'stumbling blocks' for which KBL offers the meaning 'decay, ruin'. The sing. form of the same word in Is 3 : 6 means 'ruin'. Here in Zeph, the MT can best be translated 'and the ruins with the wicked'. Some suggest that the text should read a verbal form built on the same stem as the noun form of the MT. This would give a translation such as the RSV has 'I will overthrow the wicked'. It might be possible that the consonants of the MT *m k š l w t* could be interpreted as a fem. plur. part., in which the translation could be 'and the things by which the wicked are made to stumble' or 'and that by which the wicked are overthrown'.

: 4 (B) The DNV has followed the MT literally in translating 'the remnant of Baal, the name of the idolatrous priests with the priests'. The word *'im* would thus mean 'together with'. The RSV, however, has followed the LXX in omitting the final phrase 'with the priests'.

: 5 (C) The MT vocalization indicates that the last word should be translated 'their king'. Another pointing that has been followed by some is *Milkom* (cf. the RSV). This is found in a few mss of the LXX. Sometimes it has been read as 'their Moloch' but this is uncertain. Moreover, it means that one definite interpretation of the Moloch worship is followed.

: 14 (C) The RSV has 'the sound of the day of the Lord is bitter', but this is an uncertain rendering. Another possible translation is based on an interpretation of the Hebr *qōl* as an interjection, i.e. 'listen, the day'. As for the Hebr word *mar* 'bitter', it may be a predicate of the preceding nominal sentence with the 'day of the Lord' as subject, i.e. 'the day of the Lord is bitter' (RSV). But *mar* may also be an adverb that modifies the sentence that follows, i.e. 'bitterly cries the hero' (DNV).

: 2 (B) The Hebr reads literally 'before a decree is born; like chaff a day has passed away' (cf. the RSV margin). The DNV follows the MT except that it renders 'the decision'. Though the Hebr article is not present, yet it is possible to translate the word as definite. Note that the verb *yālad* in this context means 'to carry out'. Thus, the text, in making the invitation to repentance more urgent, affirms that a day disappears as quickly as chaff is scattered. The RSV text has 'before you are driven away like the drifting chaff'. This translation is based partially on the LXX and partially on guess work. The first occurrence of the word 'day' is omitted in both the LXX and the RSV.

2 : 5 (C) Besides the DNV and RSV translations, the following rendering is possible:

'Woe to you inhabitants of the seacoast,
you nation of the Cherethites;
the word of the Lord is against you!
O Canaan, land of the Philistines,
I will destroy you till no inhabitant is left'.

There is a question as to whether one adds the words 'the word of the Lord is against you' to what precedes this clause or to what follows it.

2 : 7 (C) The RSV (cf. also the DNV) renders 'on which they shall pasture'. The words 'on which', *'ălē(y)hem* (more literally 'upon them') undoubtedly refer back to the sing. noun 'sea-coast' that is found in the preceding line. The plur. suff. 'them' can be explained from the fact that in v. 6 'sea-coast' is described by the plur. nouns 'pastures' and 'meadows'. Since v. 7a seems to break the connection somewhat between 6b and 7b, some have conjectured *'al hayyām* 'at the sea' instead of *'ălē(y)hem*. But in view of the fact that the MT contains an understandable sense, it is better not to accept this change.

2 : 14 (B) Following the LXX, the RSV and others have altered the MT *gōy* 'nation' and translate 'beasts of the field' or 'beasts of the earth'. On the other hand, the DNV has adhered to the MT considering the word *gōy* 'nation' to be a qualification of 'beasts'. Thus it obtains the somewhat uncertain rendering 'all the beasts that live in groups'. Later in the verse, the RSV has made two other changes. In place of *qōl* 'voice' it reads *kōs* 'owl', and instead of *ḥōreb* 'desolation' it reads *'ōrēb* 'raven'.

(C) Cf. Hab 1 : 8. The translation 'evening wolves' has been strongly questioned in recent times. One proposal is to read *'ărābā(h)* 'desert, wilderness' instead of *'ereb* 'evening' (the LXX has 'wolves of Arabia'). In view of the word *bōqer* 'morning' that follows, Humbert (*op. cit.*, pp. 35 f.) feels strongly that 'evening' is the correct reading. Elliger (*Festschrift für Alfred Bertholet*, 1948, pp. 158 ff.) has discussed the text in detail, preferring to speak no more of 'evening wolves'. Since the discussion on the subject is not at an end, it is too early to make a change in Bible translation at this point. Perhaps the sense is 'her judges are wolves of the evening' or 'in the evening'.

(C) If the MT is retained, a translation of it should be close to that of the DNV 'then her dwelling will not be cut off according to everything with which I will visit her'. However, if one reads *mē'ē(y)ne(y)hā* 'from her eyes', instead of the MT *me'ōnāh* 'her dwelling', the translation takes on more meaning 'nor shall disappear out of her eyes everything that I have instructed her' (RSV = 'she will not lose sight of all that I have enjoined upon her'). The verb stem *pqd* means 'to visit' or 'to instruct, charge'.

17 (B) The DNV renders the MT literally 'he will be silent in his love'. Supported by the LXX, the RSV has read a slightly altered text 'he will renew you in his love'.

19 (B) The verb *'āśā(h)* should here be interpreted as *'āśā(h) kālā(h)* 'deal fully with'. The RSV has 'I will deal with all your oppressors'.

HAGGAI

15 (C) The RSV has accepted two slight changes at the close of the verse. First, it has added the first word of v. 16 *mihyōtām* to the end of v. 15, and then, on the basis of the LXX, it has changed the form *mihyōtām* 'since their being' to read *mah hĕyītem* 'how did you fare'. There is much to be said for the LXX translation. As it stands, the MT is difficult. However, since a little earlier in the verse, the prep. *min* is combined with *ṭerem*, i.e. *miṭṭerem* to mean 'before', it is possible that the prep. *min* is combined with *heyōtām*, i.e. *mihyōtām* to give the same sense. The DNV has built its translation on this basis since it

renders 'before stone was laid on stone in the temple of the Lord, before these things happened' (literally 'before they were').

ZECHARIAH

2 : 8 (B) (MT, 12) The words *'aḥar kābōd* 'after glory' are difficult. What does the literal phrase mean 'after the glory hath he sent me unto the nations' (AV)? Both the AV and RSV have taken the prep. *'el* 'unto' with the verb *šālaḥ* 'to send'. This is possible. It is quite possible also to read with one Hebr ms the prep. *'al* 'concerning' instead of *'el* and to connect the prep. with the verb 'to say'. Thus, the DNV has rendered 'the Lord says concerning the peoples'. It also has chosen the reading *'ăšer kebōdō* making it the subject of the verb *šālaḥ*, i.e. 'whose glory sent me'. Similarly the RSV has read *kebōdō*, taking *'aḥar* in a temporal sense, i.e. 'after his glory sent me to the nations'.

4 : 12 (C) The MT has 'from which the gold is poured out'. By 'gold', oil is meant and it is usually translated thus. One can, of course, alter the text to read 'oil'. It is better, however, to retain the MT as it is and understand that the oil is here called 'gold' because of its yellow color.

5 : 6 (B) The MT *'ē(y)nām* 'their eye' is rendered in the DNV 'they look like this'. The RSV has 'the iniquity' which in the main follows the reading underlying the LXX, *'ăwōnām* 'their iniquity'.

6 : 3 (C) In verses 2 and 3, red, black, white, and dappled horses are mentioned. The word 'dappled' (RSV = 'dappled gray' here but 'dappled ones' in 6 : 6) is the Hebr *bārōd*. The word is also used of animals in Gen 31 : 10 where the RSV has rendered it by 'mottled'. The usual translation is 'spotted'.

6 : 6 (C) The black horses go to the north and the white horses go 'after them' (the dappled go to the south). The phrase 'after them' might indicate that the white horses go to the north also. Or it might mean that they leave 'later than they', i.e. after the black horses have departed, in which case nothing would be said about the direction they took. However, it is possible by a very slight textual change in the clause *'el 'aḥărē(y)hem* 'after them', to read *'el 'aḥărē(y) hayyām* 'to

the west'. This is certainly more probable than the suggestion of some that the text should read 'to the east'.

6 : 7 (C) The RSV renders the word *'ămuṣṣīm* 'steeds' which agrees with the DNV translation 'strong horses'. The same word at the end of v. 3 is rendered 'horses' in the RSV. The DNV translates the end of v. 3 'for the fourth (chariot) spotted; strong horses', thus indicating that the phrase 'strong horses' refers to all four groups. KBL prefers to translate *'āmōṣ* as 'piebald' which would mean that it is a kind of synonym of 'spotted'.

6 : 11, 14 (B) The Hebr plur. 'crowns' should be translated as a sing. 'crown'.

9 : 1 (C) The prep. *bᵉ* may indicate here locality, i.e. 'the word of the Lord *in* the land of Hadrach' (a town in a small Aram kingdom), or it may signify opposition, i.e. 'the word of the Lord against the land of Hadrach' (cf. the RSV). The sense of 'against' reproduces the meaning well. The text continues 'and Damascus is its resting-place' (RSV more freely 'and will rest upon Damascus'). The next part reads literally 'for to the Lord belongs the eye of the people and all the tribes of Israel'. It is hard to make sense out of this. In order to retain this text, one needs to paraphrase 'because to the Lord belong all people, and (not only) the tribes of Israel'. However, this is an interpretation and not a translation. To resolve the problem, two textual changes have been proposed. One change is to read *Aram* in place of *'ādām* 'man, people', and the other is to read *'ārē(y)* 'cities of' in place of the MT *'ē(y)n* 'eye'. Thus, the RSV has obtained the rendering 'for to the Lord belong the cities of Aram, even as all the tribes of Israel'. The translation makes sense in this context but it involves textual change.

9 : 15 (C) The Hebr text reads literally 'the Lord of hosts will protect them, and they shall devour and tread underfoot the sling-stones; and they shall drink, thrive as from wine, and become full as a bowl, as corners of an altar'. To say the least, the verse is puzzling. First of all, one should probably read *bᵉnē(y) qela'* 'slingers' instead of *'abnē(y) qela'* 'sling stones'. Then in place of the *MT hāmū* 'they thrive' it is preferable to read *dāmām* 'their blood'. Thus the RSV renders 'and they

shall devour and tread down the slingers; and they shall drink their blood like wine'. The text would mean in this case that the people of God will achieve a great victory through God's protection: they will devour and drink blood! The 'slingers', then, are the enemies of the Jews. A completely different interpretation gives the following translation 'the Lord of hosts will protect them (i.e. the Jews); the sling-stones devour and tread under foot; they drink blood like wine'. Here the 'sling stones' are the subject and the text as a whole expresses the action of God. It is God who gains for the people a complete victory, for the sling stones are in His hand. However one may interpret the text, the idea remains quite puzzling.

10 : 3 (C) The MT has the word 'he-goats' which the RSV has rendered 'leaders'. It is clear that the word denotes notable men. Since, however, the figure of the shepherd and the flock permeates the verse, it is perhaps better to retain the literal translation 'he-goats' (cf. Ezek 34).

10 : 11 (C) The Hebr has 'and they (he) shall pass through the sea of distress'. Since the sea of Egypt is meant, many have read *miṣrayim* 'Egypt' instead of *ṣārā(h)* 'distress'. Nevertheless, the MT reading is firmly established. Perhaps the sense is 'they shall pass through the sea Distress', thus considering the word 'distress' as a kind of personification.

10 : 12 (C) For the MT reading 'and in his name shall they walk', some have suggested on the basis of the LXX the reading 'and they shall glory in his name' (RSV). This means the difference of one consonant in the Hebr—from the stem *hālak* 'to walk' to *hālal* 'to glory'. But it is not at all necessary to deviate from the MT since its makes very good sense. It means that the journey of those who are brought back (cf. v. 10) shall be undertaken in the name of the Lord.

11 : 13 (B) Instead of the MT 'the potter', the RSV adopts the reading of the Tg and Pesh 'the treasury' thereby making a connection with the temple treasury. But it is not at all likely that the temple treasury is in view in this context. It is better with the DNV to keep to the MT which can also be translated as 'metalfounder'.

16 (B) The Hebr reads 'the youth'. With a slight change in text one can read 'the wandering'. The RSV has 'the wandering' and the DNV 'the scattered'.

: 10 (B) The RSV translation (cf. also the DNV) 'when they look on him whom they have pierced' is based on Th and it forms a fitting parallel to the following clause 'they shall mourn for him'. The MT 'they shall look on me' does not give any clear sense here.

: 5 (C) The MT literally translated has 'because someone has let me buy since my youth', i.e. in order to cultivate the field. The Hebr form can also mean 'because someone has caused me to possess since my youth', namely a field, so that I must look after it. Thus, the text yields somewhat of an acceptable meaning. The RSV rendering 'for the land has been my possession' is based on a change of text, i.e. from the MT *'ādām hiqnanī* to *'ădāmā*(*h*) *qinyānī* or *'ădāmā*(*h*) *qānītī*.

: 5 (C) In the final part of the verse the MT reads 'my God shall come and all the saints with thee'. The prophet who proclaims can surely speak of God as 'my God'. Thus the change to 'your God' suggested by the RSV is not really necessary. The other change in the RSV 'with him' in place of the MT 'with thee' is necessary. The reading 'with him' is reflected in the LXX.

: 6 (C) Literally, the MT reads 'on that day there shall be no light, precious things, they shall stiffen'(?). The meaning of 'precious things' is not clear. The idea of 'planets' is only a guess. Since the text is obscure it is probably best to understand three nouns—'no light' (i.e. no warmth), 'but cold', i.e. *w*^{e}*qārā*(*h*) or the plur. *w*^{e}*qārōt* in place of the MT *y*^{e}*qārōt*, and 'stiffening' or 'frost' (i.e. *w*^{e}*qippā'ōn*). Thus, the translation becomes 'on that day there shall be no light, but cold and frost'. This might imply that a miracle of God occurs since v. 7 says there will be light. The RSV has omitted the word 'light' and hence, has rendered 'on that day there shall be neither cold nor frost'. This makes v. 6 fit in better with v. 7 and provides an understandable text. On the other hand, it is not possible to prove that such an omission is correct.

14 : 18 (C) According to v. 17, the 'families of the earth' which do not go to Jerusalem to celebrate 'the feast of booths', do without rain as a punishment. Egypt, however, is not dependent on rain but on the flooding of the Nile which gives fertility to its land. Thus v. 18 apparently means that even though the withholding of rain does not seriously affect Egypt's rural economy, yet if it fails to observe the feast of booths it shall be punished with the 'plague of the nations' in some other way. Therefore, one should be careful to retain the negation *lōʾ* 'not' in v. 18. With this negation the translation can be 'and if the family of Egypt does not go up and does not come, then upon them shall there not be the (same) plague with which the Lord afflicts the nations'. This interpretation can be supported. There is obviously a good reason why Egypt comes in for special mention. But this reason is difficult to explain if the negation is omitted as the RSV has done.

MALACHI

1 : 7 (C) The 2nd masc. sing. suff. in the MT word *gēʾalnūkā* refers to Yahweh. According to Johnson (*Supplements to VT*, I, 1953, p. 75), the verb *gāʾal* here and in v. 12 is used in order "to condemn the Jews of the post-exilic period for the poor quality of their offerings, and the resultant 'degrading' treatment of Yahweh and His altar." Johnson, therefore, retains the 2nd masc. sing. suff. as the DNV has done in its translation 'you bring unworthy fare to my altar. And then you say, how have we treated you unworthily'. The RSV, however, has changed the suff. to a 3rd pers. masc. sing. referring to the altar, i.e. 'how have we polluted it'.

1 : 12 (C) The MT reads literally 'its fruit . . . its food' which can be taken to mean 'what it produces, its food'. Usually, however, the word *nībō* 'its fruit' is omitted from translation.

2 : 3 (C) The Hebr has 'the dung of your feasts, and he shall bear you to it', but to whom does the subject 'he' refer? Perhaps one should translate 'thou shalt be carried (dragged) here'. There is no further light on the subject of *nāśāʾ*. There is a question as to where the persons are carried. Is it to the 'dung'? Is the RSV correct in translating 'your offerings' instead of 'your feasts'? The LXX implies that God is the subject of the action described since it translates the verbal form in the 1st

pers. The RSV has adopted this change and has further altered the text to read 'and I will put you out of my presence'. This translation is very uncertain.

(C) The MT has the form *'ēr* 'the awakening one'. It is possible, however, that the combination *'ēr wᵉ'ōne(h)* provides the sense of 'everyone', literally 'the one who is awakening and the one who answers' (cf. the BSG 'awaker and answerer'). The translation can then be 'may the Lord cut off from the tents of Jacob, the entire generation of the man who does such a thing, even if he brings an offering to the Lord of hosts'. Such a possible translation makes unnecessary the textual change the RSV has adopted when it reads *'ēd* 'witness' instead of *'ēr* 'the awakening one'.

The MT reads literally at the beginning 'and not one he has made and a remainder of spirit to him'. This conveys no sense. The 'one' might mean God as the RSV concludes in its rendering 'the one God'. On the other hand, since the negation 'not' seems to be closely linked with the word 'one', the translation could be 'nobody'. A question surrounts the meaning of *rûăḥ* here which might signify 'Spirit' or 'life' or 'passion'. The DNV has 'not one does likewise', but in this case, one would expect a demonstrative here. Again, the DNV takes the words 'in whom is a rest of spirit' as qualifying 'one', translating 'not one does like this, who possesses a sufficient spirit'. The meaning is not clear.

Elliger (*Das Buch der zwölf kleinen Propheten* II, ATD, 1956 p. 189) retains the the MT as it is and translates in agreement with the DNV. The RSV has rendered 'has not the one God made and sustained for us the spirit of life', a translation that involves still a different idea. Word for word rendering here is probably the best policy in order to avoid expressing in translation a biased exegesis. In the final clause the MT has 'woman of your youth'. The suff. does not fit into this context and can easily be explained as influenced by v. 14 'wife of your covenant'. Thus, in v. 15 read 'wife of his youth' (cf. the AV, DNV, and RSV).

(B) The first three words should not be rendered 'he hates divorce', but rather the MT perf. 3rd pers. should be vocalized as a part. *śōnē'* '(I) am hating'. It could also be understood as a perf. form 1st pers. sing. *śānē'tī* 'I hate'.